# VICTORIAN POPULAR FICTION, 1860–80

*By the same author*

ANTHONY TROLLOPE: The Artist in Hiding

# VICTORIAN POPULAR FICTION, 1860–80

R. C. Terry

MACMILLAN PRESS
LONDON

*First published 1983 by*
THE MACMILLAN PRESS LTD
*London and Basingstoke*
*Companies and representatives*
*throughout the world*

ISBN 0 333 25958 0

*Typeset by*
*Wessex Typesetters Ltd*
*Frome, Somerset*

*Printed in Hong Kong*

*For Judith*

# Contents

# List of Plates

# Preface

We know a great deal about what was provided for the working man to read and what the working man chose to read, what was given to him for his improvement by the missionary-minded, and what the entrepreneur gave him to do himself good.[1] Surprisingly, though, we have bothered less about what the middle-class book-borrowing Brown, Jones and Robinson chose to read – or were persuaded to read – by the powerful new industry, the book trade.

By the late fifties the Browns in their hundreds of thousands were inundated by all kinds of reading-matter – sermons, diaries, memoirs, travellers' tales, and novels of all shapes and sizes. Novels in three volumes mostly, but novels in part issues, novels serialised in periodicals, novels in cheap reprints, novels in lurid covers on railway stands. David Masson observed, in the magical year which is my starting-point, that the novelist had become the truest wizard of modern times.[2]

It is a vast subject, even with the twenty-year limitation I impose and my choice of novelists for detailed study. To begin with my title, the word 'popular' represents what satisfied a middlebrow public seeking entertainment, the 'comicalities' and 'light literature' which beguiled the travelling and leisure of Thomas Arnold's 'Reading Class', and not what a contributor to *Macmillan's Magazine* in 1866 coyly termed 'that literary provender which satisfies the lower classes of our country-men'.[3]

It is unhelpful to produce a historical guide and it is always dangerous to use novels as social history, yet at the same time the student of so vast and neglected a field must give some sign of the diversity of material and relate the fiction to its cultural milieu. This is the concern of my first chapter. Although popular fiction is short on ideas and enduring literary values (yet it can surprise occasionally on both counts), it should be considered as part of the scene in which great writers did their noble work, and its role in the commercial and critical sphere is worth exploring. These are the subjects of my second and third chapters. For criticism I rely chiefly on the leading middlebrow magazines, such as the *Athenaeum*, the *Saturday Review* and the *Spectator*, as indicators of the variety of responses, blind spots and bizarre judgements on popular writing. The first part of my book is therefore a broad survey of what the mid-Victorians read, what working-conditions were like for the professional man of letters, and what the mass-circulation periodicals thought of it all.

The larger portion of the book studies such matters in relation to three minor novelists whose work is of sufficiently engaging quality to establish the point that not all kings and queens of the circulating libraries fell into a well-deserved oblivion. The possible choice of authors is enormous and several have been dropped along the way as my own tastes have changed, until three came to seem most representative of cultural moods, fashions and methods. Happily my trio of Mrs Oliphant, Rhoda Broughton and James Payn fit well into three schools of fiction denominated by Alfred Austin in 1870 as 'Simple', 'Fast' and 'Sensational'.[4]

In the course of examining a corner of the vast treasure-house of Victorian fiction I see one constant thread of inquiry, and that concerns the more eclectic nature of Victorian middlebrow reading, and possibly the more flexible criteria we need to do it justice. Of course, it is of little purpose to rescue forgotten novels unless they have something still to say to us, but equally there is a justification in many of the novels under review for insisting that they do possess certain intrinsic values as well as illustrating perspectives on mid-Victorian manners and thought. We might do well to re-examine our attitudes to what after all satisfied a sizeable public. Interesting questions may be posed similar to those raised when we approach modern popular amusements in film and television. Beyond this invitation to compare aspects of culture now and then this study is primarily intended to illustrate the pleasure afforded by some minor Victorian novelists of 1860 to 1880.

I wish to thank the University of Victoria for a period of leave to undertake research for this book and the Social Sciences and Humanities Research Council of Canada for assistance. I am grateful to many libraries for information and access to minor fiction and manuscript materials, notably the Humanities Research Center, University of Texas at Austin, Texas, and the Joseph Regenstein Library of the University of Chicago, Illinois, particularly with regard to James Payn. To the National Library of Scotland, Edinburgh, I am indebted for information regarding Mrs Oliphant, and I also wish to acknowledge assistance from the libraries of the Universities of London, Essex and Exeter and the London Library; I am particularly grateful to the staffs of the British Library and the University of Victoria Library. Among many individuals my thanks are especially due to Mr William Payn for talking to me about his grandfather and giving me access to his private collection of novels. In addition I wish to thank many friends in Victoria who have helped in various ways, including Shelley Hunt, Tracy Cameron, Helen Edelmeier, Sarah Baylow and Helen Harris. My final acknowledgement goes to my wife, Judith, for unfailing encouragement and practical help when the byways of mid-Victorian popular fiction seemed unending.

*Victoria*                                                      R.C.T.
*British Columbia*

# 1 Reading Mania

*Do not speak slightingly of the three-volume novel, Cicely.*
Oscar Wilde, *The Importance of Being Earnest*, Act 2 (1895)

Embarking on the subject of Victorian popular fiction is like that favourite Victorian occupation of mapping the source of the Nile: the dark continent beckons, but the explorer soon begins to feel like Captain Speke without a compass, for ever following tempting channels that wind up in swamps, for ever in danger of being lost in vast, unmapped regions, and not sure what he will find when he gets there. Two large, menacing rocks loom out of the water immediately. Who were the readers? What were they reading? To attempt to negotiate these obstacles will be the business of this chapter, before my exploration plunges deeper into the jungle of commercial publishing, criticism, and three examples of mid-Victorian popularities – Margaret Oliphant, Rhoda Broughton and James Payn.

That the audience for novels was a large one by the 1860s and 1870s is a commonplace; just how large is difficult to say for sure. If it did not reach into the millions, as Wilkie Collins and others had speculated hungrily at mid century, it was at any rate to be numbered in the hundreds of thousands.[1] 'We have become a novel-reading people,' said Anthony Trollope in 1870, 'from the Prime Minister down to the last-appointed scullery-maid.'[2] This is an interesting observation from an author who had his finger on the public pulse and whose practice will be taken from time to time in this book as a yardstick of middlebrow fiction. The novel-reading public was more socially broad, less exclusive than one might perhaps think, and its appetite for fiction gargantuan. People were always sticking labels on this generation, wrote Alfred Austin in 1874 – the age of gold, the scientific age, the age of humbug – but one thing was certain: 'It may be the

1

age of anything else people like; but assuredly it is the age of Novels.'[3]

Numerically it is unwise to be too dogmatic. There had been phenomenal population growth in England and Wales, from some 6¼ million in 1750 to 18 million by 1850. Add to these statistics the increase in the second half of the century, particularly of the middle class: 357,000 in 1851; 482,000 in 1861; and 647,000 in 1881.[4] Picture this restless, upwardly mobile population, engulfed by change they did not understand, riven by anxieties about social status, prey to deep disturbance about living conditions, perplexed by the break-up of old orthodoxies, excited by the prospect of material progress and already feeling the groundswell of more evolutionary scientific advances. The problems of the individual and mass society begin here, ·and the paths to diverge between literary culture and popular fiction, both important aspects of this book.

In their higher levels the middle-class readers are Arnold's philistines, rioting on the milk of Tupper and the water of Hain Friswell, terrified of intellectual struggle and abstract ideas and capable of appreciating art only on Mr Podsnap's terms utilitarian and photographic, and devoted to getting up at eight, shaving close at a quarter past, breakfasting at nine, going to the City at ten, and so on. This condescending attitude has largely coloured our own view of Victorian middle-class readers, but they had their defenders. An essay by James Payn called 'The Midway Inn' puts very well the essence of middlebrow taste and the brand of lighter fiction it cultivated. This is a sly, subversive piece of work, in Payn's best manner, written in 1879 for *Nineteenth Century* with a touch of *fin de siècle* cynicism about it as well as nostalgia for a bygone literary era.[5] Payn makes a case for the modern man of letters as entertainer without glossing over his faults, and is spokesman for a level of middle-class taste well above the Podsnap and Veneering level and a range of fiction important to our broader understanding of the Victorians.

Mine host at the Midway Inn is 'the quintessence of the commonplace'; he has no more at the back of him than at the back of a looking-glass, and like the looking-glass he reflects bourgeois taste. This is Payn's narrator, an admirable device for ironical comment. The inn stands halfway between home and school, where the horses were changed in days of yore, and from this midway point Payn voices a Thackerayan melancholy, tinged with asperity, at the changing world. Midway days are middle age, doubt and depression, discontent with the new, and loss of contact with the old. Religious faith is on the wane; even the clergy 'faintly trust the larger hope', and philosophers voice 'unwelcome doubt respecting the divine government of the world', while the average man shrugs and walks away. Dullness at home has increased public entertainments. 'There is no such thing as high spirits anywhere.' Instead of the lively, boisterous talk of our fathers, 'we have drawing-room dissertations on art, and dandy drivel about blue china', although two pleasures never fail, even among the young – business and making money. At his best in table talk and occasional essays, Payn draws the middlebrow figure as Trollope would: solid, down to earth, practical. New literature has arisen, extolling money-making and thrift; its heroes are all self-made men. Since poetry is all gloom, the public craves fiction. People are glad to find themselves 'anywhere, anywhere, out of the world', and are generally gratified, 'for anything less like real life than what some novelists portray it is difficult to imagine'.

In this, as in other essays he wrote for *Nineteenth Century*, published as *Some Private Views* (1881), James Payn voices an articulate, independent stance that embodies the middlebrow reader for whom Victorian popular fiction provided reasonably intelligent and amusing fare, not without stimulus to thought and reflection. It is too easy, Payn argues consistently in this and other essays, to patronise 'light literature'. As he says in 'The Literary Calling and its Future', in much of it there is a reasonably high standard, a healthy individuality and abundant talent:

> Persons of intelligence do not look for such things perhaps, and certainly not in magazines, while persons of 'culture' are too much occupied with old china and high art; but to humble folks, who take an interest in their fellow-creatures, it is very pleasant to observe what high thoughts, and how poetically expressed, are now to be found about our feet, and, as it were, in the literary gutter.[6]

Payn's persons of intelligence, however, were quite likely not merely to know what was to be found about their feet, but also to enjoy it, even though he does not quite like to say so. Catholicity of taste can be inferred from contemporary evidence of various kinds. On the undiscriminating and uniform reading-practice of the mid-Victorian middlebrow public Kathleen Tillotson has observed that novels crossed all boundaries. People took in their stride *The Woman in White, Great Expectations, East Lynne* and *Lady Audley's Secret.* Tennyson said he was steeped in Miss Braddon – 'I am reading every word she ever wrote'[7] – and there were many readers like Edward Fitzgerald who struggled with George Eliot's prose more out of duty than enjoyment. Abandoning *The Mill on the Floss* Fitzgerald lamented, 'I couldn't take to it more than to others I have tried by the Greatest Novelist of the Day; but I will go on a little further.' This was followed by a heartfelt, 'Oh, for some more brave Trollope!' More bluntly, R. D. Blackmore admitted he much preferred Miss Braddon's golden-haired homicidals to Gwendolen Harleth, and dubbed Meredith the 'great unintelligible'. Later in the century one reader turned from *Jude the Obscure* with 'Thank God for Kipling, and Stevenson, Barrie and Mrs Humphry Ward.'[8] It is clearly necessary to resist compartmentalising both audience and reading-material: the audience for *Daniel Deronda* was not always separate from that for *Good-bye Sweetheart!* any more than today's television audience for *Brideshead Revisited* is necessarily separate from that for *All Creatures Great and Small.*

Huge quantities of novels of all kinds were devoured, certainly without the critical sophistication we bring to the subject, but in some cases with far more freedom from exclusive and sometimes inhibiting criteria. Refreshingly, it seems to me, the Victorian bookworm, whether highly educated and leisured or with the minimum of knowledge and of humble status, could move comfortably from classic to bestselling sensation novel, deriving from each kind certain values and ideas, and the inestimable (though usually ignored or discounted) boon of recreation. The Winkworth sisters, Catherine and Emily, were a pair of devoted readers for pleasure who certainly knew the difference between 'literature' and commercial fiction. They had been taught by the Rev William Gaskell in Manchester, were friendly with Charles Dickens, and fortunately left diaries of what they read. Catherine appreciated *Jane Eyre*, but found it infinitely below *Mary Barton* or *Deerbrook*; *Alton Locke* puzzled her. She seems most to have enjoyed books by Mrs Oliphant like *Mrs Margaret Maitland* (1851). Her sister concurred, noting her particular enjoyment of Mrs

Oliphant's *Neighbours on the Green* (1871). Ranking novelists did
not occur to them. For Emily the most agreeable aspect of all
fiction – the greatest asset a writer could have – was to help the
reader see 'the life in life we all long for'. She wanted someone to
collect bits of R. H. Hutton, Miss (Anne) Thackeray – above all
George Eliot – and make them into one book 'to turn to, like
sermons, when one gets pushed and down-hearted'.[9] The yoking
of such dissimilar arts and attainments is a striking example of a
typical response of readers still able to share spontaneously in the
common pursuit and untroubled by the aestheticism of a later
generation. What is also noticeable in the Winkworths' response
is a commonly shared assumption about the general moral
efficacy of novels and the simple artistic criterion which I find the
single most important preoccupation of the middlebrow novelist
of the sixties and seventies: a good story well told in realistic
terms and in a spirit of useful, energising commitment to life and
people. James Payn and his contemporaries grasped this essential
need of the mid-Victorian public.

Diaries and memoirs add to our understanding of the eclectic
reading of the period. Even Mr Gladstone solaced his leisure
hour with a popular novel or two, as S. M. Ellis reports:

> I remember a friend, who was a member of the same club as
> W. E. Gladstone, relating that on one occasion he saw the
> statesman in the library, deep in the perusal of a book.
> Gladstone read on for a long time, and when eventually he put
> the book down and left the room, the engrossing volume
> proved to be not a work of philosophy or classical history but –
> *Red as a Rose is She*.[10]

Another indicator of the reading public's unwillingness to
categorise is found in the periodical reviewing of fiction, which
refuses to discriminate between major and minor writers, and
quite cheerfully lumps together some books we now acknowledge
as classics with popularities long since forgotten. And this is not
entirely a matter of the state of novel-criticism, which, like Joe
Gargery's education, was still in its infancy, but stems in part
from an acknowledgement of novels for sheer amusement.
Similarly, literary surveys which appear in increasing numbers at
the end of the century show fascinating preferences and
juxtapositions. *Women Novelists of Queen Victoria's Reign* (1897), for

example, pays tribute to George Eliot, Mrs Gaskell and the Brontës, but is not beyond praising Mrs Craik, Mrs Henry Wood, or even lesser lights like Julia Kavanagh.

That Mudie's and other circulating libraries stocked huge quantities of biography, history, travel, philosophy, religion and general science as well as fiction is evidence that readers wanted knowledge, breadth as well as entertainment. In fact the surest guide to the make-up of the mid-Victorian public and what it read is found in the catalogues of Mudie's Select Library of Fiction. Charles Edward Mudie's command of mid-Victorian book-circulation and his consequent role in the fiction industry can hardly be exaggerated. As John Sutherland has remarked, by the late fifties his library controlled a major section of the market in London, in the country and overseas; at the height of his power in the 1860s he earned up to £40,000 a year in sub-scriptions.[11]

Starting on a small scale in King Street, he rapidly expanded in 1852 to premises in New Oxford Street. These were enlarged in 1860 in what Trollope called Mudie's great flare-up, and thereafter the firm dominated all aspects of the book trade for another thirty-five years. Fiction accounted for 44 per cent of the stock in the boom years. Between 1858 and 1860 Mudie acquired 165,445 novels, and by 1861 the library held 800,000 volumes (according to Guinevere Griest 960,000, nearly half of them fiction, acquired between 1853 and 1862) and by 1900 the library holdings were 7½ million books. A popular novel of 1880 (unremarkable in every way except for this view of Mudie's magnificent emporium) shows how the patrons were under its spell:

'To Mudie's'!
    The footman touched his hat, put into the carriage a packet of books, a purse, card-basket, and court-guide, the para-phernalia necessary to a lady's afternon in London, and then jumping up beside the coachman, gave the word, and the trim little brougham was soon swallowed up in the gloom of the December fog that hung over the city.

The lady's carriage is followed through Piccadilly, which under the feeble gas lamps seems to the authoress like 'one of the circuses of the Tuscan poet's hell, with its rows of lost souls wandering disconsolate through the *aura morta*'. Mudie's Library, by contrast, is a literary elysium:

> a large gray building which, with its high windows and swinging glass doors, was evidently the emporium of a brisk business of some sort. The occupant of the little brougham, taking up the books that lay on the seat in front of her, descended. As she entered, her eyes rested with a grateful sense of repose on the rows of richly-bound books that lined the walls, and she inhaled with pleasure the atmosphere of the place, that seemed to be impregnated with the odours of learning and leather.
>
> The counters for distribution were surrounded by rows of eager people, some looking at the catalogues, others opening up books that stood in front of them, whilst the rest waited impatiently until the volumes they had inquired for were brought by the indefatigable attendants, who ascended as occasion required, to the dizzy heights of the iron gallery, running round the top of the room, or descended by the winding stair in the centre to the depths below; but always returned, like the gnomes of the German fairy stories, laden with the golden treasure that is supposed to make glad the heart of man.

Despite this flattery, Mudie did not find a place for the book on his shelves.[12]

In an age of machines Mudie transformed what traditionally had been a fairly leisurely trade into a commercially efficient business with exquisitely calculated profit margins and ruthless exploiting of the market. Mudie was the tycoon – some said the tyrant – of the book trade, and soon had publishers, booksellers and authors eating out of his hand. Perhaps because his prejudices were largely those of his public, his exercise of censorship – sometimes quite inconsistently – was not resented, except among authors like Reade and later George Moore (who bitterly attacked him in the 1880s); but, to give Mudie his due, he did offer a wide range of reading – safe, wholesome and entertaining – at prices the public were willing to pay.[13] That was his masterstroke. For a guinea a year a client would take one volume and change it as often as he pleased. Many of course took out several subscriptions, one factor in Mudie's fight to maintain the three-volume novel.

Mudie's Library, then, is the microcosm – and a pretty large one – of what Brown, Jones and Robinson permitted in the sitting-rooms of Maida Vale, or what her ladyship tolerated in the boudoirs of Belgravia. To reduce this outpouring of print into anything like manageable terms I must pursue (with Mrs Malaprop in mind) my allegory on the banks of the Nile and point to many rivers flowing inexorably into a vast lake of fiction. One major course is the historical novel, from Scott's mountainous heights with tributaries from W. H. Ainsworth and G. P. R. James; alongside it, adventure stories on land and sea from Smollett and his successors down to Captain Marryat. This river acquires a European cast from Dumas and Hugo, is naturalised in R. D. Blackmore and William Black, but grows more international and exotic in Ouida, Marie Corelli, Rider Haggard and Anthony Hope. The religious novel runs straight and slow, high and low, on its course from Charlotte Yonge into shoals and eddies of unbelief; the sensation novel erupts from underground from an eighteenth-century Gothic source amid a landscape clearly Brontë-esque, bursting its banks in the sixties with work of Wilkie Collins, M. E. Braddon and their imitators. Between it and the novels of religious doubt or non-belief runs a powerful flow of the supernatural and unseen and the occult.

Then at last we come to the Nile itself, the domestic novel, or what Vineta Colby calls the 'home and family centred novel', which has been at the heart of English fiction since Fanny Burney, Maria Edgeworth and Jane Austen.[14] Here there is the greatest diversity from the discursive currents of Miss Mitford's *Our Village* (1824–32) to more subtle interaction of character and place in Mrs Gaskell or the robust social comedy of Anthony Trollope. Somewhere into this flood comes a Victorian updating of Mrs Gore's novels of fashionable life in the 'silver-fork' fiction of Bulwer Lytton and Disraeli; the equestrian, military and sporting novels of Charles Lever and George Whyte-Melville; and the tales of school and university life which flourished from the forties and combined with comic material (the legacy of the *Punch* journalists) to provide stories which were really jokes and anecdotes strung on a thin line of plot. But, whatever the variation, love shall be lord of all. There must be love in a novel, declared Trollope, and the mainspring of the English novel has been the study of community, family, boy meets girl, against a familiar landscape.[15] In the days of Boot's 'Book Lovers'

Library', I recall the most often heard request across the counter was for a good family story, which meant a love story among recognisably average people in grandly improbable circumstances, or highly glamorised individuals in credibly ordinary settings. In the days of Mudie's Library it was much the same, and to meet demand a forgotten army – mostly female – drove their pens: Katherine Macquoid, Hesba Stretton, Florence Marryat, Annie Thomas, Lady Wood, Amelia Edwards, Dinah Mulock (Mrs Craik), Holme Lee (Harriet Parr), Anne Manning, Emma Marshall, Lynn Linton, Mrs J. H. Riddell (Charlotte Elizabeth Lawson Cowan), Julia Kavanagh, Matilda Betham Edwards, Sarah Tytler, Helen Mathers, Emma Worboise. Mrs Oliphant's recipe for the novel may stand for the genre: 'a happy circle with subtle flavour of incipient love-making'.[16]

There is as much demand as ever for the 'good family story', but today it is most often satisfied by television. The technique of domestic realism characteristic of *Coronation Street* or *Upstairs, Downstairs*, which has enthralled millions, was essentially that of the Victorian popular novelists. Both with varying degrees of sophistication copy from the life; the novelists, indeed, prided themselves on the veracity of their scene and characters drawn from life. Both hold, as the saying had it, the mirror up to nature; and, of course, no one who looks in a mirror ever sees himself in the glass.

A word on the 'domesticity' of the English novel, from Arnold Bennett in a comment on Rhoda Broughton's *Foes in Law,* published in 1900, shows how the term eventually became a stick to beat the Victorians with.[17] Miss Broughton, he says, is the typical novelist of our domesticity, and continues in what appears to be a tone of genial flattery:

Endowed with wit, sentiment, and a discerning eye for some aspects of character, she has during thirty and three years given a modest and refined pleasure, not only to the *petites âmes conjugales*, but also to the great intellects philosophic, scientific, and economic, which in hours of slippered ease graciously 'unbend' themselves over a novel.

What Bennett is out to do is first to patronise, then to annihilate this staple ingredient of Victorian fiction: 'The domestic novel is so called because it is written for, not because it is written about,

domesticity. . . . It is part of the artistic furniture of the home,
like the ballad on the piano and the water-colour on the wall.' It is
always gratifying to see how writers of the Edwardian era reveal
themselves in their scathing treatment of the previous generation,
and as Bennett warms to his task we can appreciate what deep
down was a sense of loss. The Broughton image of life, he says, is
safe and apt for the English home, 'one of the most perfectly
organized microcosms on this planet'.

> It is the fountain of refinement and of consolation, the nursery
> of affection. It has the peculiar faculty of nourishing itself, for it
> implicitly denies the existence of anything beyond its doorstep,
> save the Constitution, a bishop, a rector, the seaside,
> Switzerland, and the respectable poor. And its exclusiveness is
> equalled by its dogmatism. . . . This is right: that is wrong –
> always has been, always will be. This is nice: that is not nice –
> always has been, always will be.

Bennett does well to bring Mr Podsnap to mind, for what would
bring a blush to the cheek of the young person had been
(especially in the 1860s) a significant limitation on what authors
felt free to write about, but in an odd way Bennett tells us more in
the touch of envy he shows towards the domesticity he now
proceeds to debunk: 'The domestic novel was born in the home,
and it has never been past the porch. When its time comes it will
expire of neglect in the attic.' Trivia, superficiality,
sentimentality, smugness – though not hypocrisy – Bennett
concludes, are the hallmarks of the Victorian domestic novel.
This and similar attacks are part of the debunking that Trollope
and his contemporaries also underwent, but it serves to remind
us of a certain wholeness and solidarity about the Victorian age
which the domestic novel embodied.

The authors at the heart of my study are certainly representative
of such strengths as well as some of the indulgence Arnold
Bennett condemns; they are not conspicuous for innovation, art
or depth of insight, but they illustrate levels of interest we do not
customarily take note of in our preoccupation with the first rank
of nineteenth-century novelists. They stand in that ambiguous area
between the novel as art and the novel as commodity; and their

work and attitude raise interesting questions about the commercialisation process, the division of art from entertainment and the emerging problem of cultural standards, of 'us' and 'them', élitism and popularism.

Margaret Oliphant, Rhoda Broughton and James Payn were, of course, stars of the circulating library, and it is to the Mudie empire that the focus of this chapter returns for some conclusions as to who the public was and what it wanted to read. As an index of middlebrow taste, no better guide is available than the annual catalogue of Mudie's Select Library, so I have undertaken surveys at regular intervals from 1861 until the end of the century.

In the first year of my survey, among writers of the lesser rank, the largest holdings are in W. H. Ainsworth (7 titles), Wilkie Collins (7), G. P. R. James (26), Holme Lee (7), Charles Lever (12), Lord Lytton (20), Mrs Oliphant (12) and Charlotte Yonge (6). All except James, who appears to go briefly out of favour in the 1870s, continue to rise numerically, the most dramatic being that heroic drudgery of Mrs Oliphant, whose listing numbers eighty-nine items in the year 1898. Only Emma Marshall's score beats her the same year, with ninety-two.

New stars are continually being introduced, such as G. M. Fenn who reached his peak of popularity at the end of the century, having issued his books anonymously throughout the bulk of his career. As one would expect, a characteristic the more popular novels share is their rapid rise and sudden departure from the catalogues, while better authors, like Trollope, Collins or Lytton, remain consistently in demand. Lever, for example, levelled off in the early seventies with twenty-two titles. There were twenty-six against his name in the 1888 catalogue and twenty-seven in 1898.

A few of Mudie's prejudices show up. Rhoda Broughton is apparently unacceptable until the mid-seventies, although by the end of the century the Library carries sixteen of her books. Miss Braddon, on the other hand, despite her sensationalism, seems to have had her place from 1865, when the catalogue lists seven of her novels. She continues to rise in favour, with thirty-two titles in 1884 and fifty-eight by 1898. Lady (Emma Caroline) Wood, whose novel *Sorrow on the Sea* (1868) caused howls of moral outrage (see p. 59), was represented by six titles in 1876. *Sorrow on the Sea* joined them by 1884, perhaps an instance of Mudie's commercial instincts overcoming his moral scruples.

Examination of the catalogue for 1888 gives a fair sample of what fiction was probably most in demand. To start with there are extensive holdings of children's books, notably those of R. M. Ballantyne (39 titles), Thomas Mayne Reid (23) and W. H. G. Kingston (20). There are the classics: Jane Austen, Charlotte Brontë and Dickens. Thomas Hardy and George Meredith tie with eleven titles. Hardy's inclusion shows greater tolerance in Mudie than might be expected in view of current criticism or Moore's attacks on Mudie's prudishness. American fiction is well represented by Fennimore Cooper, Howells, Twain, Harte, Irving and Hawthorne.

In minor fiction the major interests lie in the sensational novel, the romance or domestic love story, and the adventure tale, either historical or geographically exotic. Miss Braddon with forty-six titles is obviously the queen of crime. Mrs Henry Wood and Edmund Yates also command an audience. Light, wholesome, morally edifying, innocuous romance, often with a religious tinge, must always have been a mainstay of the circulating library, and is evident in the consistent appearance of authors such as Charlotte Yonge, Mrs Craik, Anne Thackeray, Mrs Oliphant, George Macdonald, and a host of imitators.

The third popular sector of reading embraces the adventurous outdoors novel with military, sporting or school and university settings. Ainsworth and James represent the continuity of the historical tradition, but they are topped by Alexandre Dumas, who is represented by thirty titles. Lever's boisterous style of hunting and country-house novel is maintained by James Grant (35 titles), Whyte Melville (22) and Henry Kingsley (16). In a somewhat similar vein Captain Frederick Marryat, star of a much earlier period, continues to attract the reader of adventure and travel. The increasing jingoism as Britain extended its empire is reflected by novels written by ex-officers and old campaigners such as Colonel Philip Meadows Taylor. Rudyard Kipling's reign is just about to begin.

The range of choice is evident and underlines the eclectic nature of the reading public. Middlebrow taste took a good deal in its stride: even continental fiction has its shelves, and while periodicals are constantly lamenting the deplorable flood of French novels Mudie's foreign department stocks Balzac, George Sand, Flaubert and Victor Hugo, although it draws the line at Zola. The latest bestseller jostles with established classic, while the solid core of the library affords a solid, entertaining and sometimes better-than-average body of work that deserves better than Moore's derisive term 'nuvvles'.

Any student of minor fiction must vindicate a task many specialists dismiss as irrelevant to literary criticism. The very terms 'popular fiction' and 'light literature' seem themselves to invalidate serious consideration: if criticism is restricted to a concern with the best that has been thought and expressed, then what have we to do with a fiction by and large conventional and second-rate? The *raison d'être* of the popular novel, after all, is that it address the multitude and by definition not disturb or profoundly engage or break new ground. On the other hand, as I have already begun to indicate, should not different criteria be applied? Does it not, in a similar way to the literature of new, young cultures and the Third World, call for concepts of evaluation different from the traditional literary criticism vocabulary and aesthetic? Quite apart from this methodological question, the value of what the purist might discount as literary exhumation lies in extending knowledge of the literary context in which the great novels existed. As for historical and sociological value, it may be claimed that minor novelists, making up in reportage for what they lack in genuine creativity, offer a view of manners and event that can enlighten us. They are often sound on what lies in front of their eyes – Trollope was long thought major quarry in this respect – and it is notable that Rhoda Broughton is cited in many surveys of the period.

Gordon Ray observed that the great novels were usually studied in English courses at the university as if they were unrelated to anything except other great novels: 'Yet in fact all of them grew out of a tangled undergrowth of minor fiction. An awareness of these initial surroundings often enables the reader to view the surviving masterpieces in an unfamiliar and revealing perspective.'[18] This is particularly so of novels in England during the 1860s and 1870s and the explorer must take this kind of open-minded approach on his map-making journey. It is significant that the *Wellington Index of Victorian Periodicals* among its many virtues is performing the service of broadening the spectrum of inquiry into the Victorian literary landscape. It is salutary for the scholar to be reminded of the legions of half-forgotten names beyond the familiar figures, of writers who may well have had a more immediate impact on readers' outlooks than those most

often cited. Who truly had the ear of the middle-class public who
read the periodicals? The same might be said of the minor
novelists between 1860 and 1880, and thus the scope of this study
suggests a similar kind of broadening of the spectrum of inquiry.
One result of such interests is the growing number of reissues of
minor novels.

An eclectic approach, one attuned to the cultural ambience of
the age in which these popular works appeared, one alive to the
psychological aspects of recreation, one aware of the complex
forces which surround the making and the receiving of a book is
appropriate. As opposed to the exclusiveness of attitude revealed
in Q. D. Leavis's pronouncements on popular fiction in the
1930s, it is pleasing to see that her contemporary Bonamy
Dobrée was not above putting Ouida alongside an essay on
Thackeray.[19] 'It is sinful to take the novel too seriously', as
Anthony Burgess has observed, and it is as well from time to time
to remind ourselves of Virginia Woolf's advice on turning from
'the purer truth of fiction' to the so-called literary rubbish-heap.

> The greater part of any library is nothing but the record of such
> fleeting moments in the lives of men, women, and donkeys.
> Every literature, as it grows old, has its rubbish-heap, its
> record of vanished moments and forgotten lives told in
> faltering and feeble accents that have perished. But if you give
> yourself up to the delight of rubbish-reading you will be
> surprised, indeed you will be overcome, by the relics of human
> life that have been cast out to moulder. It may be one letter –
> but what a vision it gives! It may be a few sentences – but what
> vistas they suggest![20]

Equally, of course, some novels have undoubtedly been
condemned to unmerited oblivion. Where are the books of
yesteryear? The fate, good or bad, of many Victorian novels was
the result not always of sound critical judgement but often of
mere chance, some trivial, adventitious circumstance. Disraeli's
*Lothair* (1870) was a bestseller the day after publication largely
because of speculation as to whom the ex-Prime Minister had
thinly disguised in it. Likewise, a generation earlier Newman's
*Loss and Gain* (1848) gained from its author's name and the
possibility of a few intimate confessions. It is said that *East Lynne*
(1861) was launched on a *Times* review, and Stevenson's *The*

*Strange Case of Dr Jekyll and Mr Hyde* (1886) cannot have been harmed by the Canon of St Paul's basing a sermon on it. *Lorna Doone* (1869) did not take the public fancy at first, but Sampson, Low's one-volume issue in 1871 coincided with a press report linking it to the Marquis of Lorne's family, and sales perked up enormously. A catchy title increased a book's chances of being noticed, then as now. Samuel Warren's *Ten Thousand a Year* (1841) focused upon the magic sum considered feasible for a gentleman's existence. Bulwer Lytton's *What Will He Do with It?* (1859) is one of the many question titles that enticed the public – this one in particular, for Mudie ordered 1000 copies when it appeared.

Such considerations as these emphasise the perils of exploring mass-circulation novels and middlebrow tastes and these are only minor details. Advertising, puffing, which Trollope satirises in *The Way We Live Now*, and the complex organisation of the book trade in general all played their part in making one book stand out over another, with literary merit hardly part of the picture at all. Thus in the sphere of minor novels of the Victorian age, just as with today's fiction, vagaries of the trade present us acutely with the problem of what to look out for and what to pass by; the very presentation, as well as the marketing, of the novel assumes great significance. To take one example, consider the growth of illustration, from the artwork on the covers of yellowbacks, luridly enticing railway travellers to buy something for the journey, to illustrations accompanying serialisation in magazines. What effect this had on widening a book's currency (though book issue was not always accompanied by the original pictures in the serial version) is incalculable, but publishers evidently thought it profitable to engage famous artists, and collaboration between author and illustrator -- Dickens and Hablot Brown ('Phiz') in the thirties and forties, Trollope and Millais in the sixties, come readily to mind – became standard commercial practice.

There are good reasons for seeing 1859–60 as a watershed in popular fiction as well as in other things Victorian.[21] Year by year dynamic changes in science, philosophy, religion and social studies came with startling rapidity, beginning with Darwin's *Origin of Species*. Consider, alongside that earthquake, the after-shocks of the following: Mill's *On Liberty* (1859) and *Utilitarianism*

(1861); Thomas Huxley's address on the progress of science to the Royal Society in 1860, followed by *Man's Place in Nature* (1863) and Spencer's *First Principles* (1862). Samuel Smiles produced *Self Help* in 1859, a secular bible of individual striving, as sacred to the aspiring lower class as *Burke's Peerage* to the gentry. Henry Mayhew's pioneering studies of working-class existence proceed from 1861 to 1863, culminating in *London Labour and the London Poor*. Literature also addressed urgent social questions. Ruskin's essays *Unto This Last* appeared in the *Cornhill* (1860) until editorial squeamishness caused their abrupt cessation, and Matthew Arnold began his inquiries into literature and society with *Culture and Anarchy* (1859).[22]

The harvest of new books is truly phenomenal: in 1859 *Adam Bede*, Dickens's *A Tale of Two Cities* in his new periodical *All the Year Round*, Thackeray's *The Virginians*, Meredith's *The Ordeal of Richard Feverel*, Trollope's *The Bertrams* and his travel book, *The West Indies and the Spanish Main*. In addition came popular works: George Alfred Lawrence's *Guy Livingstone*; Mrs Craik's *A Life for a Life*; James Payn's *The Foster Brothers*; Charles Lever's *Davenport Dunn*; Henry Kingsley's *The Recollections of Geoffrey Hamlyn*; Bulwer Lytton's *What Will He Do with It?* The following year Wilkie Collins's *The Woman in White*, serialised in *All the Year Round*, launched a flood of sensation novels; and also in 1860 came Mrs Henry Wood's *Danesbury House*, Payn's *The Bateman Household*, and Mrs Oliphant's *Lucy Crofton*. Henry Kingsley's *Ravenshoe* was serialised in *Macmillan's* (1861–2), *East Lynne* ran in the *New Monthly Magazine*, soon to be followed by Ouida's *Held in Bondage* in 1862, the year also of Miss Braddon's *Lady Audley's Secret*.

It was as though the melancholy mad elephants of *Hard Times* had discovered even more profitable uses of power in a fiction industry.[23] Appropriately, in 1859–60 Mudie enlarged the premises of his library at New Oxford Street. A rather pathetic coda to this age of glory is recalled by an acrobat in 1861 who like many of his profession was falling upon hard times, the chief cause of which, he lamented, was books and reading mania: 'Nowadays, so many magazines, papers, and cheap books are printed, that the workmen have a taste for reading, and they despise tricks.'[24] Alas, poor Sleary.

A period of greater stability and prosperity lessened the appeal of practical knowledge and information prominent in the fiction of the thirties and forties, and, although a strong market continued for the work of religious authors like Charlotte Yonge and Mrs Craik, reviewers certainly got more impatient with them, and readers sought more of what Altick calls 'comicalities' to solace their evening hours or the tedium of train journeys. Novels High Church, Low Church and No Church claim many Mudie adherents, but the climate of fiction in general is to embrace a more secular morality and, indeed, a more openly epicurean physicality.[25] Popular fiction moves decidedly from Sunday Morning Fervour to Saturday Night Fever.

For all that Miss Yonge's version of the popular hero, Sir Guy Morville in *The Heir of Redclyffe* (1853), established a pattern of Christian virtue and remained one of the most influential novels of the age, and her patient Griselda heroines models of feminine delicacy, a good many female readers with more on their minds than the obligations of Sunday schools and charity visits turned to freer and more challenging avenues opening up around them. They could find in the work of Miss Braddon, or the so-called 'fast' school, an escape from the domestic cage and the role of angel in the house. Even the exoticism of Ouida was preferable to a fiction that saw drama in clergymen wearing beards or smoking or that extolled the Dorcas meeting. Trollope's churchmen grow away from cloistered Barchester until in the *Last Chronicle* his perpetual curate is embroiled in the sensational matter of a forged cheque.

A robust and fleshly materialism is the hallmark of mid-Victorian fiction, underpinned by a generally moral tone, basically decent, vulgar, conservative and unfailingly cheerful. Its quality is best expressed by James Payn's 'high spirits', whether in the tempting borderlands of vice, as Trollope described the contemporary atmosphere of romance, or the opulent world of the adventure story.[26] Much of that high-spirited and heavy merriment in the sphere of domestic fiction derived from the *Punch* model and its sporting parodies, vignettes, cartoons and the facile humour perpetrated by Richard Doyle, Douglas Jerrold, Mark Lemon, Shirley Brooks and Gilbert à Beckett, aided by artists such as George Cruickshank and John Leech. Dickens's own career, after all, was launched on the broken back of a scheme to add copy for a series of comic drawings, while vignettes accompanied by cartoons are at the basis of Thackeray's. Comic sketch, parody and cartoon in prose

were major elements of middlebrow taste in fiction, and even in
the 1880s Bradbury Agnew's list offers reissues of the Handley
Cross sporting-novels, comic books by F. C. Burnand and many
others of the *Punch* school.[27]

The vogue in the forties for school and university tales
continues, no doubt because it presented an opportunity to
exorcise the humiliations of childhood (Thackeray's memories of
Charterhouse as Slaughterhouse, for example, or Trollope's of
Harrow), while it presents a form of *Bildungsroman*, placing the
child in a closed society with its own rules and power struggles,
and seeing him grow through adolescence. The brilliant handling
of this theme by F. Anstey (Thomas Anstey Guthrie) made *Vice
Versa* a bestseller in 1881. It is also a narrative structure
admirably suited as a peg on which to hang picaresque incidents
and anecdotal fragments, as both Frank Smedley and Cuthbert
Bede use it.[28] Bede's tales of Mr Verdant Green published
between 1853 and 1857 caused much amusement in their day,
and its eponymous hero was dubbed 'a kind of undergraduate
Pickwick'. Taine cited it with *Pendennis* and *Tom Brown at Oxford*
as source material for his 'Notes sur l'Angleterre', while Thomas
Seccombe wrote of Bede, 'we can scarcely refuse a certain
measure of genius to the author'.[29]

Concern for higher education as part of the Reform era
acquired even greater urgency among the new middle class with
which this study is concerned, and interest in school stories also
undoubtedly stems from the new wealth. At last merchants and
ironmasters could educate their sons at exclusive academies and
tread the hallowed ground of the ancient universities. Such snob
appeal continued into the school stories of the 1920s and 1930s,
notably the Bunter and Greyfriars books of Frank Richards,
though by this time they were almost exclusively read by
children.

Many of the comicalities people took to read on long railway
journeys or their holidays in Brighton portrayed a cheerful
brutality and anti-intellectualism that leads us to another
important strand of popular reading. The brand of slapstick in
the sporting-*cum*-education stories of Frank Smedley found
a wide public in the forties and fifties and acts as a useful link
with the hearty manliness of Charles Kingsley's muscular
Christianity, as well as its opposite, the muscular blackguardism
of G. A. Lawrence and his successors.

George Alfred Lawrence[30] specialised in heroes mad, bad and dangerous to know. In the same year as Kingsley's *Two Years Ago* (1857), in which the hero, Tom Thurnall, is a gentle giant of a doctor who rescues a Cornish village from cholera, came Lawrence's *Guy Livingstone or Thorough*, which set the public by the ears with its deification of brute strength and selfishness.[31] That it offered something people hungered for is evident in the six editions called for in ten years. Largely forgotten now, this novel is one of those minor landmarks, like Mrs Craik's *John Halifax, Gentleman* (1856) – though entirely opposite in values – remarkable not in itself but for the change of direction it marks. After Guy comes a whole series of attractive brutes, in Rhoda Broughton, Henry Kingsley, Ouida, and the gamut of bestselling authors down to Harold Robbins, Ian Fleming and George Macdonald Fraser, who has taken that notorious cad, Flashman, from *Tom Brown's Schooldays* to play the lead in some immensely popular adventure stories.

'The virile novel', as S. M. Ellis dubbed *Guy Livingstone*, spends much time rippling its pectorals, but is still domestic romance even if it has an aroma of late-night brandy and cigars.[32] What at first sight sounds daring turns out to be rather tame and conservative. The link is perhaps more with Disraeli than Kingsley in this respect. Lawrence's heroes are Young Conservatives no longer in the bloom of life, keeping up a vigorous jogging programme, as it were, but losing the battle of the bulge. That is to say the programme, if there is one, is the quixotic revival of seigneurial values peddled by Disraeli and the Young England movement: strictly conservative, class-conscious and snobbish. Indeed, as one critic has said, 'some looked upon Guy as a medieval hero out of place in the modern world'.[33] Perhaps this was the secret of Lawrence's success after all. Readers of popular fictions like the comfort of the familiar and old-fashioned while being hoodwinked into believing it saucy, daring and entirely up-to-the-minute.

As E. A. Baker says, G. A. Lawrence is at times 'a novelist of no mean dramatic power'.[34] *Guy Livingstone*, indeed, positively drums with horses' hoofs. The theatrical flavour of the story is sustained by its presentation of the 'Dramatis Personae', and like the well-made play it unfolds in a series of events written with great verve but almost entirely without reflection on life or motive. As is generally true of popular fiction, action is all. A consumptive storyteller directs the narrative, first describing Guy's public school, where he defends weaker boys and reads Homer. The Tom Brown atmosphere is enlivened, however, by the hero at seventeen being credited with great 'knowledge of feminine psychology' from flirting with the headmaster's pretty young wife. At Oxford Guy hunts three times a week and despises the scholarly men 'creeping into morning chapel jaded and heavy-eyed, after a debauch over Herodotus or the Stagyrite' and doomed 'to pine, slowly but very surely, in remote curacies' (ch. 3). A high point in the early chapters is a battle between town and gown, Guy's right hand hitting home 'with a dull, smashing sound, which was bad to hear' (ch.4).

What Guy is fighting for remains a mystery except that it represents resistance to the foe, in this case the ugly proletariat, and to the modern reader it looks suspiciously like the sheer joy of fighting as an end in itself. This is an indication of the confusion at the centre of Lawrence's view of life: however much he vaunts the chivalric and heroic basis of his hero's attitude, the overriding emotion conveyed to the reader is exhilaration at hearing bone crunch on bone. Lawrence goes to some lengths to establish a feudal context for his hero's shenanigans, but unfortunately Guy has no Saracens appropriate to his crusade and no Christian ethic to sustain his actions; he is a Victorian rebel without a cause, dangerous and thereby destructive in a way quite at odds with Lawrence's ideas about him.

We follow Guy from Oxford to his estate at Kerton, Northamptonshire, where the hall is decorated with 'countless memorials of chase and war, for the Livingstones had been hunters and soldiers beyond the memory of man' (ch.5). The prose rises exultantly: 'Look at the helmet, with the clean even gap in it, cloven down to the cheek strap – the stout old Laird of Colonsay struck no fairer blow.' Guy himself is magnificent in the uniform of the Life Guards and astride his black charger; his dense moustache 'fell over his lip in a black cascade'. Such a picture and the kind of action that occurs, here and in other Lawrence novels, is most interesting from a cultural standpoint. Surely the readers of the day responded to the anachronistic portrayal of such a man in an age of commerce and machinery. Looking at *Guy Livingstone* in this way one can see how popular literature deals with concerns of the time no less than work by the acknowledged masters; only it presents problems in a simplified, more highly coloured form, more easily accessible, therefore, to the majority and certainly as important for that very reason. On all sides, in the poetry of Tennyson and Browning, or in pre-Raphaelite art, a visionary world of action, heroism, spiritual resolution and fulfilment made more tolerable a world of sordid gain, intractable social problems and the widespread malaise of religious schism or, worse, no religion at all. The average man had begun to face the paradox of greater material well-being for the majority, increasing technological mastery of his environment, and a growing sense of isolation and loss of unity, wholeness, direction. Essentially the twentieth-century *angst* is formulated in mid-Victorian popular literature, in *Guy Livingstone* and its like as well as in *Great Expectations*.

The plot of *Guy Livingstone* centres on Guy's relations with two formidable women, Constance Brandon, to whom he becomes betrothed, and Flora Bellasys, who tries to steal his affections. Flora has 'the provocations of a myriad of coquettes and countesses concentrated in her marvellous eyes' (ch.20), especially as she sinks onto a convenient *causeuse* in the conservatory surrounded by camellias and broad-leaved tropical plants. When Constance stands before the guilty couple, 'calm and pale as the Angel of Death' (ch.21), Guy for once is bereft of speech. The marriage is off and Guy heads for Paris, the rest of the novel being one long penance and descent to death enlivened by occasional punch-ups and a supererogatory subplot.

This is the obvious flaw. Once Othello's occupation is gone, so to speak, Guy has little *raison d'être*. Although he still fights, his heart is not in it, and when called back to the dying Constance, consumed by remorse, Lawrence even tells us his manhood was shattered and he wept; Constance's loyalty had triumphed over Flora. 'Try to grow better' she whispers on her deathbed (ch.28) and, true to the subtitle of the novel, Guy is thorough. Only his mother's lips ever touched Guy's again and that not until 'he had been a corpse an hour' (ch.28). In other novels too, Lawrence tries to bring about the main character's reformation with similarly unsatisfactory results.

An earlier thread of narrative is revived at this point for a touch of sensationalism, but the novel has run out of steam and Guy lasts out in listless apathy and solitude. What Lawrence is attempting to do is graft some kind of noble renunciation and stoicism onto his hero, but in doing so he undermines the integrity of a figure of titanic emotions and Byronic indifference to the storms of fate; the cup of hemlock might have been more appropriate. All the same, it is precisely by scaling down his hero to long-suffering pain and recognition of his former excesses that Lawrence made such appeal to his audience. While ranging over forbidden ground during the course of the story, popular fiction conforms in the resolution of its plot to the moral convictions of its audience; indeed *must* do so if it is not to leave its audience shocked and disapproving. At the last, all must be brought under control, according to conventional attitudes.

In many ways Lawrence typifies certain admirable qualities of the Victorian *zeitgeist*. His heroes are the pattern adventurers of generations of later popular entertainment, his heroines the forerunners of many rebels and *femmes fatales*. His books are romantic parables of daring and conquest in reaction to the mediocrity, muddle and moral complexity of his age. They are lurid prose versions of some of Tennyson's poems. Lawrence himself was something of a Ulysses, dreaming that

> something ere the end
> Some work of noble note, may yet be done,
> Not unbecoming men that strove with gods.

His was that restless yearning that took men like Henry Kingsley and Laurence Oliphant abroad as special correspondents, that sent Speke to search for the source of the Nile, and hundreds of younger men to the goldfields of Australia and the backwoods of British Columbia. A Tennysonian note is often present in his work. As he puts it in *Sword and Gown*: 'Shall we stay sullenly at home when all the world is flocking to the tournament? . . . A corner in the cushioned gallery is left to us still' (ch.3).

Sustaining this high style with panache he sounds like Alexandre Dumas or such writers of heroic drama as Dryden and Otway, and at this level it is easy to see why he caught the public imagination. He satisfied, as the best popular writers do, a hunger for emotion, action and uncomplicated response. It is not real life, but life as the harried, bewildered and unsophisticated reader would like it to be – simple, shaped and intense. Other authors dealt with in this study conform in their different ways to the formula, but before examining their work in detail it is time to study the mechanics of the fiction industry and critical responses in general to popular authors between 1860 and 1880.

# 2   The Fiction Industry

*There's writers and there's authors. The writers are the ones that make the money.*

Mickey Spillane, *Dick Cavett Show* (28 May 1981)

The Victorian fiction industry is a consequence of population growth, social progress, printing technology, and the visionary drive of many bookmen. The glittering prizes of bestselling novels had begun to be won early in the century by Sir Walter Scott, but Scott in all his glory, noted the *Saturday Review* in the mid-1870s, was not to be compared with Dickens for popular success. We did it, said the *Review* in awe, as though eyeing some monster devouring its genius; we made him, we the public, and we helped destroy him.[1] The book revolution had by now reached alarming proportions, said another gloomy *Saturday* reviewer in 1878, and was growing in such ratio that within a generation or two Russell Square would need to be annexed to the British Museum.[2] Sir Walter Scott, according to James Payn, observed to a fellow author, 'You and I came just in the nick of time'.[3] Scott foresaw, amongst other changes, the formidable competition of the market place (though he had no reason to fear it at the time). Would he do so well today? Payn asks. In his essay 'The Literary Calling and its Future' in the December 1879 issue of *Nineteenth Century*, Payn concluded that for all the difficulties 'light literature' is still a pleasing calling: 'Its promise is golden, and its prospects are boundless.'[4]

While the older men adapted slowly, younger booksellers and publishers were ready to seize their opportunities. The 'retailers', as Scott once loftily referred to them, were now a new breed, adapting methods of the factory system, raising capital, advertising, marketing, vying with one another, streamlining with new machinery to meet a potential market of colossal dimensions. William and Robert Chambers, John Cassell and

23

Charles Knight were the pioneers of cheap literature. Henry Colburn and Richard Bentley launched cheap editions of both standard classics and contemporary novels by authors of note, and their example was followed by Hurst and Blackett, Routledge and others. As the industry got into high gear in the fifties and sixties the broad thrust of major houses – Blackwood, Macmillan, and Smith, Elder – greatly to the health of the trade and of authors, was largely in the hands of innovative young businessmen. This chapter is concerned with aspects of this remarkable phase of industrialisation and its effects on popular fiction.

Reprints and cheaper issues were one means by which the book trade expanded, although initial printings were generally small (except for the biggest names) and the expensive three-volume novel dominated the market for most of the century. Colburn's fortunes were founded on the three-decker retailing at half-a-guinea a volume, 31s. 6d. the set, and Colburn had in his stable profitable authors like G. P. R. James and Lord Lytton and was always seeking out bestsellers. Besides operating a library in New Burlington Street, he speculated in periodicals such as the *New Monthly Magazine*, whose editors included W. Harrison Ainsworth. Publishers had to diversify and constantly look for new talent and new outlets. Many, like Colburn, offered cheap fiction in select libraries or works of modern novelists. Revenue was also available from reprints, retailing generally at six shillings after the three-volume publication, a practice established with Bentley's Standard Novels in 1831. This series alone had 126 volumes by the fifties.

Richard Bentley was another highly successful businessman with a gift for talent-spotting. One of his shrewdest strokes was to secure Dickens as editor of his magazine, *Bentley's Miscellany*, which made the serial story its principal feature and launched many popular novelists, especially after 1859, when the magazine became *Temple Bar* under the editorship of his son George, tireless promoter of many bestselling authors, including Trollope, Wilkie Collins, Mrs Henry Wood, Mrs Riddell, Hawley Smart, Rhoda Broughton and Marie Corelli. While older houses such as Longman's adapted more slowly to the aggressive business methods required by the age, Bradbury & Evans, Chapman & Hall, Blackwood, Macmillan, and Smith, Elder vied for larger shares of the trade with varying degrees of caution. Authors' fees rose in consequence. George Smith's fairness to his authors became legendary: launching the *Cornhill Magazine* in 1860 he was so delighted by sales that he doubled Thackeray's salary as editor. Smith has his place among the triumvirate of mid-Victorian publishers along with John Blackwood and Alexander Macmillan.

Attempts to reach the new public for whom the guinea-and-a-half book was too dear led to enormous growth of periodicals from 1859.[5] The *Cornhill*, launched in January 1860, closely on the heels of *Macmillan's Magazine* (and the weeklies *All the Year Round* and *Once a Week*) had a host of imitators: *Good Words* (1860), *St James's Magazine* (1861) *Victoria* (1863), *Temple Bar* and *Argosy* (1865), *Belgravia* (1866), *Tinsley's Magazine, St Paul's* and *Broadway* (1867). Magazines were often vehicles for the stories of their editors: Trollope in *St Paul's*, Miss Braddon in *Belgravia*, Mrs Henry Wood in *Argosy*. Well established journals like *Chambers's*, the *Dublin University Magazine* and *Blackwood's*, which had greatest prestige, promoted not only stories but useful general discussion about fiction.

Horse-trading among publishers enlivened the trade considerably. Richard Bentley published the *New Monthly* for Colburn and from about 1863 Ainsworth's *New Monthly* as well. George Bentley was miffed, though, when Helen Mathers, whose *Comin' thro the Rye* his firm had launched, set up the *Burlington Magazine* to compete with his own *Temple Bar* (one of his most valuable properties), adding insult to injury by using in her title the firm's street address.[6] Like Bentley, the Tinsleys knew full well the spin-offs from their journals in the form of cut-price advertising, even if the magazine ran a loss: 'What cheaper advertisement can I have for twenty-five pounds a month', boasted Tinsley.[7] He himself had his stable of authors, including as editor Edmund Yates, prolific writer of sensation novels. With sales among the better journals of about 10,000, the publishers tapped a valuable market.

George Smith's *Cornhill Magazine* provides a touchstone of the magazine market and its rise and fall an interesting commentary on changing tastes.[8] A cut above *All the Year Round*, it set its sights on a cultivated general readership. Although fiction was its staple commodity, when Thackeray invited a story from Trollope he indicated that it would also be a journal of ideas and comment offering more solid fare than the sweetmeats of the novel trade.

But it was serialised fiction that kept the magazine afloat and helped widen the reading public. Its soul, said Sir Edward Cook at the time of its jubilee in 1910, was the spirit of that humane culture Arnold believed in.[9]

The *Cornhill* had a succession of distinguished editors after Thackeray, including a committee comprising G. H. Lewes, Frederick Greenwood and Edward Dutton Cook with Smith as chairman (1864-8), Leslie Stephen (1871-82), James Payn (1882-96), John St Loe Strachey (1896-7) and Reginald Smith (1898-1900). Stephen tried to maintain the original level of information and discussion, but the seventies already reflected a change in public taste towards the gossip and personality journalism of the *World* (edited by Edmund Yates) and the illustrated papers. When Payn took over, circulation had fallen to around 12,000, a decline he attributed to 'the failure of the literary and especially the classical essay to attract the public'.[10] Payn, like Yates and Sala, was a shrewd journalist with a fairly low opinion of public intelligence, but even he could not halt the drop in sales. Lowering the price from a shilling to sixpence did not help either. Tit-bits journalism was on the rise as the gulf between novel and commercial fiction widened. Payn himself, ever adaptable, ended his career writing a weekly column for the *Illustrated London News*.

In the heyday of the magazines providing what Walter Bagehot called 'the light frivolous style of merely amusing literature',[11] the serialisation of a good novel in a leader such as *All the Year Round*, with a circulation at 120,000 (300,000 for Christmas numbers), or the *Cornhill*, averaging 84,000 in its first two years, could do wonders for an author's reputation. Trollope's career really began to take off when *Framley Parsonage* came out in instalments in the *Cornhill* from January 1860 to April 1861. It was a mutual benefit. James Payn's *Lost Sir Massingberd* (1865) increased sales of *Chambers's Magazine* by 20,000.[12] In 1870 *Cassell's Magazine* raised its circulation dramatically to over 70,000 with Wilkie Collins's *Man and Wife*.[13]

James Payn lived through all these changes and saw the emergence of other outlets for the journalist authors in serialised novels in newspapers, and country journals buying rights of stories already published. The literary industry, he declared by the end of the century, had many branches:

Travels are 'gutted' and form articles in magazines, illustrated by the original plates; lectures, after having served their primary purpose, are published in a similar manner; even scientific works now appear first in the magazines which are devoted to science before their mission of 'popularizing' their subject.[14]

At the end of his career, busily involved with Besant and the *Society of Authors,* Payn dreamed of new conquests. A scribbled note among his papers is a blueprint for a grand literary journal, for which he planned the support of an array of big names including Hardy, Rider Haggard, Blackmore, Barrie and Conan Doyle.[15]

The growth of illustration in periodicals is also part of the pattern of popular fiction, although to what extent it increased readership is a moot point. Certainly it rapidly increased after the great era of wood engraving associated with the forties and fifties, and, with developments in printing technology and artists readily available, commercially minded publishers obviously found it worthwhile to add illustration even to the most ephemeral novel appearing in *Good Words* or *Temple Bar, Chambers's Magazine* or *Macmillan's.* Artists such as Frederick Leighton, Arthur Hughes and William Orchardson were quite willing to illustrate for the popular magazines, while publishers found they could provide pictorial accompaniment to text more cheaply as mass production cut costs. Where in the forties and fifties a publisher might see roughly £120 of the £400 spent on a 30,000 run of a monthly serial going for illustrations, by the sixties his costs were cut by one-third.[16] Electrotype casts were capable of rendering the artist's original with little loss of clarity. In the case of John Everett Millais's work, for example, his illustrations to Trollope's novels for the *Cornhill Gallery* (1864) are by no means inferior to the wood-block originals.[17]

Although publishers anticipated a vast public, the high cost of novels kept buyers down, so it was by serialisation in periodicals, part issues, and the circulating libraries that readership grew prodigiously in the sixties.[18] From some 50,000 in the 1830s (Walter Besant's conservative estimate), the reading public may certainly be considered to have quadrupled within thirty years.

Mudie's income from subscriptions amounted to £40,000 a year.[19] Walter Houghton notes too that over 25,000 journals of all kinds were produced to satisfy the Victorian craving for the printed word.[20]

Still, actual book sales were quite low until the eighties.[21] Scott's success was remarkable for its date: *Waverley* (1814), 11,000 in collected editions of his romances, 1820–9; *Rob Roy* (1818), 10,000 in its first appearance and over 40,000 by 1836. *Adam Bede* (1859) achieved 3350 in three-volume issue and 11,000 in the cheaper two-volume issue. *The Mill on the Floss* (1860) sold 6000 in its first three months. Only when considering a novel's reissues over a long period can sales be reckoned in six figures, unlike today's instant millions for bestsellers. Among the stars of the popular market a century ago, however, Mrs Henry Wood's novels were said to have topped the 2½ million mark by 1898, *Danesbury House* selling 100,000 copies in her lifetime, *East Lynne* 1 million. Mrs Craik's *John Halifax, Gentleman* had sold 250,000 by 1897.[22] An interesting case of the value of keeping a minor bit of merchandise alive and waiting out the market is to be found in the case of Cuthbert Bede. The Verdant Green novels, bound in one volume, had sold 100,000 by 1870, although Bede had had a hard job finding a publisher until Nathaniel Cooke of the Strand took it for one of his 'Shilling Books for the Rail' in 1853. The book ran to five editions between 1900 and 1912 and was still around in 1925. The author himself received £350 in total, a not unusual situation in dealings between author and publisher.[23]

Railway bookstalls did wonders for the trade. Pioneered by W. H. Smith in 1846, they covered the country's principal railways by the early sixties, and publishers like Chapman & Hall were quick to capitalise on another market with cheap reprints known as yellowbacks. George Routledge, who had founded his firm on second-hand books, started a Railway Library and others followed suit. Apart from the standard novels, parlour libraries and collective editions, pioneered by Bentley, Colburn, Longman, Chapman & Hall, and Routledge, there were ventures like Ward and Lock's Shilling Volume Library offering books by M. E. Braddon, G. A. Sala, Percy Fitzgerald and Hain Friswell. Even the smallest firms, like Groombridge & Sons, cashed in on the cheaper market, with a series at 2*s.* 6*d.* pushing the much-read *Footsteps to Fame: A Book to Open Other Books* by Hain Friswell, and similar gems. Their Magnet Series 'For Summer Days and Winter Nights' comprised eight volumes cloth bound, with seven stories in each for 2s. 6d. Among its treasures were stories by Mrs S. C. Hall and Mary Howitt. On all sides then, the market boomed for men with new ideas for costing and marketing.

Edward Tinsley, like many of his contemporaries, came into publishing via bookselling. By 1866 he saw the future in 'books appealing directly to the million, rather than in the publication of books intended mainly for the Circulating Libraries', but on the verge of throwing in his lot with James Virtue he died suddenly, and his brother (with £4000 of debts in the company) decided to follow the library route.[24] Typical of the more buccaneering businessmen of the time, William liked working in his shirtsleeves and, according to George Moore, conducted his business as he dressed himself, sloppily: 'a dear, kind soul, quite witless and quite h-less'.[25] For all that he dropped his aitches, he took Moore's first novel, *A Modern Lover* (1883), and his flair for collecting popular writers brought the company M. E. Braddon, Trollope, Mrs Henry Wood, Wilkie Collins, Rhoda Broughton, G. A. Sala, William Black, Ouida, James Payn and many more. Edward, an enthusiast for Thomas Hardy, had published his first novel, *Desperate Remedies* (1871).

The Tinsley brothers may not have been the soundest businessmen, but they are a good example of the thrust of the new commercial publishing in which hunches were played, risks taken and deals with authors set up in ways that shocked the older men. By astute bargaining the Tinsleys secured G. A. Lawrence's copyrights on *Guy Livingstone*, *Sword and Gown* and *Barren Honour* from the Parkers (John W. Parker, Son and Bourne). Edward Tinsley desperately wanted Lawrence's next book, and, since the Captain was always short of money, took him for drinks at the Gaiety bar, where he dangled a cheque for £900 in front of him. He got the contract. Tinsley later said that he actually paid Lawrence £1000 for the novel.[26]

A good deal of flexibility in bargaining (to give it a euphemistic interpretation) was practised in the scramble for authors and sales. For example, in the case of Hardy's *Under the Greenwood Tree* (1872), Edward Tinsley bought copyright for £30, publishing in two volumes which did not attract much attention. Next he tried it with illustrations, and again it failed to catch on. Nor did a two-shilling edition, despite good reviews. With Hardy's next book, *A*

*Pair of Blue Eyes*, he tried serialisation in *Tinsley's Magazine*, followed by three-volume issue in 1873. Once more results were disappointing, so when Hardy came and told him he had an offer of £300 for *Far from the Madding Crowd* (1874) Tinsley let him go. As luck would have it, it was at this point that Hardy's career began to improve.

Publishing at mid-century, given the competition and risks, put a heavy burden on the businessmen. There was little means of forecasting a hit or a miss. Royal Gettman observed, 'More often than not bestsellers just happen', although then as now some publishers developed a technique for protecting their investment and others had the enviable flair of recognising what would catch on.[27] As Victoria Glendinning has put it, what the successful popular author and publisher have is 'the wit to feel the tug of kites flying in the common imagination, to pull on the strings and haul them in'.[28]

The degree to which an author should be nursed along in the hope of an eventual bonanza brought out the gambling-spirit in publishers. William Black is a case in point. Tinsley suffered losses on *Love or Marriage* (1868), broke even on *In Silk Attire* (1869), but lost again on *The Monarch of Mincing Lane* (1871). Over lunch at Simpson's he gingerly put up a proposal that the next book, assuming it succeeded, should be contracted in such a way as to soak up the loss on the earlier novels. Black replied, 'I'll see you damned first', and they parted on bad terms. 'Just my luck!' Tinsley said, for *A Daughter of Heth* (1871) gave Sampson, Low a profitable author henceforth and put Black on the high road to success.[29]

Equally, where luck was with the publisher and the book turned into a runaway success the author might have lost copyright for a modest sum. This was the case with Helen Mathers's *Comin' thro the Rye* (1875), for which George Bentley had made a standard payment of £200. After sixteen editions by 1898 it had realised some £3000 for the publisher.[30] The authoress thought it only fair that some kind of bonus was due to her, so she asked for financial help towards her son's university education. Richard Bentley answered sternly, 'If I sold a horse or a picture tomorrow for an agreed amount I should never receive another penny even if it won the Derby or was discovered to be an Old Master.'[31] Unanswerable logic. Yet it underlines the plight of the novelists, particularly women, at this time.

Then, as now, much hung upon the judgement of editorial readers. Miss Geraldine Jewsbury, herself a minor novelist, caused the firm to lose Ouida's *Under Two Flags* (1867), when the opportunity had arisen to win the tempestuous authoress from Chapman & Hall. On the whole, however, Miss Jewsbury was a shrewd adviser. She at once saw the potential of *East Lynne*, which George Meredith for Chapman & Hall twice rejected (he also turned down *Lady Audley's Secret* and Samuel Butler's *Erewhon*).[32] Towards other female novelists she seems sometimes to have been a trifle waspish. She completely failed to see anything original in Rhoda Broughton, declaring that *Not Wisely, but Too Well* was *Guy Livingstone* without the talent, and as a result the novel went to Tinsley Brothers. George Bentley followed his own judgement when *Cometh Up as a Flower* was brought to his notice. In 1875 he paid Tinsley £250 for the copyright and stock of *Not Wisely*, and henceforth had Miss Broughton under his wing. Altogether he issued twelve of her novels, which brought the firm considerable profit.

Tinsley had his lucky breaks too. When Miss Jewsbury caused Bentley to haggle with Miss Braddon over prices he lost her to Tinsley, who was confident enough to offer her £2000 each for a two-year right to two of her novels. He made a fortune from *Lady Audley's Secret* and commemorated this extremely lucrative murderess by attaching her name to the mansion he acquired.

Both as reader and editor James Payn furthered the careers of several writers, but he too made his gaffes, one of which concerned the extremely successful *John Inglesant* (1881) by J. H. Shorthouse, published by Macmillan after Payn on behalf of Smith, Elder had rejected it. One day long after the novel had gone through fifty editions, Payn happened to come across a gossip item announcing that Smith, Elder had missed a valuable commodity. Having by now completely forgotten his own responsibility in the deal, Payn stormed into George Smith's office suggesting that he would write to the perpetrator of this gross libel. Smith calmed him down and then told the truth, sparing his feelings as much as he could by adding, 'I don't blame you; I think it even now a dullish book.' Payn said later, 'I have never heard a more creditable story, even of a Divine', and he dedicated his reminiscences, *Gleams of Memory*, to this prince among publishers.[33]

More orthodox publishers than Tinsley safeguarded themselves with a low first printing (usually about 1000 copies) and, as John Sutherland points out, the three-decker offered a built-in chance of survival through the chain of supply, including trade allowances to booksellers, the Mudie bulk-purchase system, and the stable commercial framework under which marketing was carried on.[34] With copyrights often sold outright, a publisher could risk a loss, calculating that in the long term he would eventually back a blockbuster or recoup his investment on reissues of an average, or even initially poor, starter. Economics apart, most publishers played fair, putting up with tantrums, nursing talent and even at times offering sound advice. Certainly George Smith, Alexander Macmillan and John Blackwood are outstanding in this respect.

As an example of one such friendly collaboration between author and publisher consider Mrs Oliphant's career.[35] Her long association with Blackwood's began with her third novel, *Katie Stewart* (1852), of which she received the proofs appropriately on her wedding-day. At twenty-eight she was, she said modestly, 'a sort of general utility woman' to Blackwood's, but the firm's generosity towards her was considerable and she was eventually to repay it by her tribute *Annals of a Publishing House: William Blackwood and his Sons* (1897). Four early novels appeared in *Blackwood's Magazine*: *Katie Stewart* (1852), *A Quiet Heart* (1854), *Zaidee* (1854) and *The Athelings* (1857). None sold well and at least one proved a distinct liability. *Zaidee*, which had a printing of just over 1500 at a cost of merely £400, sold only 496 copies. John Blackwood covered his costs, but half the edition was still on his shelves six years later.[36] Undeterred by a string of unsuccessful books, he offered her £1500 for the relatively short novel *The Perpetual Curate*, an extravagance some of the firm thought, but it proved the turning-point in Mrs Oliphant's career, and the timely help when her life was miserably beset so heartened her that while *The Doctor's Family* was running in *Blackwood's Magazine* she wrote cheerfully to the publisher in November 1861 promising enough stories to make the series Chronicles of Carlingford.

Mrs Oliphant's struggle to make a living by her pen reflects the odds against women, odds over which so many of them nevertheless triumphed. At the start of her career her work was done amid the household chores and her mother's ceaseless chatter. She once said, 'I don't think I have ever had two hours undisturbed (except at night, when everybody is in bed) during my whole literary life.'[37] A lifetime's drudgery of book-making and hack work due to the tragedies of her life undoubtedly damaged her talent and gave her a jaundiced view of her contemporaries' success. Although she was scrupulously fair towards them, the rewards obtained by Trollope, Payn and Mrs Craik puzzled her:

> I saw Anthony Trollope's table of his earnings in his memoirs, it gave me anything but an agreeable sensation, for his worst book was better paid than my best. . . . Mr Payn, you know, speaks in the same large way of what he gets. I can't for my part understand why he should get two or three times as much as I do – but I suppose simply it is because the public likes him better.[38]

Mrs Oliphant was doomed to unceasing toil without ever achieving financial security. Even her journalism failed to turn out as well as it did for Miss Braddon or Mrs Henry Wood, both of whom had magazines to edit. Tired of the burden of constant writing she approached G. L. Craik of *Macmillan's* on Christmas Eve 1880, almost begging for permanent editorial work:

> But as I am growing old I have more and more desire for a regular quarter day, a regular occupation, and so much money certainly coming in. . . . This is where men have such a huge advantage over us, that they generally have something besides their writing to fall back upon for mere bread and butter.[39]

In 1881 there was talk of a weekly paper from Macmillan to fill the gap caused by journals increasingly devoted to gossip. Once again Mrs Oliphant was disappointed, and she had to turn to another book, the charming *Makers of Venice* (1887).

Certainly Mrs Oliphant was right about the advantages men had, although it often seems to be a case of male novelists more forcibly driving home their advantage. William Tinsley found himself facing a draft contract for *The Moonstone* which he found 'a regular corker; it would pretty well cover the gable of an ordinary-sized house'.[40] He was to pay a sum down for the first printing and so much for every 250 copies thereafter. Tinsley admitted he did fairly well by that, though 'nothing to shout about in those days'. When Collins thought the three-volume sale was about over he asked for another edition on the same terms. This Tinsley declined. Then the printer came along suggesting he would break up the type, but Tinsley, well up in tricks of the trade, pointed out that he could recognise his own type and would make sure that no other edition used it. A few days after this, he noted gleefully, Master Wilkie's people came back to accept *his* terms for a new edition.

James Payn was also a sound businessman greatly respected on this score by authors and publishers alike. Like Trollope, whom he greatly admired, he followed a long apprenticeship before he reached a comfortable eminence. In the first year of his marriage, he recalled, his income from writing had been £32 15s.[41] An early lesson came from W. H. Ainsworth, to whom as editor of *Bentley's Miscellany* he sent some 'Ballads from English History'. Ainsworth thanked him but regretted the magazine could afford no *pecuniary* remuneration; Payn speculated what other form remuneration might have taken.[42] W. H. Wills, the assistant editor of *Household Words*, was more generous, offering three guineas for Payn's first published article in prose, a somewhat pugnacious first-hand account of life at the military cadet school at Woolwich.[43] The irate governor demanded that Dickens release the name of his contributor, presumably with horse-whipping in prospect. It was just the sort of situation Dickens relished. He was politely adamant in safeguarding anonymity, and on meeting Payn delighted with the high spirits of his new recruit.

Years of steady novel production made Payn a celebrity and late in life he reckoned his income had averaged £1500 annually for over thirty-five years.[44] His inside knowledge of the trade made him an astute but always fair-minded negotiator, whose name to a contract was a guarantee of punctuality and good value. William Tinsley said of Payn, 'there never seemed an atom of selfishness in his nature'.[45] No publisher, said Tinsley, had cause to regret a business transaction with him. He was particularly watchful about overseas rights, and was shocked to learn of Charles Lever's confession that he had never received sixpence from sale of advance sheets abroad. Payn noted,

To me, whom circumstances compelled to look after such

matters pretty keenly, and who, if I had not 'surveyed mankind from China to Peru' with an eye to advanced sheets, had 'placed' them on occasion even in Japan (at Yokohama), this neglect seemed inexplicable.[46]

Even Trollope, it surprised Payn to hear, 'never got a farthing from the Americans' save £50 for *Ayala's Angel*. But Payn became adept at placing stories, and immersed himself in professional issues, especially Walter Besant's campaigns for authors' rights.

A large correspondence at the University of Texas concerning the Authors' Syndicate includes many of Payn's letters to W. H. Colles, who was in charge of the Syndicate's business from offices in the Strand.[47] While editor of the *Cornhill* in the 1890s, Payn is always urging Colles to get his stories published in America. On one occasion he is keen to secure Harper's interest but anxious not to upset his English publisher: 'I would not like to leave my friend, Chatto, except for material reasons. He gives me £50 for a collection of stories.' In another letter he reports a short story of some 3000 words completed for *Vanity Fair* and already placed in America, but he wants it marketed in the colonies. He advises Colles of a new magazine promoted by Baron Tauchnitz and says, 'the Authors' Syndicate might like to have this new string to their bow'. On another occasion he expresses anxiety over a novel for Heinemann: 'What I want is £1,200 down for the whole rights: this gives me a bit more than I got for *A Word to the Wise*, before the American copyright was originally prepared, but I am sick of these delays and doubts.' Payn thought himself hard done by in the counter offer of £1000, including royalties on an American edition, and the inference is that he wanted American rights negotiated separately.

Ouida's dealings with publishers were notorious, but the extent of her tergiversation has never been fully documented.[48] Her first novel, *Held in Bondage*, went to Tinsley for £50 after Chapman & Hall had turned it down, but at some stage she offered the manuscript also to Smith, Elder.[49] Ouida began her career with 'Dashwood's Drag; or the Derby and What Came of It' in *Bentley's Miscellany* for April and May 1859, and basking in Ainsworth's praise went on to produce seventeen more tales, with racy titles like 'The Donkeyshire Militia', 'Belles and Blackcock' and 'The Two Viscounts'. On 2 December 1859 she wrote to George Smith offering her services for the new *Cornhill*. Two years later, when *Granville de Vigne* was appearing in the *New Monthly Magazine*, she wrote again to George Smith on 25 February 1863 offering it to him, and two months later advised him that sheets were being despatched after much delay due to printers' procrastination. She had marked passages for abridgement 'which, while in no wise injuring the work will I have carefully calculated bring it within the orthodox limits of the 3-volume issue'. She continued, 'The highest opinion has been formed by many literary men upon "de Vigne" who have pronounced it certain to make a hit. If you should consider the title not a good selling one I should be happy to add another at your suggestion.' The title was indeed changed, to *Held in Bondage*. As to terms, she wrote

> this being the first lengthy work I have put forth (having hitherto limited myself to magazine papers, all of which I may mention met with the most signal success with the Press and the Public;) I would suggest that we should follow the usual course; – £50 paid down to me at once, not to be returned in any event; and a half share of the profits to me afterwards. The copyright of the Work to be yours for one or two years, during which period however you should never issue it in any cheaper form than a shilling edition, into which form I should wish it to pass as soon as the Library Edition has been sold off; at the end of that time the copyright to revert back to me.

Assured of fame after *Held in Bondage* appeared, Ouida attached herself to a repentant Chapman, who published her next fourteen novels, including the highly acclaimed *Under Two Flags* (1867). The fourteenth, *Ariadne* (1877), was issued jointly with Chatto & Windus, which caused the authoress to explode with anger at what she took to be publishing chicanery. She distrusted publishers henceforth, writing to her literary adviser and friend, J. Anderson Rose, on 27 July 1884, 'I am very distressed about everything and in these days publishers play sadly into one another's hands to get novels cheap. Has Chatto replied to you about the difference of his present offer with last year's terms?' She was then having a battle with Chatto over the phrase 'American newspaper rights' in a contract, which she feared would jeopardise book publication in America. She asked Rose to oversee the sale of a manuscript to Tillotson and Sons which she had negotiated at £15 per 1000 words. She had worked out that she was due £220, but warned Rose not to hand over the manuscript without getting the cheque, imploring him to make haste as her situation in Florence was desperate: 'if I do not obtain some money at once I shall be turned out of this house as my rent is long overdue and Italians have no mercy where money is in question.'

Ouida constantly jousted with Chatto over contracts, often taxing him with injuring the sale of her three-volume publications by bringing out cheap editions too soon. Chatto would not put up with that and once replied tartly (18 April 1883),

> We can assure you that so far from injuring the sale of the Library editions of your novels by issuing the cheap edition too quickly the 12 months interval which we allow on your stories is longer than generally allowed by other authors. We do not see that the issue of the cheap edition after so long an interval as 12 months can be blamed for the fact that three months after the publication of the library editions of *Friendship* [1878], *In Maremma* [1882], *A Village Commune* [1881] the sale entirely ceased leaving us in each case with a heavy balance of unsold copies.

Nothing daunted, Ouida set out terms for her new book in a letter of 26 July 1884, with undiminished zest. The draft arrangement shows how involved matters were becoming between author and publisher. Chatto offered £1000, payable at £50 per month for ten months with the balance on completion. Although willing to allow Ouida rights on the Tauchnitz reissue and American book rights Chatto wanted all other rights to serial publication, including American newspaper rights. Ouida balked at this, declaring that once the story had been serialised in America no publisher would issue it as a book.

Ouida was constantly irritated at the necessity of having her books appear first in serial form, and she asked in October 1877 that Chatto would write into her contract that he would never again put any of her work into serial, and that before selling her copyrights he would allow her first option. Chatto outwitted her on the serialisation matter in April 1883 by offering her £1000 for English book rights and £1350 if she also would accept serial publication. His letter continued,

As regards the American market we believe that we should not be able to obtain so much as Mr Lippincott & Co. pay you direct. Piracy is rampant there and we find by experience that the authors of very few of the most popular works of fiction make more than a complimentary acknowledgement of about £20.

Chatto went on to advise Ouida that demand for all library editions was declining and thus the publishers were obliged to fall back on the serial form. Rather sardonically he observed, 'We admire your self-sacrifice to your high views concerning the evils of the serial form.' To sweeten the pill, however, he recommended ten instalment payments of £100, 'the decrease not to be taken as a standard for future arrangements', and he threw in a bonus of £25 on every hundred copies sold of the library edition beyond the first 1500 copies.

Thoroughly piqued, Ouida set about getting back into Chapman's good graces, enlisting Rose to sound out possibilities. The prospect of *Princess Napraxine* (1884) being a disastrous loss for Chatto spurred her on, and she wrote to Chapman on 26 July 1884, with her customary arrogance:

> I quite agree with you that English Literature is much hurt by the idiotic 3 vol system and by the flood of second rate novels; but in my own case there is no kind of diminution of reputation. I do not think that my late works have been published with judgment. Mudie complained in a letter I saw of being unable to gratify his subscribers' demands for *Moths* [1880] as C. & W. had hastily broken up the type, & no copies were to be had for 'love or money'. With *Wanda* [1883] which delighted every one including your 'Fortnightly' they wholly failed to make the sale they might have done; and they hurry each work in to the cheap edition so rapidly that it is a wonder the Libraries take any of the 3 vol form.

Admitting she had been on good terms with Chatto, she could not resist adding that she would have had even better sums from them 'if you had not most unluckily for me, given them information as to the terms you made with me' – the old paranoia about publishers once more – and she concluded with a flourish, 'George Meredith is a much older writer than I and most unpopular – Would you like a serial of mine to follow his? – The new writers are all plagiarists and not one of them has any genius.' Ouida's genius, however, Chapman hardly wanted back, so she continued writing under a variety of other imprints up to her death.

As these dealings show, Ouida's confidence, tenacity and aggressiveness served her admirably. Mrs Oliphant was much too reasonable (and modest) to do so well. Rhoda Broughton survives somewhere between. She began her career with an offer of £250 for *Not Wisely, but Too Well* (1867), and for her third book, *Red as a Rose is She* (1870), received £600 (serial rights included). Bentley treated her generously, with much smoothing down when criticism rankled. He paid her £800 for *Good-bye, Sweetheart!* (1872) and £1000 for *Nancy* (1873) and his investment began to pay off handsomely.[50] By 1872–4 some 10,500 copies of *Cometh Up as a Flower* had been sold, and, even though thirteen of her copyrights were put up at £2000 when the House of Bentley sold out, her new publisher, Macmillan, derived more profits from reissues.[51]

Some of the publishing hurdles can be understood by looking at Miss Broughton's start more closely. *Not Wisely* was written some time between 1862 and 1864 (Ethel Arnold suggests from November 1863 to 1864[52]). By January 1865, at any rate, she was reading portions of the manuscript to her uncle, Sheridan Le Fanu, who serialised it in the *Dublin University Review* and began negotiations with George Bentley. Miss Jewsbury vehemently opposed publication: 'I am sorry you have accepted it & I am sorry it is going to be published at all – the interest is of highly coloured & hot blooded passion & the influence is pretended to be quenched by a few drops of lukewarm rose water sentimentality.' She criticised its poor construction, crude execution and in another blistering letter warned Bentley, 'It will not do you any credit – indeed people will wonder at a House like yours bringing out a work so *ill* calculated for the reading of decent people. . . . I entreat you *if* you have made any bargain to break it.'[53]

Not surprisingly Bentley backed off, and Le Fanu apparently advised his niece to withdraw the manuscript and offer instead another novel, *Cometh Up as a Flower*. This one caused problems – it was too short for the obligatory triple-decker, so Rhoda had to add ten chapters. Again there were passages to expunge so as not to offend Mudie's clients. With much grinding of teeth the young authoress supplied the revised version, 'hoping that *this* tale may avoid offending your reader's *delicate* sense of propriety'. The novel appeared anonymously in March 1867, dedicated to Le Fanu.[54] Sadleir guesses that Bentley paid £150 for it, while for *Not Wisely*, which also needed revisions and padding, he offered £250, a sum Rhoda snappishly refused. When *Not Wisely* did appear, in autumn 1867, it was under the Tinsley imprint, without a dedication and described as 'by the author of *Cometh Up as a Flower*'. Le Fanu confided to Bentley he would trouble his niece no further with advice on literary matters.[55] Thus, rather strangely, Rhoda Broughton launched her career with two novels in the same year with two publishers.

Print runs for unknowns and minor writers varied and exact numbers are hard to establish because of arrangements over reprints. Most agreements between 1820 and 1850, according to Royal Gettman, stipulated an edition of 1000 copies, but in the sixties editions were greater depending on the author's status. In Mrs Henry Wood's case, for instance, *East Lynne* (1861) had an edition of 2750, and on the strength of it her next book, *The Channings* (1862), had 5000. Le Fanu's *Uncle Silas* (1864) and *A Lost Name* (1868) each ran to 1000. Wilkie Collins's higher reputation would account for editions double that number for *Poor Miss Finch* (1872) and *The New Magdalen* (1873). Miss Broughton's *Red as a Rose is She* illustrates the variety of arrangements: initially the printing was 1500 copies in January, which was followed by 750 within a month. In September it was reprinted as a single volume with 1500 copies at six shillings. Eight further printings totalling 15,500 had been made by 1894.[56] For smaller fry than Rhoda, printings could be as low as 500.

How do such statistics translate into human effort and rewards of authorship? Writers at the top of their profession were certainly paid large sums. Trollope received £3000 for *The Last Chronicle of Barset* (1867) and his highest payments were £3200 for *Phineas Finn* (1869) and *He Knew He Was Right* (1869) (with no sacrifice of copyright). Thackeray was paid £3600 by Bradbury & Evans for *The Newcomes* (1855), plus another £500 from Harper & Tauchnitz for overseas publication. George Smith gave George Eliot £7000 for *Romola* (1863) and Longman parted with £10,000 for Disraeli's *Endymion* (1880). The agreement for Dickens's *Edwin Drood* (1870) specified £7500 for 25,000 copies, plus half-profits thereafter.[57] Coming down the scale, Sampson, Low, Son & Marston paid Collins £3000 for *No Name* (1862), which almost sold out its 4000 edition the first day of publication.[58] Smith was happy to offer Collins £5000 for a novel in the *Cornhill*, and Collins obliged with *Armadale* (1866).[59] But these are far larger sums than the average supplier of Mudie fare could hope to obtain; the norms of £300–500 were seldom breached by the vast majority, although enduring celebrities, as I have indicated, could reckon to hit the £1000–2000 level on occasion.[60] James Payn described his gradually increasing payments thus:

> *Lost Sir Massingberd* was, I think, my fourth book; from that time my position as a story-writer was secure, and I began to receive considerable sums for my books. Even then, however, my progress, though always upward, was slow, and it must have been at least ten years before I reached those 'four figures' which are supposed in the literary market to indicate the position of the 'popular author'.[61]

But for every moderately successful author there were fifty struggling hacks.[62]

These figures are interesting in context of the length of time it took to write a novel and other factors. Individual efforts varied of course. Rhoda Broughton took only six weeks to produce *Not Wisely*, but that was a first fine careless rapture.[63] Trollope wrote his short novels like *Harry Heathcote of Gangoil* (1874) or *An Eye for an Eye* (1879) in under a month, but reckoned his average at three books every two years.[64] That was about right, Payn thought:

> Trollope and Scott were exceptionally quick workers, but there are few men who can write a three-volume novel, worth reading, under nine months; in the same time a popular painter can produce at least three pictures, for each of which he gets as large a sum as the popular writer for his entire book. Nor does his work take out of the artist as it does out of the author. Indeed, if a man looks for wealth, the profession of literature is the very last I would recommend him to embrace.[65]

This was certainly true for the average popular novelist who, besides grinding industry faced inexplicable swings of public fancy, as R. D. Blackmore noted in a letter of 1895: 'The sale of my novels has dropped almost to the vanishing point. It is the same with William Black's and all the other Veterans who have not rushed into Pornography, or Physics, or Diabology, or Anti-Christianity, or something else that "catches on".'[66]

Partly to protect themselves from this recurrent anxiety and a certain amount of guilt over their compromises with the market, authors tended to exaggerate their philistinism or assembly-line approach to fiction. Trollope's self-disparagement, even to the misleading *Autobiography* that did such harm to his reputation soon after his death, I have written about elsewhere,[67] but it is by no means unique. Miss Braddon embraced her task with cheerful flippancy: 'I am just going to do a little parricide for this week's supply.'[68] Rhoda Broughton belittled her work as her daily tale of bricks;[69] Mrs Oliphant said that hers was an artless art, produced for the moment and written in the moment:

> I am no more interested in my own characters than I am in Jeanie Deans, and do not remember them half so well, nor do they come back to me with the same steady interest and friendship. Perhaps people will say this is why they never laid any special hold upon the minds of others, though they might be agreeable reading enough.[70]

Yet Mrs Oliphant's work was achieved by efforts of mind and heart no different from those of any author. Anne Thackeray saw her when she was visiting the Leslie Stephens at Grindelwald, keeping steadily to her task despite all temptations of company:

> I was always struck, when I saw her writing, by her concentration and the perfect neatness of her arrangements – the tiny inkstand of prepared ink, into which she poured a few drops of water, enough for each day's work, the orderly manuscript, her delicate, fine pen. . . .[71]

James Payn saw his own work in similar disciplined terms, proud of the fact that for twenty-five years he never had more than three consecutive days' holiday annually. Payn brought to the task a Trollopian pride over deadlines too, and was usually half-a-dozen articles in hand. 'I doubt if there has been any more dependable contributor as regards punctuality since the art of printing was invented', he boasted in *Gleams of Memory*.[72]

To put such hours of application and seclusion into concrete terms, consider that the median length of a three-decker was 168,000 words (although Tinsley's estimate was 120,000), and that meant, according to George Bentley, 920 pages with 21½ lines per page and 9½ words per line.[73] The three-volume novel length varied: *Bleak House* is some 380,000 words; Trollope's *The Prime Minister* (1876), his longest book, went to 418,000. *The Belton Estate* (1866), on the other hand, was 155,000, *The Eustace Diamonds* (1873) 276,000. *Pride and Prejudice*, by comparison, was 124,000. Rhoda Broughton's lengths point to the difficulty she had in reaching the minimum enforced by Mudie's demand for three volumes; indeed, Michael Sadleir argued that her best work was only achieved after the death of the triple-decker at the end of the century. It is interesting to speculate on the problems Rhoda's irregular lengths must have caused when her stories were serialised. Her shortest was *Nancy* (109,000 words); *Goodbye, Sweetheart!* was 136,000; her longest, *Alas!*, 155,000; *Red as a Rose is She*, 151,000.[74]

After the better part of a year's drudgery, then, the fledgling novelist could begin to negotiate terms with the publisher. Usually this meant making the best of a profit-sharing agreement, with very little reward for his labour: 'Profits did not accrue until overheads had been covered, and it was for the publisher to assess these, so an unscrupulous publisher could extend his costs over an entire edition until there was no profit to share.'[75] George Bentley generously offered Rhoda Broughton two-thirds of the profit from *Cometh Up as a Flower*, provided she would contribute a long serial for *Temple Bar*, but on the whole authors did not care for profit-sharing, especially since some publishers were reluctant to provide detailed statements of how profits had been swallowed up one way or another. Miss Broughton was highly suspicious about her proceeds from *Cometh Up* and almost accused Bentley of misrepresentation.[76]

Authors, notoriously poor businessmen, generally preferred payments outright; even Trollope did, and he was smarter than most, although he continued profit-sharing with Henry Colburn for *The Kellys and the O'Kellys* (1848) and *La Vendée* (1850), with some variation he obviously hoped would bear fruit. He was to receive £20 down, with a further £30 after 350 copies had been sold, and £50 more if 450 went in six months. Trollope got his £20, and no more – not even an account. William Longman published *The Warden* (1855) on the half-profits system, and Trollope had received another £20 by 1865. By the time of *Barchester Towers* (1857) he secured £100 down from Longman, and thereafter was in favour of a lump sum rather than what he called 'a deferred annuity'.

Intricate, sometimes devious, contractual arrangements were part of the trade, particularly with regard to copyrights. Having parted with *The Three Clerks* to Bentley unconditionally, Trollope was mortified to see reissues year after year (some 8000 copies in all), and when he negotiated *The Bertrams* with Chapman & Hall he obtained the important addition of joint ownership of copyright after three years. Henceforth, after about 1860–1, when reissues of his early novels were in prospect, he was assiduous in buying back copyrights.[77] Mrs Henry Wood, acting upon Ainsworth's advice, fought vigorously to hold on to hers; and with her son as business manager waged many a successful battle. But she liked half-profits, too, and did well out of them: she secured 1000 guineas for *The Shadow of Ashlydyat* (1863), while the publisher's profit amounted to £325 1*s* 3*d*. *East Lynne*, her most famous novel, sold 110,250 copies in twenty years, so by retaining copyright she made a considerable sum. Gradually her son retrieved most of the copyrights she had parted with, all but that of *The Channings*, which Bentley clung to, but even that came into her hands in 1879 for £1000.[78]

Mudie's Select Library remained the dominant influence in the book trade, forcing publishers to maintain the profitable three-volume novel. By the sixties it has been estimated conservatively that Mudie had 50,000 subscribers among what *The Times* called 'the more intelligent families', and could affect supply and demand considerably.[79] Bulk buying, for which he demanded substantial discounts, increased risks for publishers in a volatile market, and caused great discomfort. William Tinsley, who prided himself on being wide awake, gave a vivid picture of trading with Mudie. On one occasion in 1872 he had three new novels on his hands, one of which was a very successful tale called *The Golden Butterfly* by James Rice and Walter Besant, both shrewd managers of the commercial side of their affairs; Rice used to contract out printing and binding and get Tinsley to advertise and market the book. This had proved profitable with the best-selling *Ready Money Mortiboy* (1872) after serialisation in *Once a Week*, their collaborative editorial venture. 'I didn't get much out of it', Tinsley grumbled goodnaturedly, 'except the credit of publishing it.' Now he was in the same position with their latest attempt to beat the system, and felt himself trapped between the two authors and Mudie.

No publisher can keep forcing more than two or three books at a time on the Libraries, and . . . even three are sometimes too many. When I'd go to Mr Mudie on Monday morning looking for an order for my own two properties [one of which was Trollope's *The Golden Lion of Granpère*] he'd say: 'Well, Tinsley, I'm afraid I can't do much for either of them, but you can send me another twenty-five – or fifty or a hundred as the case might be – of your *Golden Butterfly. My Golden Butterfly!* Same way with Will Faux at Smith's. He'd give me an order for the *Butterfly* at any time I called, but couldn't do much with my other two books. Same way up West. I began to curse the *Butterfly*.[80]

Enjoying the joke, Rice would congratulate Tinsley on all the money he was making. It was not often that authors had the whip hand.

Mudie's patronage was sought by authors as well as publishers. Even George Eliot worried when he did not order *Scenes of Clerical Life* and heaved a sigh of relief when he added *Adam Bede* to stock, recording in her journal on 5 February 1859, that he had accepted 500 copies on the publisher's terms; she was equally pleased when he kept coming back for more. He took 2000 of *The Mill on the Floss* (1860). As Guinevere Griest noted, throughout Eliot's correspondence with John Blackwood, Mudie's runs like a *leitmotiv*. But by the time of *Middlemarch* she wanted to be out of Mudie's clutches.[81] Noting that her first novel had been taken by the Circulating Library, Mrs Oliphant declared that 'the patronage of Mudie was a sort of recognition from heaven'.[82] George Eliot thought that 500 copies was a good sale, but being in Mudie's list drummed up circulation enormously, as James Payn, who studied the market closely, well understood. His own books were well represented partly because he exactly suited public taste throughout his long career and also because he willingly conformed to the three-volume straitjacket. On one occasion, having heard that his novel *The Burnt Million* (1890) was much requested, he prodded the publisher to keep after the Library, and when Mudie, distraught after his son's death in 1879, was taking less interest in the firm, Payn was much bothered about the fate of his novel *Under One Roof*.[83]

Mudie's ascendancy was at its greatest in the sixties and seventies despite increasing opposition from publishers and authors. While Miss Braddon, Payn and lesser lights saw their best interests lay in propping up his regime, Reade and Collins opposed him, the latter once exclaiming, 'This ignorant fanatic holds my circulation in his pious hands.'[84] Mudie and W. H. Smith, who had a virtual monopoly of the railway trade, became for Collins the 'twin tyrants of literature'.[85] George Moore detected rank hypocrisy in Mudie's selection of what he thought fit for gentlefolk to read, but by the time he mounted his strenuous attacks on Mudie, notably his pamphlet *Literature at Nurse* (1885), the real issue was not so much moral censorship as length. Already by 1870 John Blackwood was saying that the days of the three-volume novel were over for profit, but Mudie clung to it. The taste sharpened for more concentrated, well-shaped single-volume novels in preference to what Reade (despite his opposition to the three-decker) called the 'great prose Epic', and Henry James spoke of the 'tyranny of the three volumes' in 1874.[86] Readers of popular fiction especially seemed to have less time for 'the good long read', and the appetite grew for the short story. The great days of Mudie were over by the nineties, when the market was flooded with cheaper and cheaper books, although the Library hung on until 1937 – a 'superbly Forsyte institution' Wyndham Lewis called it.[87] The empty shell in New Oxford Street was destroyed by air raids in the Second World War.

The most disagreeable aspect of the three-volume format was that it caused publishers to pad material by technical means or authors to work up copy to fill out the third volume. One result was bad art, the other bad business practice. Trollope was incensed by the dishonesty of such proceeding, which happened to him more than once.[88] *The Belton Estate* (1865) was in his mind a two-volume novel, but Chapman & Hall issued it in three volumes. Trollope endorsed his working-table with the words 'surreptitiously printed in three volumes'.[89] Since the novel ran to some 155,000 words Trollope was not unreasonable; it remains the shortest of his three-volume novels. He only just managed to prevent Hurst & Blackett stretching *Sir Harry Hotspur of*

*Humblethwaite* (1870) to two volumes. Of this unhappy event Trollope recorded in his *Autobiography* his cardinal sense of the honesty a publisher owed to his public:

> When I have pointed out that in this way the public would have to suffer, seeing that they would have to pay Mudie for the use of two volumes in reading that which ought to have been given to them in one, I have been assured that the public are pleased with literary short measure, that it is the object of novel-readers to get through novels as fast as they can, and the shorter each volume is the better![90]

One might have supposed that popular commercial novelists would have gone along with the 'lead and margin' strategies of the publishers, who were after all increasing profit for their authors as well as satisfying the great panjandrum of the circulating library. George Bentley offered the enticement to Rhoda Broughton of £250 – £100 more than he had paid for *Cometh Up as a Flower* – if she could expand *Not Wisely, but Too Well* to three volumes. Her refusal was typical in its forthrightness: 'I have not the slightest intention of spoiling the story by padding it out to three volumes. We will therefore if you please say no more on the subject.'[91] He continued, however, to offer her higher prices for length. For *Red as a Rose is She*, first £600, then £700, if she would write it in three volumes, which she did, although he had still some tricky spacing out to do.[92] Bentley went on urging her to write at greater length for serialisation in *Temple Bar*. When it came to her seventh novel, *Second Thoughts* (1880), he offered £1200 for three volumes or £750 for two. Rhoda was not to be persuaded: she accepted the £750 and the novel appeared in two volumes. Even Mrs Oliphant, despite her affection for the house of Blackwood, once ticked off William Blackwood for what she called the old publishing trick of padding out what was essentially a long short story into a novel.[93] Ouida, claiming the highest motives (and throwing in a disparaging remark about a fellow author) voices a similar objection when negotiating terms with Chatto for *Pipistrello* (1880):

> If I did not love *Art* too much ever to sacrifice it for money, I could easily have amplified it [the collection of stories] a little and passed it off on you as the three volume novel. But with me

you may be sure that the artistic feeling always outweighs all others; with writers like Mr Payn you would not find this.[94]

The flourish with which Ouida appeals to art is perhaps an ironical point at which to conclude this brief account of the industry's progress, from relatively simple economics to assembly-line production. As the century drew to a close the complexities of contractual and other legal responsibilities increased even as they were better understood, and the relationship between author and publisher remained subject to unpredictable market factors.[95] Success in fiction, despite the testimonies of long-term survivors like Payn and Besant, remained largely at the whim of fortune. For newcomers the chance of writing a bestseller or even making a decent living was complicated by sheer numbers of aspirants to fame. A few not inconsiderable gains were made, however – notably the loosening of Mudie's grip on the book market, the end of the triple-decker, the spread of cheap editions and the diversifying of publishing outlets by the rapid growth of smaller houses. Freer markets at home and more responsible monitoring of publishing abroad gradually came about, while public awareness of authors' rights grew as a response to government reports and the publicising of grievances over copyright by the Society of Authors.[96]

# 3 Looking-glass or Magical Mirror: Reviews of Popular Novels

*I venture to think, in spite of some voices to the contrary, that criticism is much more honest than it used to be: certainly less influenced by political feeling, and by the interests of publishing houses.*

James Payn, *Nineteenth Century* (June 1879)

The fiction industry began to benefit from the growth of periodicals in the 1860s and 1870s, not only through fresh outlets for serial fiction, but also from advertising direct and indirect. Paid advertising, which consisted of sheets of a publisher's new books with selected comments enthusiastically greeting each and every novel, probably did far less than word of mouth to send a reader scurrying to Mudie's for the latest romance; indirect advertising, however, in the form of reviews, has fascinating bearing on my subject. It is a by-product of the industry which gave a start to new writers, additional income to established authors like Mrs Oliphant or Amelia Edwards, and an impetus to taste and judgement out of which a critique of fiction would eventually grow.

An article in the *Saturday Review* for 9 December 1865, suggests in the journal's facetious vein that the reviewer's task would be easier if the merits of novels could be ticked off on a scale of Scott as 100 and G. P. R. James as nil. The offhand approach uncovers a serious question about the absence of criteria for judging popular reading, which is underlined by the statement that 'no critic . . . has yet told us what is the relative merit of a second-rate domestic and a first-rate sensation novel'. The author prompting this dilemma is James Payn, whose *The Clyffards of Clyffe* the reviewer felt should be condemned to 'critical Botany Bay'.[1]

49

What this invites us to consider, beyond the variety of fiction available, is the haphazard set of standards by which it could be judged. Commentary about fiction was very much a matter of personal whim, the cast of the journal and arbitrary application of general notions about form and values.[2] Novel criticism, then, was still in its infancy, and studies of its technique and achievement can be counted almost on one hand.[3] The first thing to bear in mind is that what we are talking about is general commentary on 'books of the season' by literature's camp-followers, much of it highly subjective, ephemeral and amateur, and much of it done, as Payn says, by the newest recruit to the light-literature brigade.[4]

Mid-Victorian debate on fiction covered ground familiar from the late eighteenth century on its demoralising effect. It moved towards specifically moral issues under the impact of evangelical hostility, and, because a crusading spirit of social reform found its way into the novel during the 1840s, the issue of the novel as instruction or entertainment became more acute. This in turn focused discussion on another historical issue, concerning the novel as a romance – largely dealing with an unreal world of fantastic happenings (the Gothic form), or sometimes 'romantic', concerned with the ideal and inspirational (in a classical spirit of depicting types and general truths) – and its modern role as a vehicle of contemporary realities, close observation of the phenomena of actual circumstances in as lifelike a manner as possible.

With the emergence of the sensation novel, dating from the appearance of *The Woman in White* (1860), these issues break out afresh, filling periodicals of the sixties and seventies with often intemperate debate as to the role of fiction in a civilised state.[5] The dominating topic is always morality and, confusingly interwoven with it, the debate between traditional modes of romance and realism. The moral debate begins in an atmosphere of shock and condemnation similar to that evangelical opposition to the novel in the early nineteenth century, but over twenty years it changes character somewhat, recognising in a more sophisticated way a certain moral autonomy within the literary work itself. Debate on realism and romance also shows signs of maturity. Beginning with a decided bias towards the documentary and familiar and at the same time a somewhat patronising air towards its photographic character, the discussion gradually shows signs of accepting a more imaginatively created world of heightened realism, while romance itself sheds something of its bad character as an escapist and extravagant form of storytelling; it begins to be generally understood that romance and realism are not mutually antagonistic.

On the whole the fiction industry was rather more of a spur to criticism than otherwise. For one thing it raised afresh the question of whether England needed some form of institution like the French Academy. This was generally not thought a beneficial direction to take, but it was increasingly felt that individual critics and book-reviewers should, as Thomas Arnold put it, 'lash what is carelessly, correct what is imperfectly done, and mercilessly decapitate what should never have been done at all'.[6] The role of the critic is to preserve language and literary traditions, but, says Arnold, the only remedy for the middlebrow reader at present undeterred by bad taste, bad English and literary crudity (exemplified most by sensation novels) is an improvement in the quality of middle-class education, not censorship from the high-minded: 'there is no kind of novel in regard to which the arguments in favour of its free circulation would not outweigh those in favour of its suppression'.[7] Milton's reasoning against censorship is unanswered, especially when it comes to the inadequacy of retrospect, foresight, insight and impartial judgement in ordinary men, and hence the impossibility of knowing what good may be achieved by a book which at first sight may seem offensive. Voltaire's *Candide* was an example from the past; *Held in Bondage* (which Arnold's article attributes to a man called 'Onida') is a contemporary example, about which he concludes, 'for the sake of the one true and forcible impression left by this book – the defectiveness of the education at our superior schools – it is good for society that *Held in Bondage*, and other works of its class, should circulate freely.'[8]

Arnold's was only one side of the argument. Many believed that increasing literacy did not inculcate a desire for high culture and that profit motives among publishing-houses brought about a greater appetite for literary pabulum. The circulating library and cheap-fiction expansion were widely regarded as damaging, and thus a central issue becomes the separation of art and popular entertainment.

Just as novel criticism is beginning to emerge, then, the rise of the bestseller and the marketing of fiction leads to renewed uncertainty. Reviewers had scarcely settled the primary question of whether reading novels was worthwhile, when they were inundated with sensationalism, religious polemic, sentimental romance, *demi-monde* literature and the phenomenon of instantly acclaimed new novels. Thus the *Saturday Review* spluttered, 'The idol of today is dashed in pieces before the end of the twelvemonth, and his shrine is taken by another.'[9] More and more periodicals cottoned on to the notion that popular fiction was widening the gap between literary culture and mass entertainment. Increasingly articles analysing the state of culture appeared, notably Matthew Arnold's on the pursuit of excellence.[10]

Arnold's discourse operated on an altogether higher plane from most people's experience. Indeed it was interpreted as an attack on just the audience the *Saturday Review* and other journals served, and his attempts 'to pull out a few more stops in that powerful but at present narrow-toned organ, the modern Englishman' met a stonily persistent advocacy of the material, prosaic and prescriptively moral. Criticism of fiction, such as it was, in the *Athenaeum*, the *Saturday Review* and the *Spectator* (although the latter is often capable of a refined and discriminating approach) made dismally flat and attenuated judgements upon the vast output of publishing during the two decades under review. Yet in its uncertain and censorious observations novel criticism was being formulated, not merely as counter-text to Arnoldian standards, but as a record of important swings of fashion in the lower reaches of novels: of the rise and fall of the sensation novel, for example; of the gradual eclipse of the religious novel; and, most importantly, of the tendency for realistic and romantic modes to coalesce, thereby gradually educating a public for the works of Hardy, Stevenson and Conrad. Arnold's ideas about values cut no ice with *Saturday* reviewers or the commuters of the Great Eastern Line, Woodford Branch, although it is to be hoped that they infiltrated, however dilute, somewhere down the line.

Reviewers in the late fifties and early sixties were as anxious about the numbers of new novels as about the moral effects of sensationalism. Writing in *Macmillan's Magazine* in April 1860, F. T. Palgrave claims that there is no reason to think the froth of this day frothier than the old – there is just a great deal more of it. The root of the wrong is that people now look 'to books for something almost similar to what they find in social conversation. Reading tends to become another kind of gossip.'[11]

David Masson provides to some extent a rebuttal of this argument the following month in 'Three Vices of Current Literature', professing that more does not mean worse. He does not lament that we live in 'the Mudiaeval era' but calls instead for a larger view of literature,

> according to which the expression of passing thought in preservable forms is one of the growing functions of the race; so that, as the world goes on, more and ever more of what is remembered, reasoned, imagined, or desired on its surface, must necessarily be booked or otherwise registered for momentary needs and uses, and for farther action, over long arcs of time, upon the spirit of the future.[12]

Masson is optimistic, and confines his criticism of current literature to bad workmanship such as awkward syntax, verbal crutches, phrase-making, mixed metaphor and the like, in which popular novels abound. These, he says, are not mere technicalities but the very context of thought itself: 'what is called style resolves itself, after all, into manner of thinking . . . all the forms of slip-shod in expression are, in reality, forms of slip-shod in thought'. George Orwell was to make a similar connection in a famous essay some eighty years later.

Triteness in facts, doctrines and modes of thought, Masson says, is a vice, although he acknowledges that wide dissemination of commonplace knowledge has its place in popular literature in order that 'these may percolate the whole social mass'. Even here, however, 'there must be novelty . . . novelty if not of matter, at least of method'. Such novelty, Masson declares emphatically, is not 'paying platitudes as they rise to the lips' – what today we would call gimmickry – but the product of thought, effort, of 'passive quietude to many impressions'. Returning to what is trite in popular writing, he instances extravagant scene-painting, grandiose character description and elaborate effects: 'the fallacy is that all great painting must be done with the big brush, and that even cameos may be cut with pickaxes'. Moreover, popular writing is always being modish:

The near then satisfies – the near in fact, which makes History poor and beggarly; the near in doctrine, which annuls Speculative Philosophy, and provides instead a miscellany of little tenets more or less shrewd; the near in imagination, which checks in Poetry all force of wing.

Masson's essay has much to tell us today about the buzz words of pop culture. Looked at in its own era, however, his remarks are squarely aimed at the materialism of his age and have much in common with those of Dickens in *Our Mutual Friend*; both attack bourgeois attitudes to art based on heavy literalism, dullness of imagination and love of novelty.

Much popular fiction flatters the bourgeois mentality, displaying a depressing tameness, an intensely practical view of life and a deeply conservative dread of experiment or individualism. Hence the popular novel, though it purports to shock its readers (and may do so by its initial events), retreats at last to safe conventionalities of custom and belief. Its realism falsifies, its mirror images flatter and consolidate the prejudices of publisher, critic and reader alike.

The narrative mode of realism which dominated the nineteenth-century novel at best mined deeply into human character and experience and transformed reality, showing what man might be or hope to be – or might hope to avoid. This Thackeray and George Eliot achieved with the utmost attention to detail of place and character and with regard to the conflicts and contradictions of human nature. But most popular novelists used realism crudely. Hence the distinction between lesser novelists and greater is that between the looking-glass and the magic mirror, an often-used metaphor in the consuming and confusing debate at the heart of mid-Victorian criticism of the novel over realism, idealism and the 'truth' of fiction.

Robert W. Buchanan, not by any means a sensitive literary critic, discussed some aspects of the issue in *Temple Bar* when sensation writing was at its height, and his views are a sound indicator of middlebrow response to literature. He begins his article 'Society's Looking-glass' by stressing the age's 'eminently practical view of life', relating it to writing.[13] Being practical, 'men no longer write for posterity'; the community of letters is a corporate one and a commercial one to boot. It follows that the novelist's path to success lies in being faithful to the interests of his audience. Thus 'the modern novelist holds the looking-glass up to society'. It is axiomatic that the favoured literary mode should be detailed realism, which is inferior art on two counts: it cannot inspire or uplift as the best imaginative art can (hence poetry is the greatest literary activity); and it has a marked propensity to record the most sordid of man's activities.

The attack on crude social realism was philosophic as well as moral; it was inadequate not only to lead men's aspirations towards higher ends but also to capture the essence of experiences. Here the argument was like Dr Johnson's on the respective merits of Fielding and Richardson: that the kind of realism the public demanded merely caught the externals of life. Buchanan turns to Scott as a standard: 'Scott, great in all things, is unquestionably the greatest modern author who ever held up the looking-glass of fiction. He is true both to human types and to Society.' Whereas society today is content with the mere reflection of her superficial features – the externals and 'realities' of daily life, Scott's realism is compounded of common life, idealism and general truths:

> His was no common looking-glass; but a magical mirror which, if it flattered sometimes, was capable of giving distinctive features to human faces – of suggesting the soul at work within, triumphant over the vagaries of convention, and aspiring to a heaven infinitely higher than that seen by respectable people through the roof of Exeter Hall.

Buchanan's equation of realism with the age's materialism is an interesting one, and it follows that the domestic fiction eagerly devoured by the middlebrow public should deploy so minutely the commonplace and familiar, succumbing to a 'detailism' that both flattered experience and was in the end mere photography. An equally popular form – the sensation novel – is also seen in the context of materialism, for, although its ingredients of suspense, melodrama and extremes of behaviour seem the very opposite of commonly shared experience, it was rooted in a taste for the factual. Its plots were largely given over to bourgeois issues of money, ambition and social status, and its character-drawing minutely detailed and faithful to recognisable people. In fact where the sensation novel so often came to grief was in the discrepancy between photographic reality of character and background and increasing absurdity of incident. Yet at bottom writers of domestic fiction and sensationalists were realistic in Buchanan's sense; both were journalists stocking up with raw material from the daily newspaper fodder of traveller's tales, heroism under fire, domestic feuds, wife-batterings, bigamous marriages, lost wills, and the thousand natural shocks that flesh is heir to. The *Annual Register* is an encyclopedia of a thousand plots for sensation novels.

Embroidering their raw material with ever more improbable devices, some sensation novelists goaded reviewers into a fury over their tricks and cheap effects. The anonymous author of *In the Dead of Night* (1875) had a scene in which the hero fabricated his own death, deluding the police into inspecting his body through a window in his coffin. What they saw was a cleverly made wax figure. This enabled the hero to unmask his villainous cousin by the ingenious ploy of a re-enactment of the crime, which caused the cousin to die of shock.

Another item in the sensationists' store which drew critical fire was the repeated pattern of a mystery solved at the end of the story. For this type of thriller the *Spectator* coined the term 'the Enigma novel', pointing out that its essential was a question to be elucidated upon which the whole fabric of the novel depended.[14] Considering Le Fanu's *Uncle Silas*, the *Saturday Review* likened the reader's role to that of detective following the clues and vicariously enjoying the solving of the crime.[15] At first this crossword-puzzle novelty held great appeal. It was refreshing, the *Saturday Review* said of Collins's *Hide and Seek*, to get away from sermons and sentimentalism and enjoy a mystery, but the drawbacks quickly became apparent.[16] The enigma novel was all plot and little else, and the journal soon speaks disparagingly of 'this reduction of fiction to a puzzle' when dealing with Collins's *No Name*.[17] Still Collins is superior to others in the genre, his imitators trapped by their own lack of ingenuity into the kind of plot which ten minutes thought could penetrate and where there is 'any amount of digression, sentiment and description'.[18] The *Quarterly Review* pointed out the limitations: 'Deep knowledge of human nature, graphic delineation of individual character, vivid representations of the aspects of Nature or the workings of the soul – all the higher features of the creative art – would be a hindrance rather than a help to work of this kind.'[19] The reader may not have been able to put it down (as blurbs today often trumpet) but, once 'the secret spring is touched', as the *Saturday Review* put it, 'the lock flies open – the novel is done'.[20]

In fact it is neither the elaborate contrivances nor the extravagant actual events they drew upon that confound the popular novelists, but their inability to transform the material with credible characters and action into fiction that illuminates human truth. They miss the distinction between show and tell. The problem is not confined to this type of novel; it is particularly noticeable in fiction with a purpose, where artistic imbalance results partly from the author's passionate desire to convert or teach. Neither Kingsley nor Disraeli satisfactorily resolves the dilemma between artist and propagandist; neither can fuse the raw material of Blue Book and evidence with the felt life of character in action. For all Disraeli's honesty about children in factories and mines, much of *Sybil* (1845) remains dead prose to which even Dickens's authorial interventions on Jo's behalf in *Bleak House* (1852) are preferable. Similar criticisms can be levelled at some of Reade's work and certainly at George Eliot's *Felix Holt the Radical* (1866).

An interesting modern parallel to this argument is the currently popular 'docu-drama' on television. The point is not so much how such programmes blur the record of what actually occurred in the holocaust or the slave trade or Churchill's role in the last war, but that they diminish, vulgarise, debase the events they contrive to depict by failing in creative imagination. William Styron's *Sophie's Choice* deals with horrors of the concentration camp far more potently than any documentary drama with its spliced footage from newsreels of the time.


Such then were the attitudes concerning imperfect assimilation of facts with a created world. There was also the perennial question of morality and the novel. On the one hand sermonising of the pious school and overt moralising prompted complaints of prudishness; on the other, perfervid emotions evoked by sensationists renewed outcries about moral pollution. Charlotte Yonge and Mrs Craik, though widely read, were sometimes ridiculed for ideals of purity. The *Saturday* declared sarcastically on one occasion that careful mothers might bring up their daughters on educational patterns of *Amy Herbert* and *Margaret Percival* while young men could be modelled on Guy Morville or

John Halifax.[21] The inference was that the novel should not be distorted for its message. One of the nice things about Miss Braddon, claimed the *Saturday*, was that she 'never confuses a novel with either a sermon, or a satire, or a paper at a social science meeting'.[22]

By contrast, Mrs Craik's *A Brave Lady* offered 'puppets on moral stilts' and 'a somewhat sickly idealization of life and character'.[23] While this points to the slackening hold of religion, the argument also suggests some advance of critical awareness. The reviewer decided that padding of a gushing and semi-religious kind destroys the *raison d'être* of a novel, its power to interest the reader in a picture of human life. 'Sermons are good things enough in their place, but a novel which is only a sermon in disguise, and that disguise as flimsy as a ballet dancer's skirt, is a fraud as well as a weariness to the flesh.'[24]

At the same time, however, demand for a pervasively healthy moral tone strengthened as the novel grew more sensational. Objections are constantly voiced to what the *Quarterly* called 'preaching to the nerves',[25] while the term 'spasmodic', borrowed from the exotic poetry of Alexander Smith and Sydney Dobell, was pressed into service. The *Athenaeum* upholds *Adam Bede* for avoiding spasmodic elements;[26] in 1865 the *Saturday*, reviewing Le Fanu's *Uncle Silas*, blames it for its 'volcanic phrases and lurid medium', and goes back to praising Scott, who balances sensationalism with picturesque description of manners and places and 'utterly disdains the spasmodic, electrical language which is the note, as Dr Newman would say, of sensational literature'.[27]

As always when casting about for a scapegoat, reviewers blamed the French: 'They have a whole mass of literature which represents the entire adult population to be thinking about nothing but how to commit, or not to commit, or to hinder or encourage other people in committing, adultery.'[28] In 1860 W. R. Greg's 'French Fiction: the Lowest Deep' in the *National Review* castigated it as voluptuous, morbid and monstrous, pointing out that its inspiration derived from 'vile morality . . . vitiated taste . . . the craving for excitement that has so long been characteristic of the nation'.[29] French influence was to blame for such outrageous novels as the Hon. Mrs Woolfe's *Guy Vernon* (1869), which was described as 'finery and foulness' since it featured bigamy (twice over), incest, illegitimacy, brutality and swindling, plus an Anonyma. The sensation novelist 'would not drape ghouls in white muslin or sugar the top of its mud-pies' thundered the reviewer over an entire page, no doubt drawing more readers to the unsavoury work than ever.[30]

Trollope's friend Lady Wood was also in hot water for her novels, especially *Sorrow on the Sea* (1868). The *Athenaeum* was particularly enraged at one scene in which Cora Noble is waylaid in a dark room at Abbotsbury Hall by Rufus Helfingham:

> Moving step by step, with the music under one arm, and the other extended to feel her way, she found herself suddenly clasped by powerful arms, and her face and neck covered with hot kisses. She dropped the book, and screaming dismally, strove to disengage herself from the forced embrace.[31]

The reviews were always grumbling about the amount of kissing, but worse is to come; having escaped from the importunate Rufus the heroine makes her way back to the drawing-room, and to her intense discomfiture the hostess observes, 'Why, Cora, what an extraordinary mark you have on your shoulder! Blue and red, the blood starting under the skin, and the indication of two teeth, or what resembles their impression!'[32] The journal draws a veil over other passages apparently too revolting to print.

Many reviewers believed that the worst crime of French novelists was to show vice triumphant. In the first instance the fault was merely one of bad example. As the *Saturday* said repeatedly, the novel reached 'many persons highly susceptible of moral contagion', and therefore should exhibit 'cleanly wholesomeness of a pure endeavour' and 'a noble aim in all that regards human life'.[33] Mrs Oliphant agreed. It was a major defect of sensation novels, she said, that so often

> the worse should be made to appear the better cause, or that it should be represented as possible that certain qualities of mind or temper are sufficient to bring a character safely through all kinds of actual and positive wrongdoing without fatal or even serious damage.[34]

Similarly, to make the criminal the subject of admiration, as in Dumas's *The Count of Monte Cristo*, said the *Saturday Review*, was a dangerous tampering with morality.[35]

Juliet Pollock maintained in *Macmillan's Magazine*, however, that, even if French novels were at fault, in some respects English fiction of the 'fast' variety was worse, one difference being that, although the French were excessive in descriptions of vice, 'one virtuous central figure is modest and dignified, and that one is generally the girl of seventeen or nineteen. In the English, the most unlimited manifestations of passion proceed from the girl herself, who is created expressly to charm the young people of good society.'[36] Rhoda Broughton is not named but clearly represents this tendency. Miss Broughton was particularly susceptible to attacks for offering undesirable patterns of female behaviour, although she could not, any more than her equally famous contemporary, Miss Braddon, be accused of preaching immorality, since both punished wrong-doing and showed in the end that irregular unions and moral transgressions produced unhappiness. This ultimate deterrent took the moral argument on another tack, for it was often detected as mere tokenism, a trick for indulging in nearly three volumes of lubricious and outrageous sentiment excused in a final act of repentance – a cynical trick to throw a cloak of respectability over the whole performance.

As early as 1859, W. R. Greg, in an article in the *National Review* on 'False Morality of Lady Novelists', had argued for watchdogs of potentially debilitating light literature. Mrs Oliphant took up the subject in *Blackwood's Magazine* in 1867 protesting that women were endangered by invitations to become more open about their feelings. The story of a young girl's flowering today, she said, was 'a very fleshly and unlovely record', and it was sad to find Trollope's charming girls calling forth not half so much notice as the Aurora Floyds of contemporary fiction, or the *Revue des Deux Mondes* citing Annie Thomas and Edmund Yates as representative English novelists when their sole contribution was to put a literary fig-leaf over the conflict of good and evil. At least Balzac and Victor Hugo were honest in dissecting vile topics.[37]

Mrs Oliphant tests her thesis against Rhoda Broughton's Nelly Lestrange in *Cometh Up as a Flower*, remarking that a new phase has arrived in portraying the modern young woman. Nelly is bold, headstrong, opinionated, and this is fair enough. Even the registering of her strong feelings is permissible, for Mrs Oliphant allows it to be feasible that a situation such as Miss Broughton creates should arise.

If two young people fall heartily and honestly in love with each other, and are separated by machinations such as abound in novels, but unfortunately are not unknown in life, and one of them is compelled to marry somebody else, it is not unnatural, it is not revolting, that the true love unextinguished should blaze wildly up, in defiance of all law, when the opportunity occurs.

What is distasteful, however, is the expression given to modern sentiments from the woman's point of view, and she cites Nelly's wondering if when the lovers meet in heaven they will be 'sexless passionless essences' and then adding 'God forbid!' What Mrs Oliphant is objecting to is the crudeness and levity of such comments, which display cynical disregard for the novelist's responsibility:

> A woman, driven wild by the discovery of domestic fraud and great wrong might propose any sin in her frenzy, and yet might be innocent; whereas a woman who makes uncleanly suggestions in the calm of her ordinary talk, is a creature altogether unendurable and beyond the pale.

The vice of current reading is 'sensual literature and the carnal mind' and it is apparent in physical description of the heroine's charms, notably her hair, which has become 'one of the leading properties in fiction'. Rhoda Broughton lets her heroine's hair down in 'splendid ruddy billows' over her lover's shoulder. In Ouida's 'very fine and very nasty books', the hair is amber. Yates's heroine in *Land at Last* has 'long, thick, luxuriant hair, of a deep-red, gold colour'.

Accompanying such emphasis on the sensual is the falsehood of depicting meanness, greed, egotism and all manner of improprieties as dominant forces in behaviour. Here Mrs Oliphant takes the usual moral stance. It is injurious to readers, she says, that Yates should give his cold, insensible and treacherous heroine 'a lofty superiority over all the good people in his book [*Land at Last*]'. Thackeray in *Vanity Fair* did not dwell on Becky solely because she was wicked, but made her 'infinitely clever, amusing, and full of variety', an uneasy begging of the question after which Mrs Oliphant lamely concludes that such heroines as Yates's are founded solely on their wickedness.

Mrs Oliphant's objections to contemporary trends can be summarised as the general reaction to fiction that purveys negative views of human behaviour and which glories in 'equivocal talk and fleshly inclinations'. The contrast in fiction today, she maintains, is between the hectic and the wholesome, and (again with Rhoda Broughton in mind) she offers some ideals for portraying women in fiction, citing Trollope's example:

> They live like the most of us, exempt from gross temptation, and relying upon human natural incidents, contrariety of circumstances, failing of fortune, perversity of heart, for the plan of their romance. . . . He gives us their thoughts in detail, and adds a hundred little touches which we recognize as absolute truth: but we like the young women all the better, not the worse, for his intuitions. They are like the honest English girls we know; and we cannot be sufficiently grateful to him for freeing us, so long as we are under his guidance, from that disgusting witch with her red or amber hair.

What Mrs Oliphant's case discloses is the inhibiting effect on criticism of the moral imperative, and how this obscured deeper questions: artistic integrity, understanding of character, and the harmonious interaction of scene, character and plot.

This kind of attitude causes further and more profound objection to the French model, that it falsified life, that it just was not true, and in many ways takes us back to Buchanan's remarks about the novel recording only the most base and sordid activities, whereas the best literature inspires and uplifts. He and a great many of his contemporaries believed that truth to life involved idealism, applying a meliorist philosophy to human affairs in a Christian way. Alfred Austin in an article in *Temple Bar*, 'The Vice of Reading' (twelve years later than Buchanan's in the same magazine), is employing essentially the same argument, blaming novels for copying from life rather than from imagination, and praising romance-writing as an invitation to lift up the heart and soul of man in the midst of so much that is selfish and cynical: 'The imagination is the true refuge against experience; its medicine, its corrective, which restores to it tone, health, and energy.'[38] The practical temperament and the sordid appetite for the realistic in fiction, Austin declares, is our real danger:

if the writer remains satisfied with portraying things just as they are, still more, if he portrays the mean and more contemptible phenomena of life, leaving it to the reader to conclude that so it is and it cån't be helped or mended, his book can certainly be an assistance to no one.

One notices a similar transcendentalism in Mrs Craik's attempt in *Macmillan's Magazine* to come to terms with George Eliot. Her statement too is based on a Miltonic concept of fiction justifying the ways of God to men, and she argues that the popular writer faces awesome responsibility, 'weaving his imaginary web side by side with that which he sees perpetually and invisibly woven around him, of which he has deeply studied the apparent plan, so as to see the under threads that guide the pattern, keener perhaps than other men'.[39] He is a Prometheus trying to reach the truth of life itself; it is 'the moral ideal, for which, beyond any intellectual perfection, a great author ought to strive'. George Eliot, she acknowledges, has such power – 'the power of creation, amalgamating real materials into a foreplanned ideal scheme' – and she is quite clear-sighted about a largeness of soul in great writers: 'the earnestness, sincerity, and heart nobility of the author' in Eliot's case. In insisting on asking what good will the novel do, however, her judgement of Eliot goes awry, for, like Mrs Oliphant, she believes that the artist's view is of necessity partial and imperfect, and therefore that by making Maggie Tulliver's end bleak and barren of comfort Eliot fails in that higher truth of serving God's design for man.

What is interesting about such debate is an inkling of understanding as to the necessity of moral substance within a unifying artistic framework in which imagination's transforming of the fact or heightened realism is one element. Mrs Oliphant goes further:

Facts are of all things in the world the most false to nature, the most opposed to experience, the most contradictory of all the grand laws of existence. The oft-repeated words 'Fact is stranger than fiction', express the very apparent truth that the things which *do* happen are in many cases exactly things which could not have been expected to happen, and, indeed, ought not to have happened had there been any consistency in life . . . for us truth and fact are two different things; and to say that some incident which is false to nature is taken from the life, is an altogether unsatisfactory and inadmissible excuse.[40]


Of course, this is the old argument concerning the imperfect and chaotic human plane of existence, the condition of fallen man destined to struggle back towards a divinely ordered ultimate truth and reality. As a criterion of literary judgement it is patently unworkable, but it does explain, for example, Mrs Craik's attitude to George Eliot, as it also clarifies Trollope's claim in his *Autobiography* that, where Anne Thackeray's characters are sweet, charming and true to human nature, Rhoda Broughton's, though so vigorous and vivid, are 'less true to nature'.[41] Such notions of a transforming idealism, despite their shortcomings as literary theory, comprehended the scope of some of the finest domestic fiction of the time, including Mrs Oliphant's own. From the time of *Cranford* (1853) for instance, Mrs Gaskell was applauded for 'the quiet, sensible kind of story, with no extravagant characters, no improbable incidents, but where the kind of people we meet in real life do the kind of things which they would do in real life'.[42] Nice things, though, it goes without saying. Mrs Gaskell herself remains true to the orthodox but embattled values of the mid-Victorians. Indeed her own appeal as novelist of commonplace domesticity, hard-won happiness and enduring values of service and companionship – the Christian underpinning without obtrusive moralising – gains strength as tension and break-up are felt in the air. The later domestic fiction of Mrs Gaskell, as of Trollope and Mrs Oliphant, however troubled by the alarms of contemporary malaise, remains fundamentally acquiescent and optimistic. Trollope ends his career with *Ayala's Angel* (1881) and *Mr Scarborough's Family* (1883), by no means soured or cynical about his world. Long into the 1870s and 1880s domestic novels exactly suited Mr Mudie's patrons, for they represented continuity and security, escape from the perplexing questions of science and philosophy, the controversies of believers and non-believers, and the social ideas of Hardy, Butler and, soon, H. G. Wells. If they occasionally subverted certain orthodoxies of male and female roles they remained true to the temper of earlier times, while the optimistic cast to their writing offered convincing assurances to an essentially old-fashioned readership (which the popular market always is) that the essential values of the British way of life would endure.

The stress of social change, radical ideas in social organisation and man's place in the scheme of things, reasserted the demand for 'wholesomeness' in a new way – that of idealism and cheerfulness. The word 'idyll' was much bandied about. For a while Hardy looked as if he might cheer up his readers with romances looking back to the vanishing rural tradition. *Under the Greenwood Tree* (1872) was touted as 'the best prose idyll that we have seen for a long while past', but his disturbing later fiction was roundly condemned by popular magazines.[43] Mrs Oliphant did not disappoint in this respect. Her novel *May* (1873) was greeted with pleasurable relief: 'If novel-writers would only go more to nature for their models, and trust less to their own sickly fancies. . . .'[44] Nature in this case is both the sunnier aspects of human behaviour among representative rural types and the more beneficent air of the countryside. The prescription for an age of headaches, Swinburne and *La Cousine Bette* is 'healthy natural books which remind one of a breezy day in the country'.[45]

It is easy to understand why popular fiction often became bland and superficial, indulging in easy tears without painful emotion, exciting adventures without real effort, and indulgent laughter without the tonic experience of great comedy. And yet 'pleasant reading', as one review of Trollope's *The Golden Lion of Granpère* put it, is not to be dismissed altogether.[46] Trollope, and after him also James Payn, represent a positive sense of life to be enjoyed, as this comment on Payn's *Like Father, Like Son* indicates: 'The world wants to be amused and we can dispense for a time with profound views of men and manners, with passionate expressions of sentiment or philosophical theories embodied in appropriate types.'[47] Praise is heaped upon him for a collection of short stories called *High Spirits*, 'those comic historiettes of which he only among living writers has the secret'.[48] In sad contrast, the same year Meredith's *The Egoist*, a masterpiece of tragi-comic writing, was greeted with puzzled approval and the comment by the *Athenaeum* that 'monstrous cleverness' was Meredith's undoing.[49]

The demand for prose idyll and entertainment, which is the hallmark of such reviewing as the *Athenaeum*'s of Payn's work, is the indicator of popular fiction to come and the cultural barometer with which I wish to draw this examination of reviews to an end. Comedy of Payn's type, genial, flattering and optimistic, later practised by F. Anstey, Jerome K. Jerome and many others, may lack the astringent quality of Meredith or Butler, and seem to turn aside with a jest from the serious issues of life, yet it represents a legitimate desire for holiday which characterises popular fiction to this day. As the *Athenaeum* put it,

> Mr Payn is certainly, his other merits apart, the most sprightly of living novelists. He is full of amiability, and his good temper, always of the jolliest and frankest type, has something contagious in it. He is not only funny and frolicsome in himself, he is also the cause of fun and frolic in others; and the man who could come within his range and not acknowledge the charming qualities of his influence would be dull indeed. Mr Payn's humour is always thoroughly good-natured and thoroughly spontaneous; it is the output of a mind that looks cheerfully on all things, and apprehends the comic in them instinctively, and by preference.[50]

This is no bad estimate of Payn's virtues as a novelist, but at the same time charm, fun, frolic and good-natured humour also measure the level of the popular fictionist's engagement with life, and the gap by now apparent between a commercial fiction offering the illusion of heroism, adventure and human conflict, and a separate 'serious' form of the novel facing up to the realities of *fin de siècle* Victorianism and a hazardous twentieth century.

It cannot be claimed from the weekly and monthly reviews between 1860 and 1880 that any systematic and coherent critical method emerged, or even that much was achieved to form an aesthetic for judging even mediocre novels – still less, the more complex art of George Eliot or George Meredith, caviare to the general as they were for years to come. This is not to say that sensitive criticism did not at times grace the *Spectator* or the *Saturday Review*. But it was after all a period of rapid writing and reading largely for the pleasure of an undiscriminating middlebrow public. Even Trollope, the best of the popular novelists, had to admit that he was not sure he had the rules sorted out, and like him James Payn and his contemporary journalists wrote as they felt, learning as they went, and with no higher aims than to tell a story, invent a character and give pleasure for the moment. As Mrs Oliphant said of her own lifetime's service to what Henry Kingsley called 'this quaint trade',

> My own stories in the making of them were very much what other people's stories (but these the best) were in the reading. . . . It pleases me . . . that I seem to have found unawares an image that quite expresses what I mean – i.e., that I wrote as I read, with much the same sort of feeling.[51]

The reviewers likewise had few firm principles to guide them other than their wish to be amused and instructed with wholesome tales. Their comments tell us little about theories of criticism, but much about the middlebrow reading public with whom they were at one. Where popular reading is concerned, fashions have changed, and yet much of the trade, much of the response, remains the same. Only a little while ago Barbara Cartland wrote something about what her public expected of her that would have been applauded a century ago:

> Of course love has been debased, sneered at, made obscene and become, through pornography, ugly and vulgar. But I am convinced that every young woman and every young man start by believing they will find in their lives the perfect love, which is both beautiful and good.
>
> If we take away people's ideals, if we accept what is called reality, which is really the mud and dirt of life, then we might as well accept that we are animals and not humans with a spiritual awareness which is only given to men and women.[52]

# 4 Queen of Popular Fiction: Mrs Oliphant and the Chronicles of Carlingford

*I might have done better work. . . . Who can tell? I did with much labour what I thought the best, and there is only a* might *have been* on the other side.
Mrs Oliphant, *Autobiography and Letters* (1899)

Mrs Oliphant is a striking example of the professional woman of letters in the mid-Victorian period. Henry James, always notable for exquisitely ambiguous judgements on his fellow-writers, called her 'a gallant woman', praising her 'heroic production' (quantity uppermost in his mind rather than quality) but expressing admiration for her perception and subtlety.[1] Queen Victoria read and admired her novels, several times calling her to audience, and at her funeral in 1897 a wreath bore a message of respect and farewell from the monarch. She was a queenly personage herself in many respects. J. M. Barrie amusingly describes his first meeting with her, in 1886, when he was 'ordered' to Windsor where she was then living. He bought his first umbrella for the occasion, but it was of little avail. The regal presence unnerved him.[2] In her obituary William Blackwood wrote, 'Mrs Oliphant has been to the England of letters what the Queen has been to society as a whole. She, too, was crowned with age and honour in her own empire; widow and mother, she has tasted the triumph of life as well as the bitterness.'[3]

I chose Mrs Oliphant as the first of my middlebrow authors simply because her natural gifts of storytelling and amazing industry perfectly represent the popular novelist's approach. She was supremely one of the 'race of middlemen'.[4] More significantly, her slavery to her pen (though she enjoyed it, and wrote as spontaneously as she talked) and the compromises forced

68

upon her for the market very well reflect the circumstances of minor writers at this time. Her output was prodigious and it is possible only to consider the best work – the Chronicles of Carlingford – of this 'considerable and original novelist'.[5] In a career spanning fifty years she produced almost a hundred novels, plus biographies of Edward Irving, Principal (John) Tulloch, Montalembert and Laurence Oliphant. She wrote over 200 articles and essays for *Blackwood's Edinburgh Magazine*, reviewing current books in 'Our Library Table' and earning distinction as a critic. As editor of Blackwood's Foreign Classics she steeped herself in European literature and herself contributed the volumes on Dante and Cervantes. She wrote a *Literary History of England* and a splendid labour of love, *Annals of the House of Blackwood*. Her energy and effort were phenomenal. As a young girl she worked, as Jane Austen had done, amidst the hurly-burly of the parlour. Later, as family tragedies threatened to engulf her, she wrote her way out of ruin and depression, as Mrs Trollope did, by working far into the night. 'As a breadwinner she began and as a breadwinner she was to end.'[6] This indomitable woman is an example of unmerited oblivion among lesser writers of the age, in many ways an unlucky victim of the publishing-system and of the vagaries of fortune that attend those who fail to reach the pinnacle of critical recognition rather than popular acclaim.

One of three surviving children, her two brothers, Frank and Willie, both proved weak characters who sooner or later depended on her for support.[7] When Willie failed as a minister of the English Presbyterian Church, it was the strong resourceful Margaret who rescued him from his London lodgings, insisting with typical spirit that they go without dinner for a week to pay off one importunate creditor. 'Mrs Oliphant could never believe in a hero',[8] remarked L. P. Stebbins. The behaviour of brothers and later sons no doubt contributed to her disillusion, although there was also a young man to whom she was passionately attached as a girl, who emigrated to America and promptly dropped her. She tells the story with wry humour, but the painful incident may well have contributed to her heroines' unsentimental attitude to love: her depiction of marriage is decidedly frosty; the men in her novels decidedly weak.

In 1852 she married her cousin, Frank Oliphant, an artist in stained glass with a small business in London, but within a few years a succession of tragic events overtook her. Prospects were bright enough at first: her husband's business went well and her early literary successes brought contact with Frank Smedley, the S. C. Halls and the Howitts. Writing in her steady, carefree way she could expect about £400 for a novel – 'already, of course, being told that I was working too fast, and producing too much'.[9] By 1856, when her first son, Cyril, was born, she had already lost two infants. Then in 1859 her husband died of tuberculosis in Italy, where the family had moved in hope of a cure. Mrs Oliphant had now to begin literary drudgery that lasted until her death in 1897. She recalled in 1885, 'When I thus began the world anew I had for all my fortune about £1,000 of debt, a small insurance of, I think £200 on Frank's life, our furniture laid up in a warehouse, and my own faculties, such as they were, to make our living and pay off our burdens by.'[10] She moved to London and, with three young children to care for, set herself doggedly to her nightly stint, often working until two or three in the morning, and producing sometimes two novels a year. But from this struggle emerged her best work, Chronicles of Carlingford, about which she said in 1894: 'The series is pretty well forgotten now, which made a considerable stir at the time, and *almost* made me one of the popularities of literature. *Almost*, never quite, though *Salem Chapel* went very near it, I believe.'[11]

At the busiest time in her career, during the early sixties, domestic burdens and sorrows accumulated. Her only daughter, Maggie, caught gastric fever and died in 1864 in Rome. She returned hurriedly to England and by the following year settled in Windsor, for she was determined that both sons should attend Eton. There was a brief period when things went well, but then in 1868 came news of her brother Frank's ruin in Canada. Now there was Frank junior to see through Eton and university. But she kept up a cheerful countenance, living for the day in extravagant style (she was not, she once said, attracted to travel second-class), and made a cosy home where all the boys' friends were welcome. Reading her autobiography, we realise what it cost to maintain both social life and her colossal work schedule. She often pauses wistfully to wonder whether her work might have been better. And, with a strong sense of puritan guilt, whether her sons might have learned habits of work 'which now seem beyond recall' (this is in 1885), had she not so pampered them.[12]

Cyril and Francis (known as 'Cecco'), who was born in that terrible year in Italy in 1859, were, she said, 'my all in this world'.[13] To provide for them was a central concern of her life and they are a focus of her autobiography and intimately bound up with the major concerns of her fiction – the intricacies of marital adjustments (usually the woman's sacrifices to the Victorian male ego), conflicts between parents and children, the pains of motherhood. Her love for her boys, A. C. Benson believed, 'had something almost morbidly passionate about it'.[14] Even her open-handedness haunted her in respect of their characters. In a pathetic footnote in the autobiography she reproaches herself for hiding her anxieties from them and thereby encouraging their idleness and extravagance. For they proved unalterably feckless. Cyril had little capacity for work and, while his mother moved to Oxford to provide him with the creature comforts to which he was accustomed, frittered away his time. Typically, she blamed herself: 'My dearest, bright, delightful boy missed somehow his footing, how can I tell how? I often think that I had to do with it, as well as what people call inherited tendencies, and, alas! the perversity of youth, which he never outgrew.'[15]

At fifty-six, Mrs Oliphant looked back on 'a laborious life, incessant work, incessant anxiety', and, although she insisted it had not been unhappy, there is undoubtedly a sense of servitude in the way she described it. She recalled that when family responsibilities piled up on her, 'I said to myself having then perhaps a little stirring of ambition, that I must make up my mind to think no more of that, and that to bring up the boys for the service of God was better than to write a fine novel, supposing even that it was in me to do so.'[16] Doubtless such thinking coloured her attitude to her contemporaries and to literary values in general. She harps on George Eliot's example with a guilty sense of her own compromises and at the same time a half-envying disdain for her protected life: 'Should I have done better if I had been kept, like her, in a mental greenhouse and taken care of?'[17] Beside Eliot and George Sand Mrs Oliphant feels 'a fat, little, commonplace woman, rather tongue-tied . . . there is a sort of whimsical injury in it which makes me sorry for myself'.[18] Anne Thackeray, far from finding her tongue-tied, said of her, 'She was one of those people whose presence is even more than a *pleasure*, it was stimulus; she was kindly, sympathetic, and yet answering with that chord of intelligent antagonism which is so suggestive and makes for such good talk.'[19] A life of suffering etched character into her features. Observing her in the chapel of Eton College in 1874, A. C. Benson noted she had an expression of endurance 'more of repression than of suppression, as if a naturally expansive and genial nature had been thwarted and baffled'.[20]

In the eighties both sons fell ill; Cyril died in 1890 aged thirty-four, and 'Cecco' four years later. Her nephew had already succumbed in India to typhoid in 1879. 'And now I am alone', she wrote, ending her fragment of autobiography, 'I cannot write any more.' Yet she had to keep on writing, partly out of habit, partly still out of need. Nine days before her death she corrected the first volume of the Blackwood history, and apologised that she could not correct the second: 'I am now lying, all possibility of work over, awaiting a very speedy end', she wrote to William Blackwood. She died on 25 June 1897, the names of her sons, it is said, continually on her lips. Anne Thackeray wrote to Rhoda Broughton, 'I have lost a life-long friend, and the world too, in that wise, tender and humorous woman whom all delighted to love and appreciate. She was to me one of those people who *make* life – so many unmake it'.[21]

The reason Mrs Oliphant caught and held her public takes us to the very heart of this study, for she is a true representative of mid-Victorian minor fiction, commercial without pandering to the market; professional without being slipshod or cynical; morally straight without being mealy-mouthed or censorious; full of feeling without being gushy; stylish without being vulgar or affected. If Trollope is, as Alexander Innes Shand claimed, 'more distinctly the family novelist than anyone who has gone before him', then Mrs Oliphant comes close behind.[22] But she is not a lesser Trollope. She has her own voice and writes unique novels. If she represents what Alfred Austin in 1870 labelled the Simple School, she wears her simplicity with a difference. Austin defines the type as

the school whose domain is the hearth, whose machinery the affections, – the school which talks to the heart without quickening its beat, yet not without moistening the eye, – the school to which home is sacred, all bad things are available only as contrasts – this we have always with us.[23]

But in Mrs Oliphant it is often a troubled hearth and an unquiet heart. Her novels have far more astringent touches than Mrs Craik's or Anne Thackeray's, for example. Shand in 1879 called her 'the salt of the contemporary generation of novelists', and it is easy to see why.[24] Justly admired for her Scottish landscapes, and winning heroines in novels such as *Katie Stewart* (1853), she returned often to Scottish characters and backgrounds, notably in *The Minister's Wife* (1869) and *Kirsteen* (1890). A more important element in her appeal is her commonsense, realistic approach that caught, as the *Spectator* said of *A Rose in June* (1874), the beauty in the essentially commonplace. In particular she tapped a vein women could respond to, reversing Jane Austen's equation of salvation with matrimony. Unlike Trollope and other male novelists, she can see that staying single – or being widowed – has distinct advantages. The jolly spinster aunts that crop up in her novels have the best of it after all.

She is questioning women's role and in her own way getting back at sexual inequality, not by showing the sensation novel's drunkards, tyrants and boors (although they are sometimes part of the picture), but by tracing the remorseless sorrows, humiliations, envies about which women were supposed to be silent.[25] She was in some respects ahead of her time, showing a disquieting scepticism in both the consolations of faith and domestic felicity. Her menfolk are often ninnies who have given up on life, as in *May* (1873), or failures in their work, as in *At His Gates* (1872). Fruits of her own disappointed life can, of course, be discerned in all this. Robert Drummond in the latter novel is an unsuccessful artist (like Frank Oliphant), and the thrust of the novel lies with the wife's combined scorn, sympathy and guilt for not being patient about it. 'When a man must not be disturbed about bills his wife must be', she writes in *A Rose in June* (1874). Heroines frequently orphaned or prematurely widowed shoulder the burden, and do so with a healthy resentment, groaning at the unfairness of it all – the social system, husbands, brothers and sons who flopped or floundered, and even protesting God's mockery of innocent women, as in *Agnes* (1866) or *Madonna Mary* (1867). Mrs Oliphant's resentment plays quietly but no doubt to sympathetic listeners at the time, and the tune is that women's life is hard. Had she had the time, or been free of the need for cash – I do not think she lacked the courage – she had it in her to come close to tragedy like Hardy's.

This is not to deny that she wrote pot-boilers with perfunctory plots and cobbled-up endings; with such an output that is hardly surprising. Nor did she escape the more baneful influences of sensation, often marring a sensible domestic study with the apparatus of ruined heiresses, impossible wills, damning letters, skeletons in cupboards, misappropriated legacies and the like, but her novels often generate genuine feelings and not the cardboard emotions of the sensationists. It was said that there were two Mrs Oliphants: the shrewd painter of domestic realities and the more lurid storyteller who in *Carita* (1877) has a sophisticated and atheistically inclined lady suffering from cancer so revolted by her condition that she commits suicide with laudanum unwittingly supplied by her ten-year-old daughter. Lurid perhaps, but as a fictional device not entirely without significance from a psychological viewpoint.

Another Mrs Oliphant emerges in a later phase of her career and deserves brief comment. Partly because of her fascination with and proximity to death, and partly in response to a vogue for tales of the occult, Mrs Oliphant produced several striking fantasies, notably *The Beleaguered City* (1880) and *Two Stories of the Seen and Unseen* (1885). In the only full-length study of the author in modern times, V. and R. A. Colby claim that the former is one of the minor classics of Victorian literature.

The Carlingford novels, however, represent the peak of her achievement. When the first appeared there was speculation that George Eliot was the anonymous author. Eliot may have flared a nostril at the comparison, but Mr Mudie's patrons perceived similarities, and it is certainly possible that Mrs Oliphant was drawn to her subject by the popularity of *Scenes of Clerical Life.*[26] Mrs Oliphant follows Trollope in creating a rural southern county, probably Berkshire-*cum*-Hampshire, with a town, not as grand as Barchester (there is no cathedral), and characters who reappear in the series, changing with the interval of years. The town of Carlingford makes its first appearance in 'The Executor', a short story in *Blackwood's* for May 1861, but the Dissenting community which made the series famous did not appear until the novels: *The Rector* and *The Doctor's Family* (3 vols, 1863), *Salem Chapel* (2 vols, 1863), *The Perpetual Curate* (3 vols, 1864), *Miss Marjoribanks* (3 vols, 1866), and *Phoebe Junior: A Last Chronicle of*

*Carlingford* (3 vols, 1876).[27] Although geographical locations are obscurer than in Trollope's Barsetshire, it is possible to place the main spheres of action: the Dissenting chapel on the edge of town, the Anglican chapel of St Roque just half a mile from Carlingford, the parish church and, nearby, the best residential quarter. There is a canal, a railway, and a new suburb representing social changes the establishment resents and within which the young clergy and doctors carry out their progressive ideas. Whereas Barchester, however, is endangered by modernism, Carlingford is still a rural backwater: 'There are no alien activities to disturb the place – no manufactures, and not much trade'.[28]

The thirty-four pages of *The Rector* make an admirable introduction to the series, its plot involving a clash between the Revd Frank Wentworth, curate in charge of St Roque's, and the new Rector of Carlingford, Morley Proctor. Mrs Oliphant establishes convincingly the predicament of the withdrawn, studious Proctor forced to compete with the sociable Wentworth, who has the goodwill of the community to sustain him as well as natural endowments as a clergyman, and when Proctor is called in off the street to minister to a dying woman and finds himself unable to make any effective speeches either to bring her peace of mind or to prepare her for the end he feels he has forfeited the right to remain in Carlingford. He resigns his pulpit and scuttles back to Oxford, a defeated man, but one who is beginning to confront his spiritual and temperamental inadequacies. Proctor's academic life can no longer shield him, and he must endure the guilt of knowing that something was demanded of him that he failed to give. The story ends with the assumption that eventually he did take on another parish, having married the elder Miss Wodehouse, and found his way out of a sterile existence.

Such a synopsis might suggest merely another dreary exercise in improving fiction, but *The Rector* is no tract in the Martineau tradition, and its merit arises from the malice and pettiness glimpsed within the individual and the family. The Rector's shyness, long a source of amusement to his aged mother, complicates his wooing. With awful skittishness Mrs Proctor teases him about bringing home a bride, and her supposition that it is the older, plainer daughter, Mary Wodehouse, rather than her sister, Lucy – 'twenty, pretty, blue-eyed, and full of dimples' – adds to his discomfiture:

When Mr Proctor saw his mother again at dinner, she was evidently full of some subject which would not bear talking of before the servants. The old lady looked at her son's troubled apprehensive face with smiles and nods and gay hints, which he was much too preoccupied to understand, and which only increased his bewilderment. When the good man was left alone over his glass of wine, he drank it slowly, in funereal silence, with profoundly serious looks; and what between eagerness to understand what the old lady meant, and reluctance to show the extent of his curiosity, had a very heavy half-hour of it in that grave solitary dining-room. He roused himself with an effort from this dismal state into which he was falling. He recalled with a sigh the classic board of All-Souls. Woe for the day when he was seduced to forsake that dear retirement!    (ch.2)

This admirable prose reads well aloud and the cadence of the sentences and good plain diction are well directed to show Proctor's prim nature, afraid of commitment either as priest or lover. The images are not striking – bordering on cliché even – but, as with Trollope, a second reading fires the imagination: phrases such as 'funereal silence' and 'grave solitary dining-room' have a special resonance and irony in a story which is about a man being brought back to life, and there is a nice contrast between his aggravated melancholy, expressed in that splendidly rhetorical 'Woe for the day . . .', and her 'smiles and nods and gay hints'.

The art of the domestic realist is to infuse plain, ordinary, commonplace routine with dramatic intensity; as Trollope was always saying, the cardinal sin was to bore the reader. Mrs Oliphant is adept at creating conflict within the domestic circle. Here, the mutual tension is low-key and comic, but it is tension none the less. Mrs Proctor uses her deafness as a weapon, forcing her son to shout his confidences into her ear, so that the servants *will* overhear. 'His dismay and perplexity amused this wicked old woman beyond measure' (ch.2). But she loves him dearly, that is plain, and the bond between them is always clear to the reader without sentimentality.

Enmity between parents and children and sibling rivalry are frequently subjects of Mrs Oliphant's fiction. There is no malice in Mrs Proctor, but one feels there is more to Mr Wodehouse's baiting of his two girls than meets the eye. Indeed his humiliation of his elder daughter touches a darker vein of parental psychology than one might expect for so tranquil a story. He is slightly caricatured in a Dickensian manner: 'Mr Wodehouse was a man who creaked universally'; 'As he came along the garden path, the gravel started all round his unmusical foot' (ch.1), but Mrs Oliphant weaves insensitivity and coarseness into the character with more subtlety than is apparent from this metaphoric insistence. His teasing is totally different in quality from Mrs Proctor's; he seems resentful of his daughter's dependence, and is rude about Mr Wentworth behind his back. In *The Doctor's Family* he is still more cynical. Mr Wodehouse has some of the unpleasant underside Jane Austen gives several of her elderly male characters.

The charm of this prelude to the Chronicles rests on the contrast pointed out between the tranquillity of the rural scene and sleepy old town with its dusty roads, walled gardens and apple blossoms and the agitated hearts and minds of its inhabitants old and young. Its skill lies in the way Mrs Oliphant evokes comedy from the plight of her central character with his 'walled up' spirit. He is a ludicrously ancient young man, as his mother recognises, she being 'let us say, a hundred years or so younger than the Rector' (ch.2). The improvement in his temper and spirits at the end of the story has a beneficent effect on the town itself, for in *The Doctor's Family* we learn that Miss Lucy Wodehouse has learned from the former Rector's example and begun to exert herself with parish visiting.

*The Doctor's Family* is a longer but slighter tale with a conventional love plot. Edward Rider is a young doctor who has set up in practice in the unfashionable quarter of Carlingford – 'a region of half-built streets, vulgar new roads, and heaps of desolate brick and mortar' (ch.18). Secretly he is caring for his wastrel brother, Fred, who has returned from Australia and sits in an upper room all day, smoking coarse tobacco and reading even coarser novels from the circulating library. Fred's wife, Susan, then appears, together with several infants, and her sister, Nettie Underwood, 'all action and haste' and 'not only slender, but *thin*, dark, eager, impetuous, with blazing black eyes and red lips' (ch.2). Nettie is one of those masterful young heroines Mrs Oliphant draws better than anyone since Jane Austen, and naturally she and Edward are destined for one another, after some stock misapprehensions.

Given the rather improbable extent of Nettie's self-imposed martyrdom (she is, at the crisis of the story, prepared to accompany her sister Susan and the children back to Australia) and the even more unlikely *deus ex machina* of an Australian who appears with a proposal of marriage to Susan, now widowed (Fred having fallen into the river while drunk), the story moves briskly and turns out to be fairly entertaining. Indeed its farcical elements are perhaps the most engaging, especially when amidst shouting and disturbance Edward arrives as Nettie is packing and preparing to leave England for ever. A reckless ride through the respectable streets of Carlingford in pursuit of Nettie makes plain all misunderstandings and offers the prospect of lifelong felicity, though as Miss Lucy Wodehouse perceives it would have been a neater ending if Dr Rider could instead have fallen in love with Miss Marjoribanks, daughter of the town's leading practitioner:

> If Miss Marjoribanks had only been Nettie, or Nettie Miss Marjoribanks! If not only love and happiness, but the old doctor's practice and savings, could but have been brought to heap up the measure of the young doctor's good fortune! What a pity that one cannot have everything! (ch.18)

With such gentle Trollopian irony does the story exert its charm, although its chief interest is undoubtedly the character of Nettie Underwood. One can even believe, because of her impetuousness, that she *will* go to Australia, but what is more interesting is the degree to which Mrs Oliphant undercuts Nettie's self-imposed duty, her determination to provide for her sister and family, by showing just how much it cloaks managerial pride, and how much it is her defence against becoming dependent. In Nettie we have an inspiration which flowered in a splendid portrayal in *Miss Marjoribanks*.

The appearance of *Salem Chapel* in 1863[29] was greeted with justifiable enthusiasm. The narrative is brisk and assured, moving immediately into a rapid tour of a more geographically certain Carlingford than we have seen before, and a subject is announced without loss of time: the gulf between Carlingford society and its Dissenting community. This is a novel about English social snobbery as a Scotswoman can enjoy it. The centre of action, Salem Chapel, is at the west end of Grove Street, where the houses are 'little detached boxes, each two storeys high, each fronted by a little flower-plot – clean, respectable, meagre, little habitations' (ch.1). Greengrocers, dealers in cheese and bacon, milkmen, teachers of day schools, form the élite of this cheerful congregation. The cream of society, on the other hand, is centred on the parish church and the chapel of St Roque's, and the big houses of Grange Lane, where the Wodehouses and the Marjoribanks live.

The new minister of Salem Chapel, Arthur Vincent, fresh from Homerton, and aflame with both social and professional ambitions, quickly feels the limitations of his flock and begins to hanker after Grange Lane. Almost as particular about the cut of his coat as Mr Wentworth, the perpetual curate of St Roque's, 'he came to Carlingford with elevated expectations' and was rapidly enamoured of the young dowager, Lady Western. But Vincent, not being a Christ Church man, or even a fellow of Trinity, feels at a disadvantage. He gazes on the curate with some wistfulness. 'A poor widow's son, educated at Homerton, and an English squire's son, public school, and university bred, cannot begin on the same level' (ch.2). Mrs Oliphant thus poses her hero in a beautifully ambiguous position; even his lodgings are at what the Grange Lane people call *the other end* of George Street (ch.1). Brought up in 'painful gentility' by his mother, Vincent is between two worlds, and the early chapters make a good deal of comic mileage out of Vincent's mistaken notions of himself and those around him, from the time his ego is punctured by the well-meant gift of a left-over jelly from Mrs Tozer's welcoming-party to his mortification at being tongue-tied at Lady Western's breakfast. Bitterly resentful at being adopted by the Tozers and their daughter Phoebe, who is 'pink all over', and recoiling from the smugness of Salem, Vincent antagonises his flock.

The chapel people are as realistic as though Mrs Oliphant had lived among them all her life, especially old Mr Tufton, his crippled daughter, the admirable Mr Tozer, the butterman, and his buxom daughter, Phoebe. Indeed, much of the zest of the novel comes from scenes involving these good folk and their surroundings. The tea meeting (ch.10), is full of fascinating detail, the blazing gas of the schoolroom, the decorations, the tables 'groaning with dark-complexioned plumcake and heavy buns', the urns, the ladies' bonnets, the fulsome speeches, and 'the triumphant face of Tozer at the end of the room, jammed against the wall, drinking tea out of an empty sugar-basin' – another jar to the sensibilities of the young Nonconformist.

Besides satirising the English preoccupation with class, birth and social mobility, *Salem Chapel* is also a growing-up story, explaining the constricting pressures of the social group against which the individual must struggle. Arthur Vincent, though naïve and self-satisfied, has many admirable qualities and gradually grows in maturity and self-confidence. This progress is underlined by the role of the butterman, Tozer, who sees himself as the minister's mentor and tries to manage his protégé's career. Vincent begins by hating his domination, but a bond grows between them as Tozer reveals a simple good nature that earns the minister's respect. Tozer is that rarity in a mid-Victorian novel, a tradesman drawn convincingly and without caricature. As principal deacon he obtrudes his opinions about the good of the chapel and meddles with Vincent's private life, but when troubles gather he grows stronger in his loyalty to the young minister, though Mrs Oliphant is careful not to lose sight of that proprietorial smugness in his attitude. 'I'll stand by you, sir, for one whatever happens', he declares when Vincent's fortunes are at their blackest, his face 'radiant with conscious bounty and patronage' (ch.25). But his counsel is sound, and when scandal breaks his advice is go into the pulpit as usual and face the flock; 'It's next Sunday is all the battle' (ch.27), and he grows in the reader's estimation. When Vincent most needs help he makes an oration worthy of Mark Antony to prevent the flock from repudiating its pastor.

The course of the solemn tribunal covers two splendid chapters of mingled pathos and comedy. Vincent's mother, disguised in her black shawl at the back of the Salem schoolroom, is the anguished witness, as Pigeon, the poulterer, declares that Vincent must go. Old Mr Tufton, the former minister, well-meaning but over-apologetic, only makes matters worse. Then Tozer rises and with his vigorous, ungrammatical, plain speaking both extols the minister's example and annihilates his enemies for their vindictiveness. His speech, some four pages long, is masterly characterisation, but it also expresses issues implicit in the whole novel: the tendency of the Dissenting community – of any social grouping – to cabal and conspire against its leader, and out of personal ambition to produce anarchy. Just as Tozer in his clumsy way had tried to show Vincent that he must conciliate his congregation without sacrificing his principles, he now makes a case against the tyranny exercised by the Salem people and calls for tolerance and understanding. When Vincent declares his intention of resigning, Tozer again enlists the reader's sympathy, groaning in his sleep with anxiety at the new cloud over Salem and poignantly expressing his vision of the ideal (far from Vincent's own imagining) of a friendly tea – 'pleasant looks and the urns a-smoking, and a bit of green on the wall . . . a bit of an anecdote, or poetry about friends as is better friends after they've spoke their minds and had it out' (ch.40).

But the maturing of Vincent cannot reside in the kind of comfortable reconciliation that would have been accepted by his predecessor, Tufton. In a passage of Lawrencean rhetoric, Mrs Oliphant has her hero take his wounded sensibility into the countryside around Carlingford: 'Here were the hedgerows stirring, the secret grain beginning to throb conscious in the old furrows' (ch.40) and Vincent decides what to do. Once more he faces the flock in the decorated schoolroom, under the text 'Love one another' amid cheers and applause, but, 'angry, displeased, humbled in his own estimation', he discourses quietly until 'the very gaslights seem to darken in the air in the silence', and with new-found spiritual authority he leaves Salem.

*Salem Chapel* also contains crudely sensational plot elements, however, involving a mystery surrounding Mrs Hilyard, whose husband has for many years kept her from her own child, and for good measure almost seduces Vincent's sister, Susan. The ramifications, involving abduction, attempted murder, and ear-splittingly falsetto dialogue – ' "She-wolf! " cried the man, grinding his teeth' (ch.9) – sit very uneasily with the dominant domestic realism, although the sensationalism can be defended in one important respect: it throws ironical light on the theme of irrationality in human affairs. People are subject to dark forces from within. Vincent's well-ordered life is suddenly overthrown by his infatuation with Lady Western; he is 'rapt out of himself' (ch.7). His sister's near ruin and madness, and the passionate hatred of Mrs Hilyard for her husband, are, like the violence and mystery, manifestations of the irregularity that threatens Salem, and they force Vincent into knowledge of the real evil and pain in the world that it is his business as minister to attend to. His journey to Northumberland illustrates well the relation between theme and sensational plot. The search for 'the lost creature', his sister, has the usual melodramatic ingredients, but the narrative makes thematic sense: the church bell's jangling reinforces the idea of the chaos into which Vincent has fallen – 'life all disordered' – and as a minister of religion he is painfully conscious of his imperilled position among the flock (whom he has temporarily abandoned) and of his responsibilities:

> As they drove along the bleak moorland road, an early church-bell tingled into the silence, and struck, with horrible iron echoes, upon the heart of the minister of Salem. Sunday morning! Life all disordered, incoherent, desperate – all its usages set at nought and duties left behind. Nothing could have added the final touch of derangement and desperation like the sound of that bell. . . .'    (ch.20)

Mrs Oliphant also shows herself adept at the kind of mounting suspense that Wilkie Collins or Miss Braddon could create. At one point Vincent is idly gazing at a train just beginning to move out of the station:

> Now the tedious line glides into gradual motion. Good Heaven! what was that? the flash of a match, a sudden gleam upon vacant cushions, the profile of a face, high-featured, with the thin light locks and shadowy moustache he knew so well, standing out for a moment in aquiline distinctness against the moving space.

It is the man he is pursuing, and as the train gathers speed Vincent struggles to open a door, until several porters seize him. Passengers stare out of windows, and in one of the end compartments he sees another familiar face, that of Mrs Hilyard, 'who looked out with no surprise, but with a horrible composure in her white face, and recognized him with a look which chilled to stone'. Over-emphatic, perhaps, but full of imaginative detail and the sudden impact one associates with a Hitchcock film.

The physical reality of a community and its environment is brought to life by a host of homely touches: Tufton's neat little house with its cabbages and huge geraniums, the green door leading to the Wodehouse villa, the cheering fire in a station waiting-room. Physical actions are highly suggestive: Mrs Vincent attending to the lamps and taking comfort from this routine activity; Tozer's hand over his empty cup and saucer eloquently conveying displeasure. Domestic details are equally exact. With Mrs Oliphant we know there is even 'Wooster sauce' on the dinner table and that beds must be well aired in January. Atmosphere is her strong card: you can smell the ham and cheeses in Tozer's shop; and, even where sensational effects are uppermost, they are often underpinned and given credibility by atmospheric touches, as when Mrs Hilyard takes her long lonely walk in the dark, rainy street.

*Salem Chapel* is the livelier novel, but *The Perpetual Curate* the more ambitious development of Mrs Oliphant's intentions with the series.[30] This was the novel for which John Blackwood risked £1500 to his associate's wonderment, and cheered by his encouragement Mrs Oliphant declared, '*The Perpetual Curate* is the sharer of my inmost thoughts'. The hero, she said, 'is a favourite of mine, and I mean to bestow the very greatest care upon him'.[31]

Care was also given to plotting a more complex work, even though the spontaneous way she wrote was not conducive to adequate anticipation of climaxes. In chapter 37 she declares her anxiety about which of her many threads of narrative shall be taken up first, and a joke about events ending for the hero 'like a trashy novel' (ch.48) perhaps betrays a certain unease about not having quite brought it off. It was apparent in her correspondence with Blackwood that the original intention was 'a little exhibition of all the three parties in the Church',[32] to be achieved by making her hero, Frank Wentworth, a Puseyite confronting the newly installed, rather old-fashioned 'high and dry' Rector, William Morgan. At the same time, Frank is badgered by his Low Church aunt, Leonora, who has the power of securing a living for him in Skelmersdale, and engaged in an unsuccessful struggle to prevent his brother going over to Rome.

*The Perpetual Curate* has much to recommend it. The larger framework enables Mrs Oliphant to have her fling at several touchy subjects: doctrinal squabbles of High, Low and Roman Church, particularly the still fascinating topic of Catholic conversion, rivalries of parents and children, prickly marital relationships, class antagonism, and that abiding Victorian preoccupation with good name. What gives it unity is the way the author shows a well-governed world turned upside down, and normally sensible, respectable and sober members of the community squabbling like pettish children. ' . . . this strange, wayward, fantastical humanity which is never to be calculated upon' (ch.24) – the phrase takes on a special resonance as the epicentre of the novel. The opening prepares us for trouble by insisting that Carlingford is a place where nothing happens. 'It is the boast of the place that it has no particular interest' (ch.1). The rule of the clergy is emphasised:

> But in every community some centre of life is necessary. This point, round which everything circles, is, in Carlingford, found in the clergy. They are the administrators of the commonwealth, the only people who have defined and compulsory duties to give a sharp outline to life.

It is the book's business to show how this order is turned upside down and how the state totters.

At first reading the novel invites comparison with one of the Barsetshire series, not least in its title, which adopts the conveniently independent though ambiguous post Trollope chose in *Framley Parsonage* (1861) for Mr Crawley, perpetual curate of Hogglestock. That element of independence is vital for Mrs Oliphant's hero, who is also of higher social standing than the new Rector, his father being the squire of another parish. So long as Frank stays within his own segment of the parish at St Roque's Chapel he is unassailable, but he has carried his muscular Christianity to the new housing-estate and the canal, forming an impromptu chapel among the brickmakers and bargemen. Pride, breeding, youth and a certain resentment at a newcomer's authority spark off an immediate clash, when Frank deliberately insults Mr Morgan by mocking the hideous architecture of the parish church, which the Rector is planning to improve. Thus a very Trollopian conflict of opposites is initiated: old ways and new, the invasion of territory, clashes of temperament and ideology, all promising a good fight. Moreover, there is enough ambiguity in both characters for the reader to sympathise at points with each. What loads public opinion against Frank is that he is suspected of having toyed with a young girl's feelings, a moral delinquency similar to that of Mr Crawley in *The Last Chronicle of Barset* (published three years after Mrs Oliphant's novel), who is suspected of misdemeanour over a cheque. In both unlikely circumstances some kind of public tribunal is involved, and it is an unfortunate sensational element in *The Perpetual Curate* that Wentworth could actually be suspected of abduction and end up before a kangaroo court of local worthies.

That dimension of clergymen in their ministry which Trollope studiously avoids is never shirked by Mrs Oliphant. Frank Wentworth gains in depth by being shown about his active ministry; he visits the sick, baptises (a flagrant invasion of his rector's parish, which adds fuel to the row), organises a Sisterhood and a Provident Society, and hears confession too. Mrs Oliphant shows him not only preparing his sermon, but also delivering it – at the Wharfside service, for example, when his text has more fervour and effectiveness than his preaching at St Roque's. Much later in the novel, when his personal troubles are at their worst, he visits the dying Mr Wodehouse and is seen to be increasing in spiritual maturity:

> Mr Wentworth came into the silent chamber with all his anxieties throbbing in his heart, bringing life at its very height of agitation and tumult into the presence of death. He went forward to the bed, and tried for an instant to call up any spark of intelligence that might yet exist within the mind of the dying man; but Mr Wodehouse was beyond the voice of any priest. The Curate said the prayers for the dying at the bedside, suddenly filled with a great pity for the man who was thus taking leave unawares of all this mournful splendid world. (ch.27)

The mixture of emotions, the recognition of human responses getting in the way of priestly ones, the gulf between the vital young man and the dying old one, and the juxtaposition of 'mournful splendid' in that last sentence convey forcefully the ambiguity of human experience.

The characterisation of the little Welsh Rector, Mr Morgan, is equally substantial. His fundamental pleasantness, resentment at having a subordinate flout his authority, uncomfortable feelings of social inferiority, and most of all his rancour towards a young, attractive man, arising from sexual envy, are all well rendered.

That the quarrel has its roots in psychological causes is understated and adds to the subtlety of characterisation, for the Rector's wife from the start shows sympathy for the curate and impatience with her husband's point of view. Indeed, the Morgans' marriage is the major achievement of the novel.[33] Some perceptive and touching comment is made upon deferred 'prudent' marriages practised among the clergy.[34] Mrs Morgan reflects drily at one point, 'how much better one knows a man after being married to him three months than after being engaged to him for ten years' (ch.5); and looking at her – 'She was a good woman, but she was not fair to look upon' (ch.20) – Frank wonders what Lucy would be like if she had to wait ten years for him. The whole problem of lost years and disenchantment is beautifully rendered in chapter 28, demonstrating what insight and restraint Mrs Oliphant was capable of at her best. The scene begins with some mild skirmishes over trivia. Mrs Oliphant, true to most domestic imbroglios, notches up a list of petty irritations between both husband and wife: the Rector is late for dinner; Mrs Morgan has already changed her dress; anxious about the fish, she wonders how cook will get her own back next morning if the food is spoiled. It is a very hot day, and Mr Morgan is somewhat put about by his wife's tranquil coolness in her muslin dress. All this is a prelude to a tantalising verbal game in which the Rector, dying to impart the latest gossip concerning his curate, is held back by a mixture of propriety and pique at his wife's command of the situation. Even the sight of his favourite All-Souls pudding fails to unlock the tongue of this righteous man, while the peaches – a special care of Mrs Morgan's – are entirely overlooked in the Rector's agitation.

> She put away her peach in her resentment, and went to a side-table for her work, which she always kept handy for emergencies. Like her husband, Mrs Morgan had acquired some little 'ways' in the long ten years of their engagement, one of which was a confirmed habit of needle-work at all kinds of unnecessary moments, which much disturbed the Rector when he had anything particular to say.

Unwisely, Mr Morgan decides it is time to administer a gentle reproof about patience: ' "I am not patient," said the Rector's wife; "it never was my nature. I can't help thinking sometimes that our long experiences have done us more harm than good". . . .'

Next, arrival of the unpleasant curate, Leeson, drives Mrs Morgan out on a charitable errand. Her thoughts as she walks down Grove Street continually return to the old sadness:

> She never could help imagining what she might have been had she married ten years before at the natural period. 'And even then not a girl', she said to herself in her sensible way, as she carried this habitual thread of thought with her along the street, past the little front gardens, where there were so many mothers with their children. On the other side of the way the genteel houses frowned darkly with their staircase windows upon the humility of Grove Street; and Mrs Morgan began to think within herself of the Misses Hemmings and other spinsters, and how they got along upon this path of life, which, after all, is never very lightsome to behold, except in the future or the past. It was dead present with the Rector's wife just then, and many speculations were in her mind, as was natural. 'Not that I could not have lived unmarried', she continued within herself, with a woman's pride; 'but things looked so different at five-and-twenty!' and in her heart she grudged the cares she had lost, and sighed over this wasting of her years.

Whenever she wrote a particular fine passage like this one, Mrs Oliphant would laughingly describe it as 'having a trot'. Here, the self-admonitory 'even then not a girl', the understated yearning for children, the oblique references to a sense of social inadequacy among the parishioners, and then the spurt of pride at the end cloaking a momentary regret for the single life, create a vivid, many-layered, sympathetic character. Soon after this Mrs Morgan meets Frank Wentworth, and her clumsy expression of sympathy, meeting with a rebuff, provokes a retort that tells the reader more about her unfulfilled longings:

> 'I don't think you would risk your prospects, and get yourself into trouble, and damage your entire life, for the sake of any girl, however pretty she might be. Men don't do such things for women nowadays, even when it is a worthy object', said the disappointed optimist.

Friendship or enmity hangs by a hair in this brief encounter.

The same tension now spills over into the Morgans' marriage, as Mrs Morgan is ashamed and angry at her husband's animosity towards his curate; he is lessened in her eyes, and it pains her deeply. The reconciliation is therefore especially touching. Mrs Oliphant, you might say, pulls off a corny trick with style. After the tribunal at which Frank Wentworth has been exonerated, Mr Morgan returns sheepishly to his wife, consumed with guilt and shame, and tells her it is time to leave Carlingford and start afresh in another living. Retiring behind her darning, Mrs Morgan senses their failure with mortification. Then he reveals that his departure will leave the Carlingford place open for Wentworth, and at once she melts, drops the stocking she was mending and begs forgiveness for her crossness: 'The excellent man was as entirely unconscious that he was being put up again at that moment with acclamations upon his pedestal, as that he had at a former time been violently displaced from it, and thrown into the category of broken idols' (ch.45). While satisfying the romantic demands of the Mudie reader, Mrs Oliphant does not sacrifice her ironical tone; Mrs Morgan falls back into the adoring posture, flattering her husband's vanity, and he kisses her, smooths her brown hair 'with a touch which made her feel like a girl again' and goes contentedly downstairs:

> Had Mr Morgan been a Frenchman, he probably would have imagined his wife's heart to be touched by the graces of the Perpetual Curate; but, being an Englishman, and rather more certain, on the whole, of her than of himself, it did not occur to him to speculate on the subject. He was quite able to content himself with the thought that women are incomprehensible, as he went back to his study.

The gulf between male and female points of view remains, and so does Mrs Morgan's wistful longing for romance.

Both *Salem Chapel* and *The Perpetual Curate* add sensational elements to what are realistic domestic studies; *Miss Marjoribanks* on the other hand is wholly in the tradition of Jane Austen and Mrs Gaskell,[35] the story nothing more extraordinary than Lucilla Marjoribanks's 'grand design of turning the chaotic elements of society into one grand unity' (ch.18), which also turns out to be her quest for a husband. It is, then, both romantic fairytale and comedy of manners, the most sophisticated and charming of the series, and a novel that can stand comparison with the best contemporary novels of its kind.

Gentility, breeding, and 'the painful pride of poverty' (ch.10) are its serious topics, and upon these matters Mrs Oliphant descants with an ironic gravity worthy of comparison with Jane Austen's. The novel moves briskly, but dramatic action centres around the commotion over who will become the next member of parliament and the death of Dr Marjoribanks, events which can be accepted as part of the everyday life of Carlingford. In fact the novel sets out deliberately to mock the breathless style of the sensationists: 'the danger came sudden, appalling, and unlooked for' (ch.14), but it is only the possibility that Mr Cavendish flirting with Barbara Lake will complicate Lucilla's plans for reforming Carlingford. And, when a more serious crisis looms, 'It was not a narrative of robbery or murder, or anything very alarming' (ch.18), but Archdeacon Beverley recognising Cavendish, one of the pillars of Lucilla's drawing-room, as the son of a trainer or 'something about Newmarket', and the possibility that he will reveal it. At one point Cavendish's sister, Mrs Woodburn, a long-time resident of Carlingford, catching his panic at social ruin, dreads that 'there might be, for anything she could tell, a little bottle of prussic acid in his waistcoat pocket' (ch.30). Thus the apparatus of sensation fiction is exploited for social comedy.

Lucilla is an outsize character, 'large in all particulars', with tawny hair 'curly to exasperation' (ch.1). In other words, she is fat and has unmanageable hair – an unusual heroine for a romantic novel. She has, however, energy and generous spirit, and has sought to compensate for her physical disadvantages by developing her intellect. One psychological insight both humorously and sympathetically conveyed is that Lucilla's self-consciousness prevents real understanding of others' needs; it is sensitivity gone inwards, with results akin to selfishness. At fifteen, she returns home after her mother's death:

In the course of her rapid journey she had already settled upon everything that had to be done; or rather, to speak more truly, had rehearsed everything, according to the habit already acquired by a quick mind, a good deal occupied with itself.

First, she meant to fall into her father's arms – forgetting with
that singular facility for overlooking the peculiarities of others
which belongs to such a character, that Dr Marjoribanks was
very little given to embracing, and that a hasty kiss on her
forehead was the warmest caress he had ever given his
daughter – and then to rush up to the chamber of death and
weep over dear mamma.   (ch.1)

Lucilla's sorrow is genuine, but it cannot subdue her sense of the
dramatic. Later in the story a character says that she is an actress,
and so she is, but at the same time she is never merely playing a
part. She is utterly sincere and that is the danger. She is devoted
to a heroic image of herself that makes her a mixture of bullying
sweetness, queenly modesty and selfish benevolence. 'I will give
up everything in the world to be a comfort to you!' she vows to
her father, at which Dr Marjoribanks recoils, seeing in her the
qualities of his late wife 'which had wearied his life out' (ch.1).
From finishing-school some four years later Lucilla returns,
determined to show her devotion by making Grange Lane the
focus of Carlingford society. Her first triumph is winning over
the cook and taking her father's place at the head of the table: 'the
reins of state had been smilingly withdrawn from his unconscious
hands', while the drawing-room which is to be the 'inner court
and centre of her kingdom' is transformed, according to her
taste, from a 'waste and howling wilderness' (ch.4).

Thus, in the first half-dozen chapters intriguing conflict extends
from home into social sphere as Lucinda pursues her masterplan
to rescue Carlingford from its social torpor. Lucinda combines
Dorothea Brooke's idealism with Emma's egotism and there are
reminders of Jane Austen in her 'well-regulated mind' (ch.14)
and that 'sublime confidence in herself which is the first necessity
to a woman with a mission' (ch.5).

Aphoristic    sharpness    enlivens    the    novel    throughout.
Carlingford's is 'the old fashioned orthodox way of having a great
respect for religion, and as little to do with it as possible' (ch.17).
Lucilla herself keeps up 'civilities with heaven' (ch.2) and
observes of the clergy, 'A nice clergyman is almost as useful to the
lady of the house as a man who can flirt' (ch.15). Everything is
for the best she reasons, 'with that beautiful confidence which is
common to people who have things their own way' (ch.9).
'Lucilla had all that regard for constituted rights which is so

necessary to a revolutionary of the highest class' (ch.10). Much use is made of antithesis and hyperbole, particularly as regards Lucilla's character and attitudes. She is a 'distinguished revolutionary' (ch.3), a 'gentle martyr' (ch.16); she shows 'artless gratitude' (ch.13), and possesses 'that serene self-consciousness which places the spirit above the passing vexations of the world' (ch.23). Hyperbole is applied to Dr Marjoribanks, with his great watch 'by which all the pulses of Grange Lane considered it their duty to keep time'. The novel sparkles more than others in the Carlingford series by virtue of such linguistic exuberance.

Lucilla's mission is matrimony, although she may not realise it, and that she misses the suitor right under her nose, her cousin Tom Marjoribanks, and thereafter attracts a succession of men – all of whom she high-mindedly rejects in noble self-sacrifice both to her father and to society – becomes the essential comic point of the novel. Lucilla's belief in her altruism remains unshaken in the weeks that follow the successful receptions in her newly decorated drawing-room and her confidence grows; even religion sanctifies her mission to be a comfort to her papa. She is 'superior to earthly delight' (ch.12), and when people fail to appreciate her sacrifices she can sigh and stand bravely to her post: 'a great soul, whose motives must always remain to some extent unappreciated' (ch.9). Providence is definitely on her side. By such rhetoric Mrs Oliphant makes Lucilla outsize, outrageous, yet thoroughly real and lovable. For, like all good comic creations, Lucilla has the trick of remaking the world to her own specifications; against all evidence of her bulldozing, she sees herself as modest, gentle, tactful, 'fluttering her maiden plumes' (ch.13), full of 'maiden candour and unsuspecting innocence' (ch.27), always 'in harmony with *herself*' (ch.28).

Even as she stands by her resolution to put off marriage for ten years, by which time she says ruefully she will be 'going off', she has moments speculating about a succession of suitors. She is a Rosalind, enjoying her freedom for the present, but looking toward matrimony. This romantic quality of the novel is seen most obviously in chapter 16, in which the motif of the garden party is that of fairyland: the night air, moonlight, twin nightingales, all indicate that, although she is no Titania, Lucilla is a creator of magic. She behaves with the serenity that makes her superior to all vexations of this world, greeting her subjects with 'sweet humility'. The garden scene is a delicately painted idyll which ironically deploys Lucilla's coronation and the now acknowledged truth that her drawing-room is 'the seventh heaven of terrestrial harmony'.

Lucilla's pursuit of power makes *Miss Marjoribanks* a feminist novel as well as popular romance, and it is interesting to speculate how many girls relished its subversive delights. Lucilla yearns for the kind of power men have and, indeed, often exercises it. She overrules her father, she bosses Tom Marjoribanks, she scorns Mr Cavendish, and even General Travers on one occasion is cut down to his proper level. She runs rings around men, two at a time if necessary, as she proves when the rival parliamentary candidates confront each other in her drawing-room, and she is patently more capable, efficient and resourceful than anyone around her. Calling on Mr Lake the drawing-master, she knows she could give him his tea as he liked it:

> And when the tea came it was all she could do to keep herself quiet, and remember that she was a visitor, and not take it out of the incapable hands of Barbara, who never gave her father the right amount of sugar in his tea. . . . She sat with her very fingers itching to cut the bread and butter for him, and give him a cup of tea as he liked it. . . .   (ch.28)

But it is not solely a matter of the domestic capabilities of women Mrs Oliphant is extolling. A serious point is being made here about the waste of womanly potential:

> Miss Marjoribanks had her own ideas in respect to charity, and never went upon ladies' committees, nor took any further share than what was proper and necessary in parish work; and when a woman has an active mind, and still does not care for parish work, it is a little hard for her to find a 'sphere'. And Lucilla, though she said nothing about a sphere, was still more or less in that condition of mind which has been so often and so fully described to the British public – when the ripe female intelligence, not having the natural resource of a nursery and a husband to manage, turns inwards, and begins to 'make a protest' against the existing order of society, and to call the world to account for giving it no due occupation – and to consume itself.   (ch.42)

Lucilla therefore goes into politics, in the only way a woman can, by making campaign favours and electioneering for Mr Ashburton. Complementing this quiet comment on the subordinate role enforced upon women, is sympathy for the difficulties of running a household. As Mrs Centum puts it,

> '. . . men are *so* unreasonable. I should like to know what *they* would do if they had what we have to go through: to look after all the servants – and they are always out of their senses at Christmas – and to see that the children don't have too much pudding, and to support all the noise. The holidays are the hardest work a poor woman can have', she concluded, with a sigh. . . .   (ch.10)

There is much understanding of the stresses and strains too for Mrs Woodburn, who had 'two men to carry on her shoulders' (ch.39).

In the latter part of the novel Mrs Oliphant boldly leaps ten years. Lucilla is twenty-nine and a new crusade to get Ashburton elevated MP for Carlingford gives her abundant energy a fresh outlet, but there is a suggestion of greater maturity and yearning for happiness. The narrative has added pathos; life has gone on, people have aged. This is beautifully captured in the Chileys, on whom Lucilla calls seeking support for her candidate. Colonel Chiley expresses his impatience with the rival, Cavendish, by poking the fire vigorously, a habit that over the years has irritated, now frightens, his wife:

> She gave a little start among her cushions, and stopped down to look over the floor. 'He will never learn that he is old', she said in Lucilla's ear, who instantly came to her side to see what she wanted; and thus the two old people kept watch upon each other, and noted, with a curious mixture of vexation and sympathy, each other's declining strength.   (ch.39)

Change is conveyed also by the town itself, in the new people and the expanding housing-estate. The novel takes on an evening air, rather like that of the closing stages of *As You Like It* or *The Tempest*. This is particularly noticeable when Dr Marjoribanks pats Lucilla's shoulder as he says goodnight – a rare physical gesture which causes her to look at him almost in alarm. The narrative is muted:

> Meantime the snow fell heavily outside, and wrapped everything in a soft and secret whiteness. And amid the whiteness and darkness, the lamp burned steadily outside at the garden-gate, which pointed out the Doctor's door amid all the closed houses and dark garden-walls in Grange Lane – a kind of visible succour and help always at hand for those who were suffering. (ch.42)

Despite this atmospheric anticipation, the news of the doctor's death next morning is shocking to the reader as well as to old Mrs Chiley, sobbing in her bed it was all a mistake, that it was she who ought to have died.

In the third volume, the discovery that Lucilla is not an heiress but must face a life of 'genteel economy' (ch.44) gives impetus to the plot, and the climax has appropriately romantic hyperbole as Lucilla faces the expected proposal from Ashburton and wonders about her absent cousin Tom: the 'very soul of good sense all her days, but now her ruling quality seemed to forsake her' (ch.49). Just as Ashburton starts his speech there is the sound of a coach rattling down the street, a door flung open, the crash of a china bowl, and Tom bursts into the house. The fairytale ending is assured: 'Fate and honest love had been waiting all the time till their moment came; and now it was not even necessary to say anything about it. The fact was so clear that it did not require stating. It was to be Tom after all' (ch.50).

The final touch is appropriate to Lucilla's character: having persuaded Tom to buy an estate near Carlingford she looks forward delightedly to work: 'It gave her the liveliest satisfaction to think of all the disorder and disarray of the Marchbank village. Her fingers itched to be at it – to set all the crooked things straight, and clean away the rubbish, and set everything, as she said, on a sound foundation' (ch.51). Thus Lucilla remains consistent, reconciles that heroic self-image with worthier objects, and to the end proves to Carlingford society that she is an exceptional young woman. What is more she succeeds in getting her own way, and can say to herself with secret delight that having married Tom she is Lucilla Marjoribanks still.

Ernest Baker described Mrs Oliphant as a 'Mrs Gaskell who has learned a good deal from Dickens and still more from Trollope'.[36] Of none of her novels is this more true than of *Phoebe Junior*.[37] It presents a more tranquil view of a society than any of its predecessors in the series, and perhaps for this reason has been underestimated. Echoes of Dickens occur in the caricature of the self-made man Copperhead, another Bounderby, a great unfeeling brute boasting of his struggle for success and bullying his genteel wife and nincompoop of a son, Clarence. But by far the greatest resemblance – or debt – is to Trollope. The subtitle, 'A Last Chronicle' immediately brings to mind its Barset predecessor. Similarly its major episode, concerning a forged bill by the incumbent of St Roque's Chapel, Mr May, and, to an even greater degree the minor occurrence of May's son, Reginald, being offered a sinecure as warden of Carlingford Hospital for the aged, are distinctly Trollopian.

This is not to say that *Phoebe Junior* is a hotchpotch of other writers' ideas. The heroine has qualities of independence that Trollope would not quite countenance, and the milieu of chapel and tradesmen's houses, the minute observation of domestic economy, are all Mrs Oliphant's own. Ursula May's awareness of the cost of an *entrée* for a special dinner party and her anxiety all the way from purchasing to cooking and eating is a case in point, and when Ursula is taunted by her father about reading novels and not her cookery book, the reader is made to feel the frustration acutely:

> Made dishes are the most expensive things! A leg of mutton, for instance; there it is, and when one weighs it, one knows what it costs; but there is not one of those *entrées* but costs *shillings* for herbs and truffles and gravy and forcemeat, and a glass of white wine here, and a half pint of claret there. It is all very well to talk of dishes made out of nothing. The meat may not be very much – and men never think of the other things, I suppose.   (I, ch.13)

'Ursula's entrées' play their part in the next chapter when father's unkind remarks about the food cause Nonconformist politician Mr Northcote to fall in love with her on the spot.

Progress has begun to affect Carlingford: the Wentworths and the Wodehouses have gone away, and the Tozers have moved into Lady Weston's old house in Grange Lane.[38] For Mrs Tozer 'the increase in gentility was questionable' (I, ch.12). For Copperhead, on the other hand, rise in status, by marrying a relative of Sir Robert Dorset, has been equally unsettling: 'Mr Copperhead felt the increase in gentility as well as the failure in jollity' (I, ch.2). Throughout the story people feel the strain of keeping up appearances or striving to maintain their superiority. Mrs Tozer secretly laments the old life over the shop in the High Street, and some of Mr Tozer's irascibility stems from his awkward social position, which makes him by turns sycophantic and belligerent towards the quality. As always in Mrs Oliphant's religious groups there is discomfort among the Non-conformists who feel their inferiority to the Anglican clergy. Not only clashes over status make Horace Northcote and Reginald May ill at ease with one another, but deep-seated divisions in religious attitudes.

Other kinds of change and displacement add to the groundswell of tension. These particularly concern the careers of the two heroines, Phoebe Beecham and Ursula May, both of whom are returned from London and experiencing the constrictions of rural Carlingford. Mr May is the voice of reaction, and both of his children are blamed, Ursula for demanding recognition as a woman and Reginald for daring to exercise his ministry in a more evangelical spirit. Reginald's opposition to his father's wish that he accept a sinecure is based on a modern radicalism challenging Victorian orthodoxies. In Ursula's case it is radicalism in the home. This is how Mr May sees the situation when Ursula wishes she could earn money:

'Do a little more in the house, and nobody will ask you to earn money. Yes, this is the shape things are taking nowadays,' said Mr May, 'the girls are mad to earn anyhow, and the boys, forsooth, have a hundred scruples. If women would hold their tongues and attend to their own business, I have no doubt we should have less of the other nonsense. The fact is everything is getting into an unnatural state.' (I, ch.10)

The question of women's status is thus implicit but unfortunately never debated; it was far too contentious for the popular market.

The roles of the novel's two heroines, however, are skilfully counterpointed to achieve greater depth and balance in the plot.

Both are intelligent and superior to the men around them, both affected in different ways by social pressures. Ursula, the clergyman's daughter, is one of the genteel poor, and at first regards the fashionably dressed and gracious Phoebe as an enviable model. Phoebe, however, has acquired her gentility by education and study, and is still the butterman's granddaughter. Her own mother, having risen in society, is painfully aware too of her past: 'the shop was still there, greasy and buttery as ever' (I, ch.5), and the reader who recalls that Phoebe of long ago (in *Salem Chapel*) appreciates the irony of the transformation. Sending young Phoebe back to relive her mother's social experience from a totally different position provides a splendid opportunity for social comment of which Mrs Oliphant takes full advantage.

Phoebe, armed with her finest wardrobe to meet Grange Lane society, is determined to be frank about the 'shop', but her first meeting with her grandparents is a shock:

Yes, there could be no doubt about it; there he was, he whom she was going to visit, under whose auspices she was about to appear in Carlingford. He was not even like an old Dissenting minister, which had been her childish notion of him. He looked neither more nor less than what he was, an old shopkeeper, very decent and respectable, but a little shabby and greasy, like the men whose weekly bills she had been accustomed to pay for her mother. She felt an instant conviction that he would call her 'Ma'am', if she went up to him, and think her one of the quality.   (I, ch.12)

Mrs Tozer, her grandmother, has put on her best cap, but, despite the sustaining power of this gorgeous creation, a huge brooch and a dress of copper-coloured silk which rustled a good deal as she came downstairs, is as apprehensive as Phoebe, feeling a thrill of excitement and 'sense of the difference which could not but be felt on one side as well as the other'. Emotion tells through the polite exchanges:

'We thought', said Mrs Tozer, 'as perhaps you mightn't be used to tea at this time of day.'
'Oh, it is the right time; it is the fashionable hour', said Phoebe; 'everybody has tea at five. I will run upstairs first, and take off my hat, and make myself tidy. . . .'

'Well?' said Mr Tozer to Mrs Tozer, as Phoebe disappeared. The two old people looked at each other with a little awe; but she, as was her nature, took the most depressing view. She shook her head. 'She's a deal too fine for us, Tozer', she said . . .

Tozer takes a more hopeful view:

'She came up and give me a kiss in the station, as affectionate as possible. All I can say for her is as she ain't proud.'

Mrs Tozer shook her head; but even while she did so, pleasanter dreams stole into her soul.

'I hope I'll be well enough to get to chapel on Sunday,' she said, 'just to see the folks' looks. The minister needn't expect much attention to his sermon. ''There's Phoebe Tozer's daughter!'' they'll all be saying, and a-staring, and a-whispering.'

Phoebe, meanwhile, contemplating her grandmother's amazing cap and her grandfather's greasy coat, and facing the vast tent bed, moreen curtains and gigantic flowers of the carpet, bursts into tears:

But her temperament did not favour panics, and giving in was not in her. . . . Now was the time to put her principles to the test; and the tears relieved her, and gave her something of the feeling of a martyr, which is always consolatory and sweet; so she dried her eyes, and bathed her face, and went downstairs cheerful and smiling, resolved that at all costs, her duty should be done, however disagreeable it might be.

Doing her duty embraces being frank about her origin, and by this Mrs Oliphant not only makes Phoebe more attractive to the reader, but also exploits further the burdens of class feeling. Ursula May, for example, is acutely embarrassed at finding out that her friend is the granddaughter of a Carlingford shopkeeper; Phoebe, though mortified by her lowly origins, faces up to the Mays and Horace Northcote with 'masterly candour' (II, ch.6) and captivates Reginald May. She teases both him and Mr Northcote with assumed fears that two rival clergymen will quarrel, and then invites both to tea: 'She carried in her two young men as naughty boys carry stag-beetles or other such small deer. If they would fight it would be fun; and if they would not fight, why it might be fun still, and more amusing than grandmamma' (II, ch.10). This happy-go-lucky quality in Phoebe seems to promise an outcome in which the heroine of humble background marries the prince, but Mrs Oliphant varies the convention. Phoebe is presented more ambiguously as the story develops. The freedom with which she brings men to her side ('in the Tozer world, who knew anything of chaperons?' – III, ch.10) provides a clue to a character not only socially but morally ambiguous.

As reviewers recognised, Phoebe was 'not quite a lady', and while disapproving of the moral tone of the novel they had to admit that Phoebe's unconventional behaviour certainly made her interesting.[39] Her independent ways become the focus of a dramatic climax when she defies her grandfather and comes to the rescue of the curate of St Roque's after he has forged Tozer's name to a bill. With great impropriety Phoebe comes into possession of the incriminating document and witholds it from her distracted grandfather, a circumstance which led the *Saturday Review* to criticise Mrs Oliphant for preaching that a pretty girl could gain any end she set before her.[40] It is precisely this realism in her portrayal that is likely to appeal to the reader. When it comes to her dealings with suitors she is ready enough to flirt with Reginald May, but knowing full well which side her bread is buttered choose Clarence Copperhead and his fortune. This is a much bolder conclusion to a romance than Trollope permits himself.

Ursula, on the other hand, remains much closer to Trollopian type, and responds to the attentions of Mr Northcote with conventional reticence. The difference between Mrs Oliphant's two heroines is ably captured in the garden scene early in the last volume, where Janey, Ursula's sixteen-year-old sister, is the innocent observer of events under the stars, her naïveté an effective prelude to the scene – 'was this how it was managed?' she wonders, as the figures move into the shadows of the laurels. Ursula feels 'a confusion strange but sweet' (III, ch.6) in the attentions of Mr Northcote, but Phoebe has no such problems when confronted by her suitors. She knows that proposals are imminent and weighs up the possibilities, concluding that she will make Clarence her career:

Yes; she could put him into parliament, and keep him there. She could thrust him forward (she believed) to the front of affairs. He would be as good as a profession, a position, a great work to Phoebe. He meant wealth (which she dismissed in its superficial aspect as something meaningless and vulgar, but accepted in its higher aspect as an almost necessary condition of influence), and he meant all the possibilities of future power. Who can say that she was not as romantic as any girl of twenty could be? only her romance took an unusual form. It was her head that was full of throbbings and pulses, not her heart.

Mrs Oliphant handles the convention with some originality, hinting at the constrictions of being the angel in the house and rightly suggesting Phoebe's need for a more active role which she will take in the only form readily available, by proxy through a malleable husband. For a while, however, it seems that Phoebe will be punished for breaking with orthodoxy and accepting Clarence with reasons other than love in mind, because Copperhead says he will disown his son.[41] Clarence speaks up with primitive eloquence for the first time; Phoebe feels proud of him and, although she shivers at the prospect of his being disowned, is prepared to accept the consequences of her decision and stand by him. Such an action reassures the reader that Phoebe is, underneath it all, the regular loving and self-sacrificing female, although Mrs Oliphant does not quite capitulate, since she has the old man repent and Clarence inheriting after all. Phoebe will have her career.

In the presentation of the Mays Mrs Oliphant is at her best, depicting the endlessly interesting complex of relationships within the family. Reginald indulges in outbursts similar to his father's and exerts his authority over the girls. Likewise Ursula is inclined to patronise Janey. All the children notch up on a mental slate their father's injustices and pay him back with spurts of malice. May himself, unlike the caricatured Copperhead, is splendidly realised.[42] Indolent and self-centred – 'He had never forgiven Providence for leaving him with his motherless family upon his hands' (I, ch.10) – he has turned in on himself, venting his subconscious resentments in spiteful attacks on the children. The girls for their part, 'having no softening medium of a mother's eyes to look at their father through', are harsher in their judgements than they should be; 'and he did not take pains to

1   Mrs Oliphant, undated photograph by [H. L.] Mendelssohn

2　Windsor, 1874: Mrs Oliphant with her sons Cyril (top right) and Francis ('Cecco') (bottom left) and her nephew Frank Wilson (bottom right)

3   Rhoda Broughton, undated photograph by Barrauds Ltd, London

4   The yellowback cover for Rhoda Broughton's *Not Wisely, but Too Well* in Tinsleys' Cheap Novels series, 1871

# GONE WRONG!

A NEW NOVEL. BY MISS RHODY DENDRON,

*Authoress of " Cometh Down like a Shower," " Red in the Nose is She,"*
*" Good ! Buy Sweet Tart !" " Not Slily, But don't Tell."*

CHAPTER IV.—*What the Author says.*

H! she has fallen below the sheer cliff, where the merry gulls sing their sweet pæans to the wind-blown, unpunctual, irregular, disappointing, unapologetic sea, and lies, her beautiful head buried kit-cat length downwards, in the muddy sand, her gleaming balmorals appealing for aid with a mighty imploring clicking of the high heels aloft, while with her lavender kid gloves she is clutching at unhappy molluscs and killing innumerable shrimps and sand-eels in her struggle for life. _ _ _ _ _ _ _

5 Illustration by F. C. Burnand accompanying his text for a parody of Rhoda Broughton's work in *Punch*, 15 April 1876

6   James Payn, undated photograph

7   Advertisement for Mudie's Select Library of Fiction issued in April 1861

(a) Miss M. E. Braddon

(b) Ouida

(c) William Black

(d) James Payn

8　Four popular authors of the day as seen by *Punch*, March–December 1881

fascinate his children or throw the glamour of love into their eyes' 'Both looked selfish to the other, and Mr May, no doubt, could have made out quite as good a case as the children did.' Quiet analysis of this kind shows once more Mrs Oliphant as a delicate student of character.

If the greatness of Archdeacon Grantly and Mr Harding in *Barchester Towers* or the Proudies and Mr Crawley in *The Last Chronicle of Barset* does not come quite within Mrs Oliphant's grasp, there is no denying the quality of her Chronicles of Carlingford and her moments of glory within the series. Vincent, Tozer, Lucilla Marjoribanks and Phoebe display the angularities and inconsistencies of superior creative imagination; they are capable of surprising, like other memorable characters of fiction. She deserves better from posterity than to be so unregarded as she has been since her death. At the very least the pattern of mid-Victorian fiction is incomplete without a readily available edition of the Chronicles of Carlingford.

That she wrote too much and too quickly remains for her as for others of her kind the penalty of commercial fiction; that she recognised how much better her work might have been was her personal anguish, as her autobiography clearly shows. What remains remarkable is what she did achieve within those limitations. 'Few writers in any age', said Herbert Paul, 'have maintained so high a level over so large a surface.'[43]

# 5 Delightful Wickedness: Some Novels of Rhoda Broughton

*She at least possesses that one touch of vulgarity that makes the whole world kin.*
Oscar Wilde, *Pall Mall Gazette* (28 October 1886)

Few novelists have mountains named after them, but to her amusement Rhoda Broughton achieved such monumental celebrity. In 1876 Captain Clements Markham aboard the explorer ship *Alert* was mapping the northern section of Ellesmere Island at the North Pole, and he and his fellow officers solaced their leisure hours with Rhoda Broughton's novels.[1] So much pleasure had she given them that they christened one icebound peak 'Mount Rhoda' in her honour. She treasured the compliment. Her fame had sprung from two novels published in 1867, *Not Wisely, but Too Well* and *Cometh Up as a Flower*, considered rather scandalous because they described with unparalleled frankness girls falling in love. They stamped Miss Broughton as a new voice and also a rather fast and dangerous one that innocent young ladies should beware of, but there was a subtext of struggle, suffering and frustration that expressed the intelligent woman's need for personal identity and fulfilment and this was undoubtedly what established her place in the front rank of popular writers. Though not by any means radical, she was in this respect a rebel.

A rather engaging picture of her at the height of her fame comes from Helen Black, who sought her out in the early 1890s for a series of articles in the *Lady's Pictorial*.[2] At this period the novelist was sharing a house overlooking the Thames at Richmond with her widowed sister, Mrs Eleanor Newcome, and 'resting' after publishing her novel *Alas!* (1890), which, according

102

to Miss Braddon, had established her title to genius.[3] Surrounded
by her Spode china, her birds, her dogs, an immense pyramid of
ferns and palms, Miss Broughton airily dismissed her fame and
showed no vanity in her role as author. She sold her books out-
and-out at once, she told her awed visitor, and after that had done
with them. This she accompanied with a rich, hearty laugh which
conveyed that 'vein of fun and wit – entirely of an original kind –
which runs through her books'.[4] Drawing upon the memories of
his father as an undergraduate at Oxford in 1883, Michael
Sadleir describes her as on the large side, with a decidedly county
air, pugnacious demeanour and rather mannish appearance; she
looked like 'a nice-looking undergraduate dressed to play a
female part in an OUDS production'.[5] No one could mistake that
firm chin and strong mouth (see Plate 3) for the docile and
retiring female offered as a model in countless popular novels.
Her conversation was 'of witty but alarming pungency', said
Sadleir, and was to land her in a good deal of controversy.[6]
Indeed she acquired a reputation as social luminary and
conversationalist which to some extent overshadowed her role as
a writer. *The Times* correspondent after her death, for example,
stated that she was better than her books.[7]

Rhoda's father, a clergyman, came of an old county family and
she grew up in conservative and sheltered surroundings; perhaps
one reason why so many of her heroines break out in rash and
usually disastrous escapades.[8] Home life for Rhoda was the
orderly routine of a country parsonage, enlivened by occasional
trips to her grandfather at Broughton Hall, Staffordshire, or to
her mother's relations in Dublin. Her father tutored his
daughters at home and Rhoda was well grounded in the classics
and English literature, acquiring that intimate knowledge of
English poetry somewhat oppressively present in her novels. One
may infer, both from her casual remarks and from the depiction
in her novels of sisterly relations in which there is often friction,
that her situation as youngest of three daughters (she also had a
younger brother) led to outbursts of temper and frustration.
There has been speculation that Rhoda had a passionate love
affair as a young woman.[9] However that may be, although both her
sisters married, Rhoda remained a spinster all her life, beginning her career in an unsettling time after the death of her parents
when she went to live with her sister Eleanor and her husband.

On a certain wet Sunday afternoon, bored to tears by a book,

*Elijah the Tishbite*, the spirit moved her to write something of her own. She also confessed that her delight in Anne Thackeray's *The Story of Elizabeth* (serialised in the *Cornhill Magazine*, 1862) and learning that the authoress was much her own age gave her confidence.[10] She wrote swiftly and secretly in an old copybook and by the end of six weeks had finished *Not Wisely, but Too Well*, keeping the manuscript by her until 1865, when on a visit to her uncle, Sheridan Le Fanu, she read him two chapters. Le Fanu accepted it for the *Dublin University Magazine*, which he edited, and is said to have exclaimed, 'You will succeed, and when you do, remember that I prophesied it.'[11] Percy Fitzgerald, Le Fanu's neighbour, who was also present, found the story really dramatic.[12] Rhoda's own account of the incident, according to Ethel Arnold (a niece of Matthew Arnold) was somewhat more prosaic: by the end of her reading, she said, 'one had fallen heavily asleep, while the other maintained a silence, blank and chilling as the grave'.[13] Her second novel, *Cometh Up as a Flower*, was written in a similar burst of creative excitement, and henceforth she maintained a regular literary output, producing a novel almost every two years. At the end of her life her writings amounted to twenty-six novels, a volume of short stories,[14] and some journalism.

At the time of her literary debut Rhoda also entered society, matching her literary reputation for being 'fast' with an asperity and social aplomb that established her as a character. Used to being noticed and saying rather wicked things in the flesh as well as in her novels, she struck one young lady in 1874 as altogether too self-assured: 'She walked about in such a "strong-minded" manner, stared at people and talked loud, and showed by every look and action that she knew perfectly well that she was the most important person there.'[15] Her table talk could be devastating; even Henry James confessed that her sharp tongue made him tremble. F. Anstey noted,

> I sat opposite to her at a dinner-party once and heard her neighbour – a middle-aged man who considered himself for no very obvious reasons, irresistible to women – say to her: 'I should like you to know my boy – he's much nicer than I am!' To which she replied 'Would you like me to say that that's impossible – or that I can quite believe it? Because I'll say either.'[16]

Not unexpectedly, repartee and sparkling dialogue are major assets of Rhoda's fiction.

In 1877 Rhoda set up house with her widowed sister, Eleanor, in Oxford. Here was scope indeed for social triumph and disaster, which followed with the ludicrous inevitability of a Feydeau farce. Matthew Arnold had promised her a warm welcome, but had apparently not reckoned on either her notoriety or academic narrow-mindedness. Lewis Carroll, whom she desired to meet, snubbed her outright: 'I shall resent it to my dying day', she later told Ethel Arnold.[17] Striding about the town attended by her dogs she was bound to cause a fluttering of academic gowns, the more so since she was not inclined to make concessions to formal pedantry or matrons jealous of their husbands' ranks and reputations. Oxford's dreaming spires buzzed with gossip and affronted dignity. She greeted the Master of Balliol with what was considered brazen informality: 'Oh Mr Jowett, I am so glad to meet you. How did you like my last book?'[18] Jowett on the whole warmed to this outspoken new arrival.

The academic community, ready for strife as ever, soon divided into pro- and anti-Broughton factions. The anti-Broughtonians were marshalled by a Miss Smith, whose brother was professor of mathematics and who stubbornly held to the belief that the newcomer was Miss Elizabeth Braddon and to be shunned at all costs. But, in circles where informed and witty conversation was prized, Rhoda's pungent eloquence won her the friendship of the Mark Pattisons, the Walter Paters, and the senior highbrow young, such as Rennell Rodd and D. S. MacColl. Mrs Oliphant, amused at her own reception in Oxford, to which she had repaired in order to be near her sons, remarked, 'I rather think I was set up as the proper novelist in opposition to Miss Broughton.'[19]

In January 1883 Rhoda's eighth novel, *Belinda*, began the usual serialisation in *Temple Bar*, and word quickly spread throughout Oxford that it contained a crude portrait of Mark Pattison as Professor Forth, Oxford Professor of Etruscan, a character several times more desiccated than George Eliot's Mr Casaubon. Privately Pattison called it a degrading caricature, but, according to Sadleir, his father had written home in October 1883 that Mark Pattison was obviously still on terms with her, sending up his name when calling as 'Professor Forth'.[20] Jowett promptly disowned the novelist. The incident had its less savoury aspect. Pattison had been enjoying the company in his wife's absence of a young lady, Meta Bradley. An anonymous letter dilating upon this singular domestic circumstance enraged Pattison, who with ill-judged rashness is said to have pointed the finger at Rhoda as the malicious correspondent. She in turn is supposed to have retaliated with the savage picture of Professor Forth. This seems most unlikely. Such a craven expedient as an anonymous letter is quite out of keeping with Rhoda's directness, and it is more probable that the novel was merely a general expression of her frustration at the hypocrisy she detected in that bastion of male supremacy. In any case, long after *Belinda* appeared the Pattisons were apparently on good terms with her. Indeed Rhoda was a guest at the Lodge in Headington following the Rector's death.[21]

In Richmond, Oxford or London Rhoda held court, 'the centre of a band of the faithful who assembled', *The Times* said after her death, 'to enjoy the rare crackle and savour of her talk'.[22] Her friends numbered men and women in every stratum of political, literary and artistic society. She had the kind of imperious, booming voice that could carry across Harrod's food hall. Sir Charles Dilke once described her as 'a very ignorant, very honest, good-hearted sort of woman with a loud abrupt country-family sort of manner'.[23] Her somewhat eccentric habit of dropping her aitches is recalled by Ethel Arnold. When her nephew, Harold Newcome, returned after a haircut one day, Rhoda cried 'in tones of shrill amaze: "Oh, 'Arold! 'ow 'orrible you look! whatever 'ave you done to your 'ead?"'[24] Her gusto was undiminished as she grew older. Percy Lubbock commented, 'her old age was never lonely. She grew very infirm, she suffered much pain, she was poor; but nobody ever heard about her troubles, which she swept aside with a high hand. The society of her friends was all she needed, and they flocked about her.'[25]

With Henry James she had a long and affectionate friendship. They met at Lord Houghton's long after he had made some disparaging comments on her work, and often at dinners thereafter, 'where Miss Broughton's sharp tongue and Mr James's wit were prized'.[26] In the winter of 1891 he escorted her to the visiting Comédie Française and the friendship blossomed. From 1900, when 'Miss Broughton's tongue was sharper than ever, her legend longer', they corresponded regularly, and Lady

Battersea claimed that through the long years of the rheumatoid arthritis which confined her to her chair James called upon her daily.[27] 'Poor dear heroic Rhoda', he said of her in 1912, and in the last year of his life spoke of her delivering 'appreciation and discriminations as straight from the shoulder as ever'.[28] She deeply mourned his death in 1916.

When she lived in Richmond, James made a habit of visiting her, and occasionally summoned her to the theatre. 'She would come refusing to be his guest and belligerently paying for her stall.'[29] James found under that brusque and domineering manner almost a kind of tutelary spirit, as Edel observes. Lubbock vividly describes their friendly bickering in the drawing-room before company:

> Henry James, massive in the centre, his great head thrown back, his wide and steady eye fixed upon the twining of his thought as he slowly uncoils it; his voice breaking out in sonority as his phrase is amplified, qualified, left suspended for an interlude, recovered and again developed; slowly, deliberately the argument is built and adorned; and you see the climax looming, you wait and wonder how he will shape its last enrichment. He talks of Shakespeare – of the portent of that brilliance, that prodigality, that consummation of the mind of the greatest of ages – all emerging out of what? – out of nothing, out of darkness, out of the thick provincial mind; from which a figure steps forth, a young man of ill condition, a lout from Stratford, to reappear presently –
>
> 'A lout!' exclaimed Rhoda, 'me divine William a lout?'
>
> 'But wait, dear lady, wait – see where I'm coming out – he reappears, as I say, this lout from Stratford' –
>
> 'I *won't* have yer call me divine William a lout', she cries; 'and that's flat'; but still she mistakes his drift, the whole tendency of the contrast to exalt, to enhance the wonder of the transformation by which this – in short this –
>
> You would as well resist the way of an ocean liner.[30]

One cannot help but think James's elevated discourse, no doubt listened to with breathless admiration (and perhaps some boredom) by the company, entirely deserving to be punctured by such earthy interruptions. Rhoda, of course, denied that she bulldozed her way through conversation or inspired timidity.

Told once that she had terrified one young man, she opened her eyes wide like one of her heroines and said, 'Frightened of me? A simple maiden of sixty summers? What, afraid of this venerable relic?'[31]

Her letters written during the Great War give as eloquent picture as any of her manner. James poured out his anguish to her in those hideous days, but unfortunately we do not have her replies. One parcel of letters to which I have had access, however, reveals something of the dreadnought firing salvos against the Hun. The correspondence is addressed to the Hon. Mrs Florence Henniker between January and December 1918, from residences in Farnham, London and Oxford.[32] On 6 January she derisively notes how Lloyd George is leaving a loophole for restoring German colonies at the Peace. On 2 February she writes enviously of her friend's country retreat – 'your land flowing with milk and *butter*', while she exists on margarine 'and soon will be sitting down to a banquet of Horse flesh! I hear a dreadful rumour that it tastes *sweet!*' On 13 February she hails the great push at Verdun and hopes the U-boat menace is in hand. On 23 August she positively gloats over a British trawler with one gun overcoming a German submarine. Later she rejoices that two Zeppelins have been shot down: 'Our Anti Aircraft Guns seem really to be beginning to have a tardy and partial success!'

She delights in gossip about her fellow writers and the war effort, noting on 19 March that Mrs Humphry Ward, in France, questioning one of the younger staff officers at a lunch 'And what are you going to do this afternoon towards your great task of winning this Great War?', received the reply, 'I am going into Amiens to have my hair cut'! She remarks that Mrs Ward is looking prosperous and pompous, and is slightly piqued that,

> Marie Corelli makes £12,000 a year with old Royalties and Cinemas! She, I also hear, announced that Kitchener is a prisoner in the Hebrides! Kept there *by Asquith's orders*!!!! Whence she obtains this remarkable information does not transpire!   (23 August)

Rhoda bears the privations of wartime London stoically, solaced by her flowers and her dogs. News is bad, she writes from Chelsea on 29 February, but she jogs along 'reading a good many books which I instantly forget; toddling as far as the Hospital;

and welcoming any friend who is kind enough to visit me'. She feels quite at home in church with the Chelsea Pensioners. 'Our Chaplain treated us lately to a sermon warning us against Adultery! so suitable to our years and opportunities!!!' She worries about her nephew, Geoffrey Broughton, wounded in France (31 May). In August she recalls entertaining a wounded officer for tea. He had been a Rhodes scholar, but 'was quite the most inarticulate person I have ever met! The one subject on which he showed any interest was what the legs of the Tea Table were made of!'

She receives gifts of her friend's novels from time to time, graciously but not sparing her criticism. Of Norris Brown's *Amber* she is enthusiastic: 'He is always so readable which I used to think a low praise but now consider a high one' (19 March). Wells's *Mr Britling Sees It Through* provokes a cryptic comment: 'I am told that Mr Britling and his amours are Wells's himself and his excursions in to the Kingdom of Paphos! So far I must own it amuses me, tho' I generally detest Wells!' (8 November). In the same letter she admits that literary taste has changed since her day, instancing a current novel: 'the highminded chaste heroine's response to her young lover's declaration of love . . . that she would like to *make him the father of her son* made my Victorian head go round!'

She is flattered at receiving a letter praising her novel *A Thorn in the Flesh* from Mrs Thomas Hardy conveying her husband's congratulations (23 August). Of Mrs Henniker's *Brenda* she notes, 'It is (what Octogenarian praise!) – such delightful big clear print.' She will have her cousin read it aloud to her sitting in her little garden where the rambler roses are hastening into flower (31 May). Flowers always delighted her. She says of stocks, 'I always think that there is no flower that is more determined not to let you ignore its scent!' (6 June). On 17 May she speaks of Henry James's fine portrait and is enraged that suffragettes tried to damage it, but she is pleased to hear it can be mended ' "equal to fresh" as the shopkeepers at Richmond used to advertise their eggs!!'

The usual grumbles about her publishers recur. She had hoped to send *A Thorn in the Flesh* as a belated Christmas card, 'but the thorn seems to have stuck so tight in the Publisher's flesh that he cannot get it out; and it has not yet been produced' (13 February). 'The world is not much the poorer. But I am somewhat so.' On 19 March she says her publisher 'maintains his Masterly Inaction'.

Rhoda Broughton's death in her eightieth year, on 5 June 1920, brought tributes from eminent men of letters, not only to her character, but also to her achievements as a writer. Andrew Lang dedicated a volume to her and affectionately parodied her style[33] and, as Barbara Silberg notes, Dobrée and Batho included her among their late Victorian novelists with Meredith, Hardy and James, and not among 'Some Best Sellers', to which M. E. Braddon was consigned.[34] Michael Sadleir praised her 'brilliant understanding of humanity' and declared she was 'that rare phenomenon, a genuine novelist'.[35] Ernest Baker described her spirited love tales as unique elements of the mid-Victorian literary landscape:

> So fierce was her revulsion from the conventionalism of most novelists of her sex, and from the reticence which she would have called prudery of such as Miss Thackeray and Mrs Oliphant, that she took her revenge by writing of nothing but love, and writing with an unrestraint that was too much for the stiff decorum of the sixties and seventies.[36]

This alone makes her worth recalling. Although she has none of the tragic weight of the Brontës she does strike a similar note, a kind of romantic fatalism also strong in French fiction of the period. In *Good-bye, Sweetheart!* for example, the European setting, the ubiquitous Roman Catholic ritual, its erotic overtones and the Gallicised hero, Paul le Mesurier, are reminiscent of *Villette*. In other novels, too, the self-destructive passions of the heroines suggest the Brontë model. Her outstanding merit is insight into female mind and character; she widened women's outlook by giving, as *The Times* recorded after her death, 'a franker view of life'.[37] Undoubtedly, for the modern reader, Rhoda Broughton's significance lies in this uninhibited directness about women's strong feelings and, by implication, their sexual needs in a male-dominated society. Her presentation of headstrong girls, albeit in lush, melodramatic terms, was an act of rebellion at an unfair and sexually explosive state of affairs. In view of the currently fashionable feminist studies of literature it is strange to find Rhoda Broughton's contribution so sadly neglected.

She is also notable for a vivid and exact rendering of manners and the mid-Victorian scene; her novels are a quarry for the social historian. Meticulous observation of seasons, landscapes, fashion, domestic interiors enlivens the most pedestrian and familiar plots. The presentation of the lodging-houses of Inkerman Terrace at the beginning of *Not Wisely, but Too Well* and the bustling activity of the seaside is a splendid example.[38] A few touches convey just the right cheerful setting for her heroine: the glistening white bathing-machines, a forest of wooden spades, goggle-eyed shrimps, mutton smells wafting from every lodging-house at meal-time, and there, sitting reading on the beach, Kate Chester, 'a pretty patch of blue on the grey stones'. All such background detail helps to frame and naturalise the more exotic elements of Rhoda's material, where it is easy to find fault. The overwhelming passions she bestows upon her heroines inevitably lead to throbbing prose. Given the nature of her narrative concerns, however, two things can be said in her favour. First, the purple passages are relatively few and are done with such bravura that most of the time they can be read with a smile and passed over; Rhoda is not afraid to take risks. Secondly, there is the redeeming property of an often tart, astringent comment that puts the more flamboyant passage in perspective. After one particularly violent love passage in *Not Wisely*, Rhoda declares she has had quite enough of talking about love; on another occasion she detaches herself from the shockingly immodest behaviour of her heroine with a rebuke to the censorious reader: 'To describe bad actions is not, as I would meekly submit to indignant virtue, to be an accomplice in them' (ch.16).

A question is posed early in *Not Wisely*: 'when does love cease to be the most ennobling and highest of our purely natural impulses?' (ch.9), and the tantalising glimpse of the forbidden territory of physical desire and wilful submission to it is at once enticingly proffered. While most novelists were evasive, Rhoda charged ahead with a frank, honest exploration of the girl's passionate, implicitly sexual feelings, even though the outcome was pain and punishment, humiliation or slow death. Most other writers of the time place the most extraordinary restraints upon their heroine's emotions; she is to be heart-whole until love is declared (and honourably) by the man. 'A girl loves most often because she is loved, – not from choice on her part', says

Trollope in *Ayala's Angel* (ch.17). 'She is won by the flattery of the man's desire.' Bosh, Rhoda Broughton would have said, with some justice. In reaction to this attitude Rhoda's heroines 'let go', and allow themselves – not actual physical desire – but the intense feeling which is partner to it. Passion becomes a euphemism for sexuality.

Kate Chester is the first in a line of self-willed heroines whose passionate nature gets them into trouble. A buxom lass with a mop of reddish hair, sensuous lips and 'eyes of the colour of sea water' (ch.8), she is ripe for initiation into life and love. To Colonel Dare Stamer, bored with all that North Wales has to offer in the way of excitement or company, she is 'a bewitching little person of twenty' (ch.7) and, of course, she falls immediately in love with him, declaring that 'his eyes scorch and shrivel up my soul', and vowing that she will love him though he were 'as wicked as sin itself' (ch.9). Stamer conforms to the sterotype of the Victorian muscular cad. Six foot two with 'herculean shoulders', white teeth and hairy countenance, he almost outdoes Guy Livingstone.[39] Kate, however is much more convincingly drawn. While it is obvious that Rhoda Broughton is content to abide within the formula, 'A woman in love thinks of nothing but her love; a man in love thinks of his love parenthetically, episodically; it shares his thoughts with his horses, his trade, his books, his dinner' (ch.6), the evocation of passion in 'poor erring Kate', together with the guilt, the torment, the moral dilemma, are done with fine understanding and credibly erotic overtones. Kate justifies gradual surrender to her feelings by scorning what she calls an 'antiquated code of propriety'. In addition, there is much talk of her rejection of religion. Prayers, we are told, were like part of her toilet, brushing her hair: at Sunday service her words may fly up but her thoughts are certainly here below. Sentiments of that sort are clearly what incensed some of Rhoda's critics. Nevertheless, the author stays circumspectly within those enticing borderlines of vice that Trollope confessed were the novelist's province: at a crucial moment, Kate's goings-on are discovered by her father, and she is spared the shame of flying with Dare to Portsmouth by his confession that he is already married. Henceforth she is to abjure men's solicitations and, to make the matter quite definite, Dare makes her promise never to marry. All this brings the first section of the book to a throbbing parting-scene.

The second part of the novel moves in a new direction. Kate, though chastened, does not waste and pine like many a lovelorn heroine, but carves out a new life for herself as a social worker under the adoring tutelage of a humble parson, James Stanley. At this point Rhoda's strong sense of scene is foremost. The description of the shabby genteel house where the Chesters live in Queenstown, the lurking dangers of the meaner streets, the smallpox and typhus, and the charity visiting on bitterly cold days, gives substance to the narrative and holds the reader's attention through the pallid love affair. One incident quite powerfully evokes the gulf between social workers and the objects of their charity, and Rhoda is honest enough to acknowledge the repulsion felt by Kate towards 'a horde of little old men and women in child shapes' and the goblin children who need food not tracts (ch.20). Once she gets lost among coalheavers and bargees and feels 'a moral fear of men of the lower orders', recoiling from one leering individual who says 'I'll give you a ha'penny for your crinoline, miss' (ch.21).

We see clearly that Kate's charity work is therapy, to save herself, as she confesses, from 'going utterly to the bad' (ch.23), while her flirtations are a means of punishing the male for Stamer's fault. Thus, while the reappearance of Dare Stamer at a concert in the Crystal Palace is merely predictable plotting, Kate's response – she agrees to run away with him – is believable. Alas, Rhoda's dialogue at this point fails to buttress the truth of her characters under tremendous stress. In the Exotic Court and sculpture room, among 'goat faces and Titan frames', Kate hears again those 'cathedral-bell tones' and all her carefully assembled defences are down. 'What's the good of kicking against Fate? It's Kismet', she admits. She is once more saved from taking the irrevocable step, this time by James Stanley, and after an attack of brain fever becomes first a hospital nurse and then, acquiring a new serenity after James's death, decides to go to Manchester as a Protestant Sister of Mercy. At this point the conjunction of a dream of marrying Dare Stamer with the words of the funeral service provides both a timely psychological insight and a prefiguring of the catastrophe which ends the novel. It is the night before her sister's wedding-day, and Kate is for once happy at a dance, when with all the brash confidence of her pen Rhoda has Dare Stamer's dogcart arrive and spill him out on the very steps. 'There he lies, like a fallen Colossus' (ch.35), and with this melodramatic contrivance the novel ends.

*Cometh Up as a Flower*, which followed closely upon *Not Wisely, but Too Well*, has a simple plot with similar elements, but more emphasis is given to social position and discord between sisters, subjects Rhoda was to pursue in subsequent novels.[40] Nelly Lestrange, who narrates the story, is the archetypal Broughton heroine, a large, red-haired tomboy, full of feminine warmth, and sexuality. She meets and falls in love with Richard M'Gregor, a tawny, moustached giant, rather like a New-foundland dog, with a sabre cut on his cheek (he had fought in the Indian mutiny), but the romance is checked by the poverty of her family, about which her father constantly nags, and also by the sneering of her elder sister, Dolly, 'the sort of woman upon whom Mr Algernon Swinburne would write pages of magnificent uncleanness' (II, ch.3), who engages in some nasty tricks to obtain Dick for herself. Between father and sister Nelly has a most disagreeable time. When Sir Hugh Lancaster comes to dine and there is nothing but a scraggy piece of mutton to put on the table she is mortified, and when Dolly presses her to make a far more advantageous match with Sir Hugh she is desolate. Her love for Dick burns all the stronger, and, although the first-person narrative is often cloying, Nelly shows a refreshing commonsense in punctuating her own romantic excess, reflecting after one of her more idyllic raptures with Dick, 'I might have been Ophelia, barring the flowers and the insanity' (I, ch.11). Such phrases are the saving grace in these very ecstacies of love. The voice of the turtle is seldom without the croak of the bullfrog. A slangy style helps the comic undertext: at one tender moment when the lovers are interrupted, Dick drops Nelly's hand 'like a hot potato' (I, ch.12).

As elsewhere in Rhoda's novels there is a strong substructure of vivid social detail, here the penury of the Lestrange household. Between the sweet interludes of Dick's caresses Nelly's life is spent trying to evade the butcher and other creditors, meanwhile being inexorably propelled towards the *mariage de convenance* with Sir Hugh. Nell at last capitulates, though racked by guilt that she is selling herself – 'so many pounds of prime white flesh' – and with painful premonitions: 'If the prologue is so terrible, *what will the play be?* (II, ch. 10). She undertakes miserable Egyptian bondage as Sir Hugh's bride, and settles into an excruciating routine with her husband and mother-in-law, whose cheeks match her yellow-satin decorated salon:

> We were so sitting one evening after dinner – Lady Lancaster, senior, click-clacking away at that eternal knitting; Sir Hugh not quite asleep yet, but reading *The Times* as a narcotic; and Lady Lancaster, junior, toiling unlovingly at a smoking-cap for her master, and glancing now and then from him to his mother, from the lean grizzling head and bristles to the yellow front and wrinkles, and crying out to herself – 'Oh how sick I am of you both.' (II, ch.14)

At this point Dick re-enters, bound for India, and Nell is horrified to learn that Dolly had forged a letter from her telling him not to write and preventing her letters from reaching him; in agony she begs him to take her away, but is saved from disgrace by her lover's honour. Dick dies abroad and Nell fulfils her destiny, falling into consumption and reaching willingly after death.

For the modern reader it is difficult to see how this novel or its predecessor could cause much offence. There is a juvenile exuberance about them, a self-conscious desire to be daring which is more naughty than shocking, and certainly not immoral. Michael Sadleir's response is on these lines, but he overstates contemporary reaction in the interest of extolling later novels he considers vastly superior. It is true that the *Athenaeum* recoiled from *Not Wisely* in horror, suggesting that it was from the hand of G. A. Lawrence and revelled in 'delightful wickedness', and its review of *Cometh Up* was devastating: the novel was the work of a man 'destitute of refinement of thought or feeling, and ignorant of all that women are or ought to be'.[41] It is not correct, however, to say that the novels produced 'a tempest of shocked indignation'. The *Spectator*, considering both novels in a long and courteous review, was obviously prepared to take Rhoda seriously, and found them no more immoral than *Jane Eyre*.[42] Moreover, the *Spectator* critic was prepared to look beneath the love, 'in each case . . . an emotion marvellously described', and see the desire to be loved to madness as an exercise of power. Here at any rate is the glimmering of appreciation that Rhoda's studies of female sensuality are part of a wider apprehension of women's roles in the climate of mid-Victorian social change.

*Red as a Rose is She* appeared in 1870 and marked a distinct advance in Rhoda's career. 'It was read and praised by everybody' said S. M. Ellis.[43] Although the *Athenaeum* attacked its bad grammar and 'vulgar railing', reviews were generally favourable and the novel caught on with the public, so that a second edition was offered in 1871. According to Michael Sadleir the book sold 11,250 copies in its first seven years.[44] The portrait of the heroine is once again at the heart of Rhoda's success. Esther Craven is affected by the current agitation over female roles, and at the same time uninhibited enough to dare all for love. 'The desire to be loved is strong enough in us all; in this girl it amounted to madness: it is the key to all the foolish wicked, senseless things you will find her doing through this history's short course' (I, ch.6).

Elsewhere *pour épater le bourgeois* Rhoda digresses on the subject of legs, 'at the rate of purity at which we are advancing *legs* will soon walk off into the limbo of silence and unmentionables' (I, ch.8). Despising such prudery she has Esther thrown from her horse after riding furiously across country, and the hero, St John Gerard, gently massage her pretty ankle (I, ch.10). By contrast, Constance, Esther's foil in the novel, is always 'shocked at whatever people ought to be shocked at – Colenso, Swinburne, Skittles, etc.' (I, ch.8). Esther is keen to read a French novel in the Gerard library, and Rhoda observes drily, 'men are always shocked that women should *read about* the things that they do' (I, ch.14). St John's sanctum, we are told, is all pipes, whips, pistols, sporting-prints – and yellowbacks 'with enticing Gallic titles, similar to the one she has just so heroically foregone'. The many such hits at inequality and male egotism in this and other Broughton novels do not reflect intellectual or political awareness of the movement towards women's rights, but the incipient groundswell of instinct and opinion that marks the beginning of change.

There are some well-aimed jokes at timid women novelists in an exchange between hero and heroine in their carriage, which also gives a good idea of the fresh, impudent, lively appeal of Rhoda's dialogue:

'What a pleasant vehicle this would be to make a driving tour in!'

'A tour of all the cathedral towns throughout England, as the

Heir of Redclyffe proposed spending his honeymoon in
making!'

She laughs.

'I remember long ago the *Saturday Review* saying of some she-
novelist's men, that they were like old governesses in trousers;
it was not a bad simile, was it?' (I, ch.13)

Rhoda's taunts at conventional social attitudes in general have
a range and terseness that earn her a place among the writers of
comedy of manners. Sir Thomas Gerard is one of the old rural
gentry who believed in the days 'when a man never rejoined the
ladies without seeing double their real number'; the Misses de
Grey are aptly pictured 'driving through a long duet' (I, ch.14).
She shows herself more savage in the introduction to the second
volume of *Red as a Rose is She*: 'The usual number of people have
had their bodies knocked to atoms and their souls into eternity by
express trains; the usual number of men and maids have come
together in *The Times* columns in holy matrimony; and the usual
number of unwelcome babies have been consigned to the canals'
(II, ch.1). The critics interpreted this as callousness and bad taste,
but the deliberately provocative offhandedness is exactly the
quality a modern reader can respond to, birth seen only in terms
of death, of a real social problem, the drowning of unwanted
infants. Rhoda writes without fulminating or exhorting, with
characteristic clearsightedness.

In the second volume Esther, madly in love with St John
Gerard and guilty about not confessing a half-engagement to a
former suitor, Brandon, burns with passion and shame. St John,
of course, discovers the truth and accuses her of throwing Brandon
over for the better catch, himself. She denies this: 'It is yourself –
your very self! Oh, if I could but tear out my heart and show it
you!' (II, ch.4). Both are obstinate and, after they have traded
insults in a kind of delirium, St John ends the relationship. No
doubt Lynn Linton was speaking for a good many readers when
she claims this repudiation scene as one of the best in the book,
and points to the growing psychological depth of Rhoda's
characterisation as the heroine is impelled towards confession and
humiliation 'consequent and dependent on Esther's self-shame
for her cowardly lies and treacheries'.[45] Unfortunately the
inescapable three volumes and a capitulation to popular romantic
expectation cause a return to a melodramatic finale. Forced into

becoming a governess, Esther finds employment at Blessington Court, where she has to endure the triumph of Constance Blessington – that 'splendid animal, sleek and white as a sacred Egyptian cow' (III, ch.1) who has ensnared St John. Already in a decline, Esther loses the bloom in her cheeks and gets hold of laudanum from the housemaid. To face her former love at dinner she seizes geranium petals and rubs them into her cheeks, producing 'a too hectic bloom' (III, ch.4). The thematic contrast between a vital existence based on authentic feeling and miserable soulless propriety is implied in the two women, but the novelist has her eye on the tragic last scene which will sell her book. St John runs into her on the first landing and his passion is renewed, especially as he hears her coughing ominously. A death-bed scene seems inevitable and is celebrated in the grand manner. 'But though the candle burns low; it is not blown out' (III, ch.14) and in no time at all Esther is as bewitching as ever, convalescent, conquered and conjoined in wedlock.

From the time of *Good-bye, Sweetheart!* (1872) Rhoda's popularity with the public was assured and her critical reception generally more cordial.[46] In 1874 Alfred Austin wrote a long appreciation of her work for *Temple Bar* claiming that her growth as a novelist had been steady over ten years, her latest, *Nancy* (1873), having all the freshness and spontaneity of the earlier books and more depth.[47] Austin's praise would have been better applied to *Nancy's* predecessor, *Good-bye, Sweetheart!*, which, despite its oleaginous title, is an engrossing romance with a firm grasp of character and a certain toughness in portraying a young girl's painful errors and ill luck. The story opens in a Breton town where the sisters Jemima and Lenore Herrick are on holiday with a clergyman friend, Frederick West, who is in love with Lenore. He has a woman-hating friend, Paul Le Mesurier, whose presence so intrigues Lenore that she disguises herself as a Breton peasant girl in order to look him over at the Hotel de la Poste. While serving him his brandy and soda she betrays her English origin and arouses his slightly disapproving admiration: ' "Girl of the Period!" says Paul to himself. . . . After all, the *Saturday* does not over-colour' (I, ch.2).[48] The novel turns on the sparring between these two high-spirited people in the old tradition of love contest. Lenore is impetuous, unconventional and determined not to be mastered according to the tyrannous English model; Trollope's Caroline Waddington announced that she would

never 'grow into a piece of domestic furniture' (*The Bertrams*, I,
,ch.9), but Lenore is even more outspoken: 'There is not a man
living that could keep me in order; I would break his heart, and
his spirit, and everything breakable about him first' (I, ch.6).
How Rhoda Broughton's hordes of young women readers,
trained to be demurely silent, and laden with cares of home and
husband, must have loved reading such sentiments. 'I maintain
that there is not a more contemptible creature in creation than a
patient grizzel!' Lenore declares. Paul wonders if she smokes too.
She professes to dislike children, defies custom by walking out at
night with Paul, sings slightly indelicate songs such as 'Oh, que
j'aime les militaires!', and flirts with Charlie Scrope. The trouble
is, as always, that ultimately she also forfeits Paul's understanding and confidence. He does indeed marry someone else,
and after a long illness Lenore dies.

The resolution is sentimental and conventional, yet Rhoda
Broughton brings the novel to life with lively characterisation and
narrative style, transmitting pain and bewilderment in both
characters, a very real exhilaration when they fall in love and the
comic interaction of their dissimilar natures and expectations. An
early scene cleverly presents the uncomfortable and yet thrilling
discovery of their mutual attraction and shows Rhoda at her best,
deploying the familiar conventions with satiric points of her own.
The newly introduced couple take to a boat for an evening row
upon the Rance; with moonlight behind chestnut woods and
opalescent water around them they float past ruined Lehan
Abbey. The narrative is charged with passionate images of water-
lily cups as white chalices, and as Lenore stretches out her half-
recumbent form a moonbeam catches her arm reaching for a lily
bud, which she offers to Paul: 'Keep it as a memento of the fast
girl who *would* go out boating with you, against your will, at ten
o'clock at night – of the girl who *may be very good fun, if one goes in
for that sort of thing, but is not your style*' (I, ch.8). Impulsively she
throws it into the water, he grabs for it and upsets the boat. The
very image is mocking, since the lily signifies the ideal girl Paul's
imagination and upbringing have fashioned, while Lenore is a
peony, the flesh and blood alternative. They come ashore and
burst into a fit of laughter. 'What a ridiculous drowned rat you
do look!' cries she politely, and when he offers to carry her points
out that she weighs over 9½ stone and might as well carry him.
She takes a nip of brandy, lets him wring the water out of her

petticoats, and comes back to the hotel minus a shoe, boasting that she upset the boat in order to pay off the old score of having been embarrassed by him when she first made his acquaintance in her disguise as a peasant girl. All this is typical of Rhoda's style. As Austin put it, 'Life *verve*, elasticity, pervade her pages.'[49] The nimbus of human spirituality is there, the glow of the flesh. From the water her shoulders glimmer, wet and shining through her transparent gown; 'the thick frame of heavy damp hair . . . cleaves so closely and lovingly to cheeks and throat', while 'her face smiles out, pale and pretty *and altered*' (I, ch.8; emphasis added). Paul, enraptured, wonders if she will turn out to be one too many for him.

Rhoda Broughton's fine power of observing the social strategies of the middle-class is also notable in this novel. She records and comments minutely on the fashions, furniture, food and games of the gentry. At a house party in volume II, Paul stands near the fire with other men 'whom he regards with the innate distrust and thinly-veiled suspicion with which every Englishman regards every other Englishman who has the misfortune to be unknown to him'. The women are described as 'gently rustling, softly chattering, about the drawing-room fire; sipping coffee, holding gossamer handkerchiefs between their pretty pink faces and the flame, and mentally pricing and depreciating each other's gowns'. The scene is sharpened by the detail of ottomans, walnuts, candied fruit and coffee, the gentlemen entering from the dining-room to a flutter of expectation. The craze for chignons even produces an item about price: Lenore insists that hers cost only £2 10*s*. And with exact use of bright small talk, Rhoda underscores the uneasy relationship between the lovers, and their mutual sexual awareness:

> 'Do you know what I have got hidden here?' asks the girl, looking up at him, while her whole face laughs – not only mouth, but eyes, dimples, cheeks – as she points to the wide spread of her gown. 'Guess!'
>
> 'I have not an idea.'
>
> She sweeps away her skirts, and discloses a tiny light cane-chair.
>
> 'Sit down! You are an unfortunately big person, but I think, judiciously sat upon, it *may* bear you.'

He had meant to scold her: well, the scolding will keep; it may be carried over, and added to the next account. He sits down, and his jealousy goes to sleep. (II, ch.4)

In another typical set-piece, a ball, Rhoda Broughton also shows her knack of accumulating appropriate detail, giving the names of the partners, the type of dance, the configurations and various habits of the dancers, the sound of the fiddles, the strategies of getting a partner, the dresses, décor, even the conduct of a fan. Against this backdrop the drama between Paul and Lenore is convincingly played out. She will dance with Scrope and flirt with him too, even though Paul begins moderately enough to remonstrate with her. The contretemps, so remarkably silly, blows up into a full-scale row, but is part of a wider issue, Lenore's independence. It is a female protest at male hegemony, his will against hers, and she defies him. 'Yes, I do dare.' Neither can go back now, and pride parts them. 'If you expect the tame docility of a slave you had better go to your cousin for it, for you certainly will not get it from me' (II, ch.9).

The melodramatic ending follows a predictably tearful downward course, though Rhoda does not entirely forfeit the reader's sympathetic interest in the inevitable separation. It is the obligatory consumption and death of the heroine which overdoes the agony. Having accepted Scrope out of revenge for Paul's jilting her, Lenore goes into a decline as the wedding draws closer. The last phase of the story brings about a meeting with Paul and the dreadful news that he is going to marry his cousin, the ideal woman. He too is bent on self-destruction. As he gazes on her face for the last time,

There is a pallor of a mad longing on his cold shrewd face, as he stands staring and stammering in the moonlight.
'Good-bye, lovely eyes!' he says, in a hoarse whisper;
'good-bye, lovely lips! you gave me no peace while I had you; but, yet I wish – oh God! how I wish –' (III, ch.3)

Despite these operatic final moments (greatly to the taste of the Mudie public) there is much to recommend *Good-bye, Sweetheart!* Terse, colloquial narration carries the story along in jaunty, often ungrammatical fashion, and conveys very well the personality of

Jemima, Lenore's elder sister, who sets this scene in a series of charming notes:

> A kingly June day: the hay-smell drowning all other smells in every land of Christendom: battling even with the ingeniously ill odours of this little drainless Breton town. People who suffer from hay-fever are sneezing and blowing their noses; all the world else is opening its nostrils wide. The small *salon* of a small French boarding-house; a narrow room with a window at each end; and in this room we two sisters, the two Misses Herrick.   (I, ch.1)

In this novel as others the seemingly careless syntax Rhoda often adopts, the grammatical lapses, ridiculous expressions such as 'the liveablest room in the house' or 'a great deal "gooder" than I was' are not accidental; they are partly Rhoda's attempt to find her own voice and partly her wish to break with convention.

After *Good-bye, Sweetheart!*, *Nancy* seems anaemic. Possibly Rhoda thought it time to exercise some of the restraint reviews had been urging upon her. At any rate Sadleir records her observing that *Nancy* was 'so much the purest in tone and so much the most inoffensive of my stories'.[50] It does not gain from being so. She tells the story with an archness meant to reproduce the voice of her nineteen-year-old heroine, and, even though Nancy admits that she is apt to gush, the style grows wearisome. It takes the heroine most of the novel to discover that she truly loves the husband she has married out of duty, and there is only one redeeming Broughtonian outburst. A hideously embarrassing dinner party provokes Nancy into saying 'I wish – I dearly wish – that I might bite a piece out of somebody' (III, ch.7). Unfortunately the rest of the novel lacks similar touches of irreverence until it concludes in the expected clearing up of mutual misunderstanding and renewed declarations of love. *Nancy* makes it clear that restraint and greater consideration of contemporary moral scruples were calculated to worsen rather than improve Rhoda's work.

*Joan* (1876) had a great deal more zest and shows a return to Rhoda's accustomed manner and material, which is perhaps reflected by the *Saturday*'s sour comment recommending it to all

'who desire three volumes of folly, flippancy and coarseness'.[51]
The *Spectator*, adopting the tone of kindly schoolmaster, tried to
give her a word of encouragement; she *was* improving, and if she
would but mind her grammar and be more genteel she would do
better still.[52] Henry James was savage. He found *Joan* immature
and crude, notable for its coarseness and vacuity, likening her
style to the gambols of an elephant.[53] *Joan*, the result of the longest
interval between one novel and another, is in fact considerably
better than *Nancy*. Although Rhoda is too heavy-footed to claim
comparison with Jane Austen, this is an occasion when she
achieves comedy of manners through irony of a more
discriminating kind. In *Joan* not only narrative style but also plot
itself has an Austen flavour, for part of the heroine's trials on the
way to maturity, like those of Fanny Price in *Mansfield Park*,
involve a shocking translation from upper-class environment to
an unruly and vulgar household. In Joan Dering's case, her
descent is sudden and painful: one day she is in a barouche, the
next in a butcher's cart, which deposits her at Portland Villa on
the London road between the Cancer Hospital and the Lunatic
Asylum.

Rhoda's charting with minute accuracy the niceties of class
distinction is never better. She gives a vivid account of lower-
middle-class villas and streets that were springing up in the
suburbs all over England. The new town of Helmsley is raw and
half-built: 'the bleak suburbs between the scaffolding poles and
the forlorn brick heaps' lead Joan to completed houses with
names such as 'Campidoglio Villa': 'Mean little detached houses
(even by this flattering starlight she can see that they are mean)
lie ahead of her; each seated in its garden plot; each with its own
small carriage drive and stone posted entrance gates' (I, ch.3).
We are noticeably in an evolving, stifling subtopia, the shape of
which would hardly change until after the Second World War.
Rhoda is visually perceptive about this, if showing little social
conscience, as she shudders with well-bred distaste when the
heroine arrives at Portland Villa, thoroughly downcast, to be met
by a volley of dogs and her aunt, Mrs Moberley. Aunt Moberley
is absolutely without any shape at all: 'her very laugh is fat' (I,
ch.4); but she is a warm soul and so are her vulgar daughters,
Bell and Di. 'Such hats!' says Joan to herself, 'such jackets! such
earrings! such beads! and with such a trolloping length of
uncurled curls down their backs!' (I, ch.4). After weak tea and

stale bread, Joan goes on a tour of inspection. The sash-window cord is broken, curtains do not draw properly, the spout of the ewer is broken: 'I shall grow like them in time', she says with horror; 'in time I shall learn to talk of men by their surnames, and to have a refreshment-room head of hair!' Just then, Diana, scarlet-faced, pops her head into the bedroom to say goodnight: 'we have, none of us, any manners', she says, and Joan immediately warms to her kind, rosy-faced underbred little cousin. Such incidents are typical of the cheerful tone of this novel, and provide their own comment on Joan's superficial judgements. A pleasing minor addition to the humour is Rhoda's inclusion of dogs in the social scene. The Moberleys' dogs are fondly done: Regy, hearing Joan returning to Portland Villa, mistakes her for the butcher's boy. A 'kind and conscientious dog', reflects the narrator, 'but not gifted with much insight into character' (II, ch.24).

Next day Joan takes stock and decides to brave whatever comes. Diana is to be seen at her window in night attire, but without 'her sausage frisettes' or her piled false hair. While her thoughts revert to the hall at Dering, its spotless cleanliness, polished silver and delicate flowers, the girls chatter about the nearby barracks (shades of *Pride and Prejudice*), the soldiers, and one officer, Wolferstan, whose ancestral home is nearby. Wolferstan, an old friend of Joan's and a return to Rhoda's caddish heroes, is a lacklustre hero, but the author has some fun when he comes to dine at Portland Villa, very aware of his condescension. She begins with the aroma of the anticipated feast: 'The whole house appears to have turned, in honour of Wolferstan, into hot mutton fat' (I, ch.15); Joan is on tenterhooks, the girls giggle in 'sugared bashfulness' and Mrs Moberley welcomes Wolferstan like 'a long-lost prodigal son'. When he goes to take a chair Joan has to dash forward: 'Not that one, that one! It is not safe, it has only three legs.' Fleeing to her room she sobs, 'It will kill me!' Three months elapse and Joan is thinner – not out of love or pining for her old home, but because the food is so bad. Such puncturing of romance and sharp comment on surroundings is the strength of this novel. All Joan can look back on is no more than mortification, onions, and purgatorial heat.

Two more lively characters are introduced in the second volume. Joan gladly accepts an invitation to spend a holiday with the Wolferstans – ten days' respite from the stained tablecloths, the foggy spoons and the lumpy bed, even if it does mean dangerous proximity to Anthony Wolferstan. His mother, a lively old lady, is an engagingly Dickensian character, desperately clinging to her youth with all that cosmetics and proper lighting can do for her. The other new arrival is Lalage Beauchamp, an old flame of Wolferstan's, who is the ultimate in sex appeal and full of 'the splendour of animal life'. Rhoda, never one to underestimate buxom beauty, declares confidently of Miss Beauchamp's appearance at dinner,

> She is the only décolleté woman in the room; but then, probably, no other woman in the room has such a bust to exhibit. If they had they would possibly be no more backward in advertising it than she. . . . What a neck it is! What a great deal of it! What a smooth set of pearl! What shoulders! absolutely unclothed but for the two tiny shoulder-straps, which alone hinder her garment from entirely taking French leave. With a sickening heart Joan takes in these luxurious details.   (II, ch.21)

No wonder Wolferstan has to reassure Joan he is quite cured from his past infatuation, and soon seizes his moment to take her in his arms. At this point Rhoda typically conveys the emotional exhilaration of falling in love and a girl's delighted reaction to physical contact: 'in an innocent tumult of great and astonished bliss, Joan gives herself to her love's new caresses' (II, ch.25); Wolferstan is equally elated and declares that he will come at once to announce his intentions to the Moberleys at large. Rhoda deflates the romantic glory of the moment with Joan's insistence that he must not come to lunch, knowing it to be that day 'a resurrection pie, in which all the atrocities of the past week hold dreadful rendezvous in one abominable pasty' (II, ch.26).

Complications follow the conventional course. Mrs Wolferstan appears at Portland Villa like Lady de Bourgh calling on Elizabeth Bennet, and Anthony shows his paltry nature by being overwhelmed by Lalage and drifting into marriage. In a climax to the third volume when everyone else is at the Abbey ball he sneaks into Portland Villa overwhelmed by guilt and misery. 'You know the sort of power that she always had over me – the dominion over all that is base in me' (III, ch.33). Joan knows well

enough, and now sees him selfishly careless of her own reputation
and feelings. She orders him to leave her, saying that they can
never meet until in the next world: ' "And if there is no next,"
he says heavily, breaking into her speech, "all the analogies of
nature – all the later secrets she has given up point one way! they
all say, 'There is no other! for you there is no other! make the
most of this!' " But Joan is adamant:

> but if there *is* no other – if this narrow bridge of life is all the
> space that we are given in which to tread down the brute within
> us, to take the satyr by the throat and lift up the God! then all
> the more – a hundred times the more – have we no time to
> lose! let us begin at once! – at once!

It is interesting to note that what in some popular novelists,
Charlotte Yonge or Mrs Craik, for example, would have been a
ringing Christian denunciation of Wolferstan's craven attitude, is
replaced by a much more uncertain statement of the individual's
duty.

Joan now becomes a tutor for the Smith Deloraine family, an
opportunity for Rhoda Broughton to return to what is best in the
novel, the comedy of manners. She introduces a new suitor for
Joan, a vulgar, shy millionaire who has bought her ancestral
home, Dering Castle, and started to modernise it with sash
windows and other material comforts. The social satire on the
*nouveau riche* is apt here – 'a wretched little Crusoe on his desert
island of hearthrug' (III, ch.2), and the pain of Joan's return to
scenes of childhood happiness is not merely padding for the third
volume, for the novel is greatly concerned with upheavals in the
social world: now Joan is a governess and the Smiths have
effloresced into Deloraines. Unfortunately, third volumes also
need romantic climaxes, so the Wolferstan plot is resuscitated by
the reappearance of Lalage, who tells Joan that her marriage has
been a failure. Joan begins to doubt her own high-mindedness in
sending Wolferstan away, and her sense of isolation and doubt is
counterpointed by a visit to a transformed Dering Castle: the
towers are shorn of ivy, 'while out of the Castle's disfigured face
the great new windows grin like glaring false teeth in a venerable
head' (III, ch.8) – an image reminiscent of Wolferstan's mother.
At this point Joan's predicament symbolises the painful
conditions of society losing its traditional anchors of religion,

class and the land – all of which are touched upon in the course of
the story – and it is evident that Rhoda might have written a
stronger novel had she sustained this social theme, but the ending
is simply Joan's noble renunciation of Wolferstan.

If some parallels with Jane Austen seem appropriate in *Joan*,
Rhoda's next novel, *Second Thoughts*, is notable, as Barbara
Silberg points out, for being planned on the same general scheme
as *Pride and Prejudice* (originally called *First Impressions*) and
divided into three parts: 'First Thoughts', 'Second Thoughts'
and 'Second Thoughts are Best'.[54] The heroine, Gillian Latimer,
like Elizabeth Bennet, is used to having her own way, and guilty
of hasty judgements based on immature perceptions. *Second
Thoughts* is, however, the genuine Broughton article, a charming
fairytale around the theme of growing up and distinguishing
reality from appearance.[55] Gillian Latimer is first seen among the
Marlowe family leaping over a dozen candles at a party one
minute and coping competently with domestic accounts at
another. She not only runs the household affairs but also finds
time to hold a class for reclaimed drunkards. Suddenly Dr John
Burnet appears, calling her back to Belgravia where her father is
dying. Her world is transformed; she is humiliated both by her
father's sarcasm and Dr Burnet's peremptory manner. Normal
values seem to be upended: her father grumbles at her attempting
to kiss him; when she offers to read to him he growls that he is
not fond of parsons in petticoats; and when he does allow her to
read aloud from a French newspaper he sneers at her accent.
Dr Burnet also seems to set himself in opposition to her, practi-
cally ordering her to take some exercise, to which she responds
with a look of defiance and goes to the library. 'What an
impossible person you must be to live with!' Burnet observes
(pt. I, ch. 7).
   Upon the death of her father Gillian is horrified to discover that
he has made it a condition of her inheritance that either she
marries John Burnet when she reaches twenty-one or the money
goes to him. Should he decline the marriage the fortune goes to
her. Understandably she declares the arrangement monstrous
and all but accuses Burnet of engineering it. 'I had rather be
flayed alive than marry a woman under such conditions!' he
declares angrily, reproving her rather like Mr Knightley in

*Emma*: 'Do not go through life attributing the worst motives to everyone you meet, and putting the most unfavourable construction upon their simplest actions! You may be cheated now and then, I confess; but on the whole you will be a happier woman' (pt. I, ch.10).

The second part of Gillian's education occurs when she is compelled to live under Burnet's guardianship with his elder, spinster sister. The thorny relationship between the three of them gives rise to dryly amusing exchanges. A certain harmony is just beginning to emerge when Gillian announces she is about to start another class for reformed drunkards in the neighbourhood. Burnet forbids it and Gillian retires to her bedroom, tears of mortification in her eyes at having her will thwarted and her judgement called in question. But gradually the knowledge of Burnet's good heart is borne in upon her.

In the next section of the novel is another echo of Jane Austen, for now John Burnet must overcome his narrow ideas of propriety and Gillian break the shell of his reserve by her own natural spontaneity, much as Lizzy does with Darcy. Although there are disputes between them they are instinctively drawing closer together, until at the end of the second phase it is time for Gillian to resume her old life with the Marlowe family. Here the final part of Gillian's education is to take place, and the author has cleverly arranged that her heroine, seeing the mirror image of her former childish self, will painfully recognise that what she had taken to be her own goodness, consideration and care of the Marlowes contained a large measure of selfishness. The school she had once taken pride in is broken up, the temperance room is out of use, and the eldest child, Jane, now sixteen, is in charge. Again a motif is introduced of a topsy-turvy world. All is chaos and uproar, but Squire Marlowe cheerfully informs Gillian that Jane reminds him of her. Gillian is thunderstruck as she regards Jane's 'insolent self-assertion, the deep-laid, high-spoken confidence in her own, and contempt for others' judgement; the rude and selfish snatching at power, and veiling it under a thin mask of filial duty' (pt. III, ch.2). In an ironic reversal of all she has imagined, she finds herself thinking with regret of Dr Burnet's airless London house with its india-rubber plant and somnolent tom cat. But, as the Marlowe household, which she has seen as the pivot of her existence, no longer exists, so the Burnet household has been left behind. It is a crisis in her search for identity. 'I am as unwelcome here as I was unregretted there' (pt. III, ch.1). Her centre is destroyed, her fortune a burden. Who is to guide her? This is the climax of the novel, for her answer must be that experience continually confounds our notions of ourselves and our roles. At this point a mature Gillian Latimer who retains a strong sense of independence while understanding herself a little better is the appropriate bride for John Burnet. The particular merit of this novel is that the typical Broughtonian heroine is subdued without being broken, the melodramatic ending is eschewed, and we are left with a sense of greater depth and development in character.

The drawing of the hero is also notable. Escaping from her cads and he-men, the author depicts a professional man of integrity and principle who is neither priggish nor dull. In addition there are amusing touches in the portrait of Gillian's other suitor, a Swinburnian poet, Chaloner, who woos her amidst the uproar of the Marlowe household with speeches like 'there are moments when you feel the inarticulate throbbings of a divine discontent' (pt. I, ch.1). Rhoda's lively dialogue is well deployed in several comic scenes, particularly when Chaloner presents his early Byzantine face at the Burnets' house in London. Rhoda felt all the bourgeois contempt for the excesses of the aesthetic movement and lampooned the worshipper of High Art who lunched on a wafer and a grape:

'What a terrible room!' he says, with a slight but perceptible shudder, his sorrowful eyes wandering round the room: the blinds pulled well up to the very top giving him plenty of light for examining the bold design and lively colours of the expensive carpet: the good strong undeniable blue of the carefully looped curtains, and the outlines of the first-class walnut drawing-room suite, disposed with stiff neatness about the apartment.

'Do you think so?' replies Gillian, coldly; 'I think I like it. One has had of late years such a surfeit of cholera blues and livid greens, that one begins to long for magenta and arsenic back again.'

But he does not heed: he is still looking, still slightly shivering:

'How ungraceful! how un-Greek!' he murmurs, half under his breath. (pt. II, ch.5)

The development of Rhoda's novels seems to be along more sober lines, but all the same they are not necessarily her best work as Michael Sadleir argued in *Things Past*. True, the single-volume format of the fifteen novels which followed *Alas!* (1890) results in more control and tightness, but with few exceptions the vitality and imaginative daring of the earlier three-volume novels is diminished. Most of such work lies outside the scope of this book, but *Belinda* (1883) must be mentioned if only for the scandal it raised in Oxford. *Belinda* shows off many of Rhoda Broughton's gifts, her vivid scene painting, snappy dialogue, the headstrong girl almost overwhelmed by romantic entanglements, but plot is non-existent: Belinda, having heard nothing from the man she loves, David Rivers, for eighteen months, throws herself into the thin arms of Professor Forth, Professor of Etruscan at Oxford. Dedicating herself to his scholarly pursuits, she declares, 'It is a marriage of the mind!' (pt. II, ch.5) and 'with a face set like flint . . . marches to her doom' (pt. II, ch.6). The parallel with Dorothea Brooke's fate in *Middlemarch* was obvious and it tickled Andrew Lang's fancy enough for him to use it in *Old Friends: Essays in Epistolary Parody*, dedicated to Rhoda, in which Professor Forth and Mr Casaubon engage in lofty disputation while their wives correspond with their respective admirers. Professor Forth is many times more arid than Casaubon, however, and Belinda many times wilder than Dorothea.

Back in Oxford where Forth's night-light burns – 'that ill-favoured Jack o'Lantern that is to dance for ever across the morass of her life' (pt. II, ch.3) – Belinda wonders if she will go mad, particularly as her sister seems to be having all the fun receiving undergraduates for tea. At this point Rhoda is eloquent about the Oxford she loved. Belinda has three consecutive days of freedom:

> three afternoons of being swiftly pulled down the river, that brave water-way alive with vigorous youthhood – of gaily drinking tea and sucking cider-cup through straws at little river-side alehouses – of picking the fritillaries in the meadows – of being towed back in dreamy languor at night-fall or star-rise – of loitering homewards with hands full of flag-flowers – of parting at the garden gate.   (pt. III, ch.8)

The reappearance of Rivers brings her to the brink of disaster, especially when, dizzy and faint with strain, she walks far into the mountains of the Lake District and he suddenly crosses her path like a sheepdog, urging her to accept his love: 'it is *all or nothing* for which I am asking'. ' "All!" she answers, whispering; and so breaks into an exceeding bitter cry of anguish and revolt: "*I will not die without having lived*" ' (pt. IV, ch.4). We are a long way from Dorothea's heroic renunciation, but in the nick of time Belinda returns to the hotel to recover the farewell note left for the professor. Tiptoeing to his room she finds him conveniently dead of a heart attack, and Rhoda breezily concludes, 'he has for ever vindicated his character from the imputation of being a *malade imaginaire*, and the Professorship of Etruscan in the University of Oxbridge is vacant!' (pt. IV, ch.6).

To the end of her career Rhoda Broughton continued to fascinate readers with studies of young girls trembling on the brink of heedless rapture or ruin, but the delightful wickedness of early days was toned down. As she herself said wryly of her career, 'when she was young she was Zola, and now she's Zola [older] she's Yonge'.[56] She wrote more now of older women, sometimes haunted by mistakes from the past, sometimes finding a second chance of happiness, and, although her old jauntiness breaks through, the prevailing tone is nostalgic and dis-enchanted.[57] Honor Lisle, the heroine of *Scylla or Charybdis?* (1899) shrimping in a saucy costume of blue-serge blouse and matching knickerbockers, seems like a fading sepia print in comparison with the early heroines. The proposal scene with the hero on his knees – 'an archaic solecism nowadays' (ch.11), Rhoda calls it – seems to betray her own discomfort with the modern age. Doubting whether to accept him on the score of bad upbringing (vaguely referred to as some acquaintance with the *demi-monde*), Honor makes to move away: 'He can think of no better answer than to unclasp the one hand she has left him and lifts its palm – a little hardened by much wielding of golf-clubs – to his lips.'

Tory lady and iron maiden as she was, Rhoda maintains a pleasing asperity and within her limitations contributed to the growing consciousness among women of their need for greater freedom, even though, as she grew older, larger changes than she could encompass had occurred. On one occasion she was vastly amused by seeing a number of her books on a stall at Liverpool

Street Station labelled, 'Rhoda Broughton. Soiled, but cheap.'[58] A quality of self-scrutiny and detachment is a saving grace of her passionate romances, but she brings to the form greater gifts: vitality, exuberance, infinite pains given to social setting, crisp, natural dialogue, and a broad comic sense.

# 6 High Spirits: James Payn, Best of the Journalists

*When he writes a novel, Payn takes a lot of trouble; and when novel-readers want some books, they take a lot of Payn's.*

Punch (10 December 1881)

James Payn is one of the strangest cases of neglected Victorian minor authors I have come across.[1] Virtually unknown now, he was a hundred years ago 'the most popular man of letters of his time'.[2] Today his fame rests largely on one quip in the *Oxford Dictionary of Quotations* declaring the elementary law of breakfast that toast always falls buttered side down. It is the kind of epitaph he would have relished, for he cherished few illusions about his achievements. Yet fate has not been entirely kind to a man who came close to succeeding Trollope in popular favour, who produced, among nearly 160 volumes, forty-six novels, eight collections of short stories, besides seventeen books of essays, and at least four memoirs full of wit and vitality.[3] Payn is the most appropriate writer to end this study, for he worked his way to celebrity in the 1860s, that crucial decade of increased commercial forces in publishing, and occupied that ambiguous territory between literature and hackwork. He is the most admirable example I can find of the talented writer who made the best of his abilities within the new demands of the system – dedicated, industrious, and professional to his fingertips – and to the end of his career commanded the respect of his contemporaries. A gentleman of Victorian letters.

When he died in 1899, his obituary notice was a roll-call of distinguished authors and publishers, and the essential qualities of the man and his work were captured by *The Times*'s comment, 'Few literary men excited so little jealousy as Mr Payn, and few indeed commanded so wide a circle of readers.'[4] Leslie Stephen, his friend since college days, described him as the simplest and least affected of men, overflowing with spontaneous vivacity and love of harmless fun.[5] Alexander Shand commented on his generous hospitality, and the bibliophile Horace Pym called him 'prince of conversationalists'.[6] Arthur Conan Doyle left this tender tribute:

> Payn was much greater than his books. The latter was [*sic*] usually rather mechanical. . . . He had all that humorous view which Nature seems to give as a compensation to those whose strength is weak. Had Payn written only essays he would have rivalled Charles Lamb. I knew him best in his latter days, when he was crippled with arthritis and his poor fingers so twisted with rheumatic arthritis that they seemed hardly human. He was intensely pessimistic as to his own fate, 'Don't make any mistake, Doyle, death is a horrible thing – horrible! I suffer the agonies of the damned!' But five minutes later he would have his audience roaring with laughter and his own high treble laugh would be the loudest of all.[7]

As Doyle indicates, Payn belongs essentially to a tradition of the anecdotal essay from Addison or Leigh Hunt, whom he regarded as a model, but, also perhaps influenced by a nearer and more facetious form by Jerrold, Doyle and the *Punch* school, he turned into the kind of writer David Masson in 1859 defined with some disapproval as Metropolitan Comic Fiction or the Novel of Cockney Fun.[8] In his heyday Payn labelled himself among the writers of what Leitch Ritchie hated to hear called 'light literature',[9] and is a useful link between the humour of *Punch* and the comedy thriller that became a staple entertainment in fiction and on radio in the first half of the twentieth century.

Leslie Stephen called him the best of the journalists.[10] This is true. He had the journalist's magpie mind and the instinct for a story sure to satisfy the public's insatiable appetite for news. He showed what it was like to descend in a diving-bell – material he turned to fictional use in *A Perfect Treasure* (1869); travel on the new Metropolitan underground railway; visit the least accessible Channel islands; hike round little-known spots in the Lake District; or see the latest murderer in wax effigy at Madame Tussaud's. Collections like *Stories and Sketches* (1857), *Meliboeus in London* (1862) and *People, Places and Things* (1865) are the best introductions to James Payn. Here is a man with his finger on the pulse. No wonder Dickens took to him immediately. He has the master's exuberance and eye for oddities. Indeed some of his pieces are every bit as good as sketches by Boz, derivative in style though they may be.[11] In one article on London's street shows, Payn's journalistic 'angle' is the free entertainment of people-watching, the 'puff boys' advertising various commodities, old men selling Crimea medallions, and vendors of song-books under their gig umbrellas sporting five candles. One such 'Mudie of the pavement' cries, 'Buy a warbler, buy a Murderous Narrative, buy a Halphabet for the Young.' A cove can be watched advertising 'Poses Plastiques' – emphatically not for ladies' eyes. Here a man is being arrested for debt, there a pretty girl cajoled into having her likeness taken. The Dickens influence is also to be seen in other early work: 'Amalek Dagon' about a card-shark working the Cambridge line, 'The Marker' about a man earning his living in a billiard hall, and 'Our Back Garden' about the pains of cultivating a London plot – still a theme for today's columnist stuck for an idea. Payn weaves the materials of his early married life into copy with essays on servant's foibles, landladies, home-furnishing, and eking out the housekeeping – all likely to find a responsive chord in readers of *Chambers's Magazine* or *Household Words*.

Journalism paved the way to domestic novels and a hybrid comic Gothic parody of the sensation novel, including the highly popular *Lost Sir Massingberd* (1865). Payn was henceforth the epitome of the professional man of letters: not only a talented novelist, but also a man who studied the business side of literature, encouraged young writers and busied himself about the welfare of the trade he loved. He became editor of the *Cornhill Magazine* after Leslie Stephen and was a reader for George Smith and Elder as well as for Chatto. He worked with Walter Besant and the Society of Authors, interesting himself particularly in its Authors' Syndicate, which acted on serial rights and overseas contracts, amongst other professional interests.[12] Payn was, said Hugh Walpole, 'one of the stock novelists of his day, a gallant, good-humoured generous figure with no illusions about his talent'.[13]

James's father, William Payn, was described by Mary Russell Mitford, a neighbour and friend, as a hero of the old English comedy. He was a JP and kept the Berkshire harriers – somewhat incompatible roles, for besides being a magistrate he was an ardent poacher whose depredations among the neighbours' pheasants involved lightning raids by fast-running gig accompanied by a brace of pointers.[14] James, born in 1830, seems to have been destined for authorship from infancy, since he abhorred hunting and preferred to be at home reading *Peregrine Pickle*. When despatched on a small bay pony into the Berkshire countryside he would sometimes dismount, smear himself with clover and mould and return mournfully, 'having met with rather a nasty tumble'.[15] A bookworm and 'a home bird in every feather', he recalled with loathing his preparatory school, where he developed the storytelling habit in order to escape bullying.[16] Eton proved equally obnoxious, and he was mortified at having a story rejected by the college magazine. He was to claim that not even Trollope at Harrow and Winchester suffered more abominably from the bullying and grinding of the public-school system, and he never missed an opportunity in fiction or essay to display this crotchet.[17] He hated the muscularity and games cult, declaring *Tom Brown's Schooldays* a veritable humbug, and his novels replaced he-men of the Guy Livingstone school with studious, slight heroes of generally retiring disposition.

For a further brief and even more fruitless period Payn attended the military academy at Woolwich, a noted cramming establishment for those intending to follow a military career. Totally unsuited to soldiering, Payn bridled at the discipline, engaging in various bohemian pursuits (some of them described in his memoirs, particularly *Some Literary Recollections*). Ill health ended his time at Woolwich and he was despatched to a private tutor in Devon, where in happier circumstances 'the meadows of manuscript which I had written began to produce their first scanty crop of print'.[18] Anything worthwhile that he learned, he later insisted, came from outside rather than inside school. Even at the age of fifteen, Payn remarked, 'I knew more of the queer side of life than many people at fifty, but I became acquainted with it of my own free will.'[19] Entering Trinity College, Cambridge, in 1849, his likable nature and gifts of conversation made him immensely popular, a regular speaker in the Union, and a favourite with his tutor, the remarkable W. G. Clark. His literary wings sprouted and he published at his own expense a volume of poems, *Stories from Boccaccio* (1852), which received a cordial review from George Brimley in the *Spectator*. More poems

followed in 1853, dedicated to Miss Mitford, which included
some well-turned lines on a friend's dog:

> A gleesome, fleasome, affectionate beast,
> As slow at a fight, as swift at a feast . . .
> Never more now shall our knees be pressed
> By his dear old chops in their slobbery rest,
> Nor our mirth be stirr'd at his solemn looks
> As wise, and as dull, as divinity books.[20]

After publishing this volume Payn went on vacation walking-
tours in the Lake District taking the opportunity to visit de
Quincey, with whom he dined, narrowly avoiding helping
himself to his host's laudanum instead of the port.

Soon after taking his degree in February 1854, Payn married
Louisa Adelaide Edlin, a match which produced a lifetime's
happiness over forty-four years, as his many tributes to her
show.[21] Payn observed,

> One indirect but important advantage to a man of letters in
> early marriage is that, if a happy one, it rescues him from
> Bohemianism. It is a charming 'ism', and he who has not a
> strain of it in his character is to be pitied; but it is *but* an 'ism' –
> a branch of dissent, and not the Catholic and Universal
> Church of Humanity.[22]

That combination of bohemianism and humanism now anchored
securely in happy marriage launched Payn in his chosen
profession.

Novels such as *The Foster Brothers* (1859) and *Married Beneath
Him* (1865) contain eloquent testimony to the neophyte's
eventual success, describing the hero's first appearance in print
thus:

> Experience of life, of course, he had not; but he had wonderful
> intuition in place of it; while high-spirits – inestimable gift,
> almost always denied to a well-seasoned writer; that virtue to
> which Dickens owed so much of his charm, but which
> Thackeray never possessed – illumined every page.   (II, ch.9)

Such was Payn's situation when, armed with introductory letters

from Miss Mitford, he went again to the Lake District to meet
Harriet Martineau. She was then gathering material for a guide
and doubtless contributed to his own book, *Furness Abbey and Its
Neighbourhood* (1858). Through her he met Matthew Arnold,
which may have encouraged him to write a series of letters for a
London paper on the school monitorial system. Also at this time
he wrote 'Ballads of the People' for the *Westminster Review*, for
which he received twenty guineas. So far his work had been
freelance and sporadic. However, in 1858 he was invited to
Edinburgh by Leitch Ritchie to become co-editor of *Chambers's
Magazine*. This brought him into contact with the publishers
William and Robert Chambers, provided regular income and
above all an outlet for novels. He became sole editor in 1861 and
held the post until 1874. Henceforth he settled into a steady
routine of book production for the rest of his life. As Alexander
Shand recalled, 'Sundays and weekdays, like his friend Trollope
he could always come to time; working still, when crippled
and confined to his chair, he may be said to have dropped and
died in harness'.[23] Ritchie and Alexander Russell of the *Scotsman*
taught him the daily routine of periodical editing, which was to
serve him well when he took over the *Cornhill*. Payn soon learned
that 'until a man becomes an editor he can never plumb the
depths of literary human nature', and this was brought home to
him when Ritchie's health finally gave way and Payn found
himself at the mercy of flat-earthers and loonies of all kinds.[24] It
gave him special understanding of Trollope's own thorns in the
editorial cushion described in *An Editor's Tales* (1870) – as
convincing a proof of his genius, declared Payn, as anything he
wrote:

> I once expressed this opinion to Trollope, who assented to my
> view of the matter, but added, with a grim smile, that he
> doubted whether anybody had ever read the book except
> myself, by which of course he meant to imply that it had had a
> very small circulation as compared with that of his novels.[25]

Payn did not care for living in Scotland, however. He intensely
disliked the Scottish sabbath, which he denounced in 'A Sabbath
Morn' in *Household Words*, and the climate did not suit him.
Shand remembered him 'always grumbling good-humouredly,
like Louis Stevenson, at the winds from the Firth, the eternal sea-

fog, and the drift of the whirling dust pillars along Princes Street, like so many "dervishes of the desert" ', and when the opportunity arose to edit *Chambers's Magazine* from London Payn accepted gladly.[26] Robert Chambers scoffed at Payn's dislike of the cold, and tried logic, maintaining that the thermal line was precisely the same in Edinburgh as in London. Payn replied he knew nothing about thermal lines, but that so far as he was aware the east wind had never blown over a four-wheeled cab in London, as it had just contrived to do outside his house in Edinburgh.[27]

He took to London with Johnsonian relish, settling in Maida Vale for the rest of his life. 'For years I studied London', he wrote, 'as a botanist studies the flora of his neighbourhood, and with unspeakable interest and delight.'[28] Within a few years he boasted he knew London better than most Cockneys born. Indeed, but for holidays in the Lake District he was never happy out of the city or away from the Reform Club, where he played his regular afternoon rubber. Novels followed one another rapidly in *Chambers's Magazine*, and by the mid-sixties Payn had a large following, particularly on the appearance of *Lost Sir Massingberd*, effervescent to the point of parody, spiced with humour and unlike the general run of sensation novels. Percy Fitzgerald met the author at Knebworth on Guild Day and recalled the journey back to town, when Dickens spoke of him with admiration.[29] Payn himself noted with pride that 'Dickens touched my trembling ear with praise'.[30] Wilkie Collins too was enthusiastic, assuring Payn he had not foreseen the solution to the mystery. Payn's friendship with Dickens began when he left Edinburgh. As a condition of editing *Chambers's Magazine* from London, Robert Chambers had stipulated that he write exclusively for the journal, which meant severing connection with *Household Words*. Dickens received the news with mingled regret and pleasure:

> I am heartily sorry to have lost you as a fellow-workman, but heartily glad to have gained you as a friend. . . . I hope that you will both [his wife and himself] come and see us at Gadshill, and compare the Kentish hops and cherries with the Scottish peachings.[31]

Payn dedicated *Mirk Abbey* (1866) to him and also wrote a short account of Dickens's childhood for *Chambers's Magazine* after his death. Together they sometimes walked the London streets swopping anecdotes and out-of-the-way information about the city. In return for gold, said Payn, he had only silver to offer.

Payn's circle widened, including all the best literary figures of the day, of whom he was to write vivid reminiscences in his memoirs. With Wilkie Collins Payn remained on the warmest terms after the midsixties. In March 1869 Collins advised him on marketing his books in America through Harper Brothers:

> Offer them – if your forthcoming book begins as a weekly serial – advance sheets of each periodical part, posted from England, week by week, six weeks in advance of the weekly date of publication here. Say that you are introduced to them by me, and – inquire what they will give.[32]

Payn dedicated his novel *Gwendoline's Harvest* (1872) to him, and Collins wrote in April 1870 'as your brother-writer and as your friend'. In July 1878 Collins reported that he was half alive:

> While I was away last year in the Tyrol and Italy I was 25 years old. Towards the end of '77, owing to my return to my native damps and changes, I became, by rheumatic reckoning, 95. And what is the moral of this? The moral is – not to pass another winter in England. As to making calls – we can't either of us do it and we both know it, and are as old friends and as true friends as ever. Keep the publishing business active – or the appollonaris water will drown it! My kindest regards to Mrs Payn.

And in typically bohemian vein he wrote from his home at 90, Gloucester Place in June 1882,

> I was indeed sorry to miss seeing you when you kindly called here. Gout, calomel and colchicum *do* succeed (when I am hard at work) in putting my tail down afterward – and my way of acknowledging that humiliating circumstance is, going to sleep! If you ever come my way again take the servant by the throat (if it is the young man) and round the waist if it is the plump parlour-maid or the small girl – and, for God's sake, step up and wake me. I got out for a walk yesterday for the

first time – with a patch over my bad eye. Why does everybody when they see you with a patch on, look as if you had personally insulted them???

In 1871 the death of Robert Chambers signalled a change of direction in Payn's career. He had never got on well with William Chambers and so after three more years of uneasy working relations decided to resign from the journal. Leslie Stephen claimed he was 'dismissed', but whatever the arrangement the connection was dissolved with relief on both sides and turned out much to Payn's advantage. Towards the end of 1874 Stephen introduced his friend to George Smith, then badly in want of a reader. Payn took on the job and discharged it conscientiously for some twenty years, bringing to it his unrivalled knowledge of the market. Stephen had other plans for Payn too; he was anxious to resign the editorship of the *Cornhill*, which was beginning to suffer from the competition of the lighter magazines, and embark on his *magnum opus*, the *Dictionary of National Biography*. A degree of enlightened self-interest therefore figured in his promotion of Payn as new editor. 'He is the best of good fellows in the good sense of the word', Stephen wrote to Edmund Gosse in November 1882.[33] Payn had qualms, but the cachet was irresistible. 'Mr Leslie Stephen has given over the magazine into my hands', he wrote to an unidentified contributor, 'and it will henceforth adopt a more popular line.' But he was taking over at an unfortunate time; the magazine had been running at a loss despite such contributors as Margaret Oliphant, William Black, R. L. Stevenson, Thomas Hardy and Henry James, and Arnold's essays *Culture and Anarchy*, and circulation had fallen from about 25,000 to 12,000. Stephen confided in his diary that the magazine was flagging not because it had got worse but because it was ceasing to be in fashion. He was quite right. Public taste was demanding lighter fare, from journals like *Argosy* and *Belgravia* and the illustrated magazines: 'a more ephemeral magazine for half-hour snatches between the games, amusements and new pastimes which the late Victorian age was discovering'.[34]

Payn, with his energy, contacts and experience, set out to give the journal a more dashing image, to attract new as well as established figures. Ruskin was acceptable, but Oscar Wilde was not: 'We do not publish translations in the *Cornhill*,' he wrote to

Wilde, 'or I should have been glad to hear from you.'[35] He decided to drop articles on popular science from Grant Allen, writing by the same post to J. Arbuthnot Wilson, an author of ghost stories for *Belgravia*, inviting contributions; as it happened they were one and the same. He chivvied Anne Thackeray on holiday in Paris for revision to a story, and was assiduous in chasing up late copy. In fact, his industry kept the magazine afloat and brought in much new talent. Wedded to the notion – or prejudice – that 'literary' material would not attract the public, he dispensed with the services of the author of *Virginibus Puerisque* among the first (although this did not prevent him hailing *The Strange Case of Dr Jekyll and Mr Hyde* as a work of incontestable genius). But if he lost Stevenson he encouraged the work of many new men, including F. Anstey, Rider Haggard, Stanley Weyman, Henry Seton Merriman, and, most notably, Arthur Conan Doyle.[36] The *Cornhill* under Payn ran Doyle's first story, 'Habakuk Jephson's Statement' (January 1884), which was followed by several more. Although he told Doyle bluntly not to waste time with historical novels, he accepted *The White Company*, which ran from January to December 1891, and, when *A Study in Scarlet* proved successful, Payn recommended Doyle's work to an American publisher, Lippincott, who published *The Sign of Four*, the second of the Sherlock Holmes books.[37] Thus indirectly Payn brought the famous detective to world notice. Doyle had good reason to be grateful, and it is hard to conceive of his repaying Payn by creating the evil Dr Moriarty in Payn's image, as has been suggested.[38] They were good friends and one of Payn's typically generous acts was to let Doyle turn his story 'Halves' into a play.[39]

Payn's celebrity increased throughout the eighties. He became a member of Besant's 'Rabelais Club', an informal dining-group begun in 1879–80 to commemorate Dickens, was sought after as speaker and clubman and much quoted as an authority on novel-writing.[40] His remarks on the discipline of writing and the tricks of the trade throw much light on the popular fiction industry and his own methods. After being a wretched schoolboy storyteller – 'miserable Scheherezade', he calls himself – he found himself, a very old boy, showing other people how to do it. Trollope once observed that a novelist should write not because he had to tell a story but because he had a story to tell. Payn agreed wholeheartedly. The basic issue, he would maintain, is what shall

I write about? It amazed him that novelists would go about the business without first working out their story. Thus plot became for Payn the primary problem. 'As the life of the body is the blood, so the life of the novel is its story.'[41] Plot was the result of 'some striking incident, which may not occupy ten lines, or minutes in the telling, but which takes the fancy by storm'.[42] He opted for novels of dramatic situation and incident rather than character, and preferred comic or happy endings to unhappy ones. It was vital to keep the ending a mystery; he once mortified Wilkie Collins by confessing in the vanity of youth that he had guessed the secret of *The Moonstone* long before the end. Foreign settings he thought should be avoided: 'the British reader is as insular as his dwelling-place, and he prefers to read of places he has visited, and of customs with which he is familiar.'[43] As to locales and characters, they could be exotic but had to be based on actualities, just sufficiently heightened or differentiated to be interesting (or non-libellous perhaps) and close enough to be comfortable.

Many of Payn's remarks about finding materials for stories reveal the journalist. He found what friends said a capital source, doctors particularly: 'He has had genuine experience of life, and has seen down to the depths of it; a sick man does not attempt to deceive his doctor, or put the best face on his character as he does with a priest.'[44] Some stories came to him through dreams, as was the case with *The Confidential Agent* (1880), but he mainly drew on real incidents. *Blondel Parva* (1868) came from a life-assurance swindle in Edinburgh, and *A Perfect Treasure* (1869) from a story of the Nancy diamond entrusted to a servant who swallowed it for safe-keeping. *By Proxy* (1878) evolved from the idea of a man not keeping a promise to his dead friend. Once the idea had taken shape, it was important to get it down and flesh it out with the right amount of incident. As a beginner, Payn reflected with the cynicism of old age, he was far too prodigal of incident. On the other hand, the novelist had to be careful not to pad his story; he had to be always marching on and not merely marking time. A good plot, as Hotspur said, was 'full of expectation'. Disquisitions were to be avoided, and when an opinion was called for it should be put in the mouth of one of the characters. Payn disliked first-person narration, probably for this very reason. Where characters indulged in reflection it was to be kept brief and pointed; nothing was so tedious in fiction as a Hamlet hero.

It amused Payn that the incidents he invented as the flesh to his skeletons were sometimes imitated by real life. This was true of his most famous novel, *Lost Sir Massingberd*, and of *Murphy's Master* (1873), of which he wrote,

> I got rid of a great number of disagreeable characters on an island in the Indian Seas, by the simple, though startling, device of submerging the island itself. . . . Some critics thought it audacious; but Nature was so favourably impressed by my little plan, that she used it herself two years afterwards, and in a more comprehensive way than I should have dared to invent; an island in the Bay of Bengal, with the Kinshra lighthouse upon it, with seven scientific assistants, being submerged in a precisely similar manner.[45]

Payn's ingenuity in this respect became celebrated. Both the *Athenaeum* and the *Review* applauded his tricks in bringing characters back to life: as Leslie Stephen put it, 'It takes a great deal to kill a person in his stories; a broken skull and a funeral attended by relations are not sufficient to prove that the victim may not revive in a very ferocious state of mind.'[46] Thus a man apparently drowned at sea reappears at an opportune moment in *Fallen Fortunes* (1876) and *Blondel Parva*. Payn had found the formula already in many sensational novels, but he gave it daring, exotic and often comic touches of the kind that the writers of modern detective stories have found so profitable.

Like Trollope he went about his planning with exactitude. Designing a novel was as necessary as having an architect's drawing before starting to build a house. The professional writer, said Payn, should have his denouement or catastrophe well in mind from the first. *Lost Sir Massingberd* came about because he had hit on a novel method of disposing of the old tyrant: 'This was obviously not a position in which to leave one's hero, but a very good way of disposing of one's villain. The wicked baronet of the story was drawn from life; but he never would have been drawn at all except for the tree'.[47]

Payn would begin with a large sheet of cardboard offering plenty of room for listing characters and incidents: 'The fictitious names of the characters should be placed side by side with the real ones, that their connection should not be lost sight of, while their idiosyncrasies and other recognizable qualities should be carefully avoided.'[48] Each character had a a column, and by a kind of grid system Payn would fill in appropriate dates and facts and bits of action until a full scheme was worked out like a completed crossword puzzle. It is interesting to note Payn's reliance on real people for characters. He said of *Lost Sir Massingberd* that the whole *dramatis personae* were taken from the circle of his acquaintance, although he contradicted himself in excepting the central villain.[49] Once all these preparations were made Payn wrote his story, using ordinary exercise books or ledgers. It was his habit to write in pencil on a 'block' and often lying down.[50]

His manuscript for *Married Beneath Him* (1865) is full of questions, germs for incidents, points to verify, changes of mind as the novel grows.[51] He often gives himself thematic heads: 'The Fatal Blow' (crossed out), 'The Trial', 'The interview in gaol'. This concerns material he worked out for the sensational events of the third volume, when the hero, Fred Galton, is to be implicated in a murder. Payn's concern was obviously with legal niceties (always the bane of novelists) and he asked himself, 'Can he be taken up on a verdict against "persons unknown"? Do they commit to Newgate for a murder committed in Hyde Park? Make Potts nobler at first. Make Meyrick more spiteful.' At this point Payn devised a plan by which the hero feigned madness in gaol in order to escape the gallows. This is worked out at some length in the manuscript headed 'Plea of insanity', underneath which is 'Devotion of Mary' and an outline of the incident he finally used, based on the hero's showing Mary, by means of a passage in his Bible concerning feigned madness, that he too is shamming. Another note indicates that he intended to check the actual psychological condition in a work on the detection of feigned insanity. His notes end, 'Ask Henry Lee', presumably to verify certain legal matters concerning the scene. Such detail is typical of Payn's careful preparation. His notes include calendar entries such as 'April 23rd. 14 chapters to write', and throughout that month and the next he notes a gradual diminution of outstanding copy. The tag line 'Not married beneath him after all' is proof that Payn put into practice his often stated principle that 'you must have distinctly in your mind at first, what you intend to say last'.[52]

It will be clear from these comments on methods the limits Payn set upon his work, and more particularly the measure of the difference between light literature and novels of real substance. Payn's dedication and industry are not to be doubted, but he is unashamedly mechanical and commercial. He says nothing of polishing, revision, or lying fallow, and there is no question of breaking new ground or challenging the reader's intellect. He is a businessman engaged in turning out saleable articles according to a successful formula, as the reviewers recognised. A just estimate was that of the *Saturday Review* regarding *Like Father, Like Son* (1870) which said that as usual Payn had produced a lively tale combining authentic backgrounds in the Midlands and Cornwall, a cleverly constructed plot involving an abandoned mineshaft murder and the villain's deathbed repentance. The book is well enough, but could be so much better.[53] Payn would not have agreed. He wrote so much and so quickly, he admitted 'because I should not get so much for one first-rate book as I do for three second-rate ones'; that is the hallmark of the popular fiction writer, as R. L. Stevenson deplored when he blamed Payn for encouraging a 'penny-wise and virtue-foolish spirit' in young writers.[54]

Some of Payn's novels are domestic love tales set among the country gentry, rather like Trollope's. Love and intrigue, flirtations and jiltings, are played out on the croquet lawn or between the potted ferns in the conservatories; vacillating young men provoke tears and tantrums; fathers disinherit and mothers plan socially advantageous marriages; mistaken identities are eventually unmasked, lost fortunes are recovered; inconvenient rivals, impostors or tyrants are drowned at sea, and love becomes lord of all. These variations on the staples of Victorian fiction, derivative as they may sound, often strike the reader freshly; his realistic scene-setting, his appetite for odd characters and happenings, his ironic consciousness of the genre and high-spirited comedy give sparkle to the commonplace romance. Much the same could be said of the main branch of Payn's fiction, the thriller. His fertile imagination produces intriguing locations redolent of mystery and adventure: potholes, fissures in rocks, hollow tree trunks, Chinese prisons, dangerous tidal beaches, abandoned mineshafts, collapsing roofs, sheer cliffs, quicksands, trackless moors and fens. His preference for events involving danger and death from the natural environment rather than from Gothic expedients of poison or ingenious weaponry give an edge that the sensation novelists often lack. Again his journalistic training stands him in good stead, for his appetite for fact gives him more in common with Reade or Collins than with, say, M. E. Braddon and her followers. Many sensation writers took themselves seriously; Payn never did. His lightness of touch saved him from accidental bathos. He is always aware of and enjoying the absurdity.One of his most ingenious twists came in *Not Wooed, but Won* (1871), in which a nasty character was given to hurling his bulldog at the door when the mood took him. Payn disposed of him by having the dog bite him so that the man died from hydrophobia. Such a writer disarms criticism.

One of Payn's 'prentice works, a fine collection called *Stories and Sketches* (1857), clearly shows him in pursuit of a literary voice. Two stories in the collection are reminiscent of Hawthorne: one turning on mistaken identity ('Blobbs of Wadham'), the other ('Change of Gold') a haunting piece about a man who wilfully abandons business, wife and friends and then reappears after many years, only to learn with bitterness how totally a man may be forgotten. The resemblance to Hawthorne's 'Wakefield' is very strong. The narrative assumes archaic style: 'No man knoweth me, whence I come or who I am. My brother met me yesternoon, and brushed my shoulder; I looked into his eyes, and he into mine, and we walked on our diverse ways like strangers. . . . To myself, I seem to have two separate beings.' That sense of insubstantiality pervades another tale about the corrosive nature of cowardice, 'The White Feather'. The model is Poe even to the rhythms: 'I have earned it with sweat, and with toil, and with terrible fear.'

Dickens is, of course, Payn's major model, and he is all-pervasive, from the facetious naming (an army officer becomes Lieutenant Bullseye, a headmaster, Mr Sackem) to vigorous metaphoric zest in description. Mr Sackem is 'a scholastic blacksmith; he was of a coaly complexion and enormous bulk, had some little knowledge of mathematics, and was famous for hammering out scintillations of intelligence from the very densest masses'. Payn has caught Dickens's dry, amiable tone, and learned something of his daring with image. He certainly has a flair for the particular in rascally or bizarre character. A German tutor in a piece about ushers speaks beautifully fractured English: 'Now, if he does it ein time more, so vill I give this up for gute.'

Most pieces in the collection are like this, an amalgam of reportage, memory and imaginative working-up, peppered with

jokes. 'The Railway Companion' is typical of such short
mood pieces or shaggy-dog stories of the kind Dickens and his
circle – and the periodical audience – loved. It purports to be a
memory of Payn's Woolwich days, when as a lad of fifteen he
found himself passing Hanwell Asylum, alone in a train
compartment with a very strange-looking man to whom he
observed, 'How well Hanwell looks from the railroad sir!' The
anecdote continues: 'At this he placed his hands upon his knees,
stared at me straight in the face, and replied, very deliberately:
"Ah, you should see how the railway looks from Hanwell!" '
The volume clearly shows promise. The more journalistic essays,
such as 'Sark', 'Under the Sea' and 'On the Downs', have that
warm, discursive quality Payn was to develop into a pretty fair
copy of the essayists he so much admired, Charles Lamb and
Leigh Hunt.[55] As for the short stories, no study of James Payn's
work can ignore his undoubted talents in the form which most of
all demands concision.

  One of the best and most typical collections is *High Spirits*
(1879), three volumes of chatty, semi-biographical short stories,
which captured a wide audience.[56] Among them is one long story
that shows Payn's versatility very well. 'The Fatal Curiosity' is
science fantasy, a form that was already becoming popular
(attracting even Trollope, whose feeble effort, *The Fixed Period*,
was to appear in *Blackwood's Magazine* during 1881–2). Payn
chooses the year 1979, with the Raymonds' family Christmas an
opportunity for some regretful looks at the past. Mrs Raymond
prefers the old ways, despising automatic tea-makers, mass-
produced tasteless bread made from cowcorn, and ersatz
flavourless marmalade. The eggs she serves are 'laid by live hens,
one at a time', and she brews her tea following the method
described 'in one of old Anthony Trollope's domestic novels'.
Payn's vision of 1979 includes spectacles that act like telescopes
when worn high on the nose and like microscopes when
depressed, as well as pandioptic spectacles which enable the
wearer to see through anything. Air-conditioning is so
sophisticated that one can dial a choice of Swiss mountain air or
Brighton breezes. Postal deliveries from Australia arrive twice
daily, and a rapid crossing to France is possible via the Channel
tunnel. Houses have controlled climates and lawns can be
covered in bad weather with vast canopies of gold-beaters' skin.
On Sundays there is no need to go to church, since services are

relayed from St Paul's or Westminster via speaking tubes in the family chapel. Burying the dead has ceased; it has become barbaric 'to dibble them in like potatoes', and cremation is practised everywhere. Although the sun is losing its powers, huge air fleets transport surplus food for the hungry throughout the world in concentrated forms such as 'sheep lozenge' or 'pork lozenge'. The family transport is a 'wind wagon' and entertainment includes 'wall pictures' showing whole plays and pantomimes. What remains unresolved in this utopia is the Sunday opening of museums and the Tichborne case.

Payn's faintly Peacockian satire in this tale concerns the eccentric inventor Mr Raymond, who amuses his house party with his collection of curiosities from a century ago. His wand, a fragment of birch used at Eton, gives Payn a chance to air one of his crotchets: 'No allowance was made at any of those great seminaries for individual character; a boy of genius was made to grind at Latin verses just as if he had been a fool; thus the great principle of that epoch, the repression of ideas, was maintained in its integrity' (p. 181). Mr Raymond also has figures rather like Tussaud's waxworks. One is of a labour agitator, of whom the lecturer says, 'Where there was discontent, he fostered it; where there was none, he begot it; where there was hope of reconciliation between man and master, he stepped in and trampled it out' (p. 183). This was the not-surprising fungus, Raymond declared, of a rotten soil – antagonism between capital and labour because of lack of co-operation and understanding, born of the iron law that 'self-interest was the only rule of life' (p. 185). Another figure is of an exceedingly well-dressed man with a languid air, 'surveying universal nature through a race-glass' (p. 188) – a hereditary legislator. By lifting the skull of this figure Raymond can display the brain, which reveals total absence of humour, a gap where Latin quotations had been, traces of arithmetic by which he made up his betting book and some few clichés like 'the small end of the wedge' used to prevent any kind of social reform. Amongst other models is the Girl of the Period, tottering along on high heels and likely to fall on her nose, but for the centre of gravity being restored to its proper place by the weight of her chignon. Such perceptive glimpses into our world and mildly corrective glances at his own age constitute the charm of this story.

All of Payn's novels appeared initially as serials, and until *Lost*

*Sir Massingberd* (serialised in 1864) were published anonymously. His first, *The Foster Brothers, being a History of the School and College Life of Two Young Men* (1859) attracted little attention in *Chambers's Magazine.*[57] Drawing on his university experiences, Payn produced a rambling narrative about two sons from differing social backgrounds, and vaguely toyed with the question of what constitutes a gentleman – birth and pedigree or environment and training. The *Athenaeum* received it as an attempt to show the comparative chances of success in a career for those born in aristocratic or plebeian circumstances and applauded its message of stern training and self-discipline.[58] Such underlying seriousness is, however, badly undercut by the convention whereby the two young men turn out to have been exchanged at nurse. There are a few amusing squibs directed at both brothers' schooling. The collegiate school of Sunbury so prides itself on its antiquity that it administers a Latin oath adjuring the pupils not to throw missiles or discharge cross-bolts at the cathedral windows. A pecking-order among the students is rigidly upheld; the newcomer, Robert Birt, brought up as the poor relation, is accosted at once, 'Are you a nob or a snob, young 'un?', nicknamed 'Coachey' and sent to the ancient burial ground by bullying pupils to collect a skull. The principal, Dionysius Tertle, is given to such orotund phrases as 'You do not lithoballize', which Payn translates as 'Not to chuck stones'. The brothers finally meet at Cambridge, and the novel turns into a paean for university days and lost youth, ending with the astonishing revelation of 'the damning spot' which proves that Adolphus is really the working man's child, and Robert Birt the gentlemen. The youth brought up to rank and prosperity cannot bear the thought of losing it, while the democratic yet true-born gentleman, who has espoused a life of prudence, frugality and scholarship, disclaims the title that has fallen due. There Payn leaves the reader to draw the moral that good habits and a lucky dispensation of genes, regardless of blue blood, are what make a man a decent human being. Payn continued drawing on youthful experience, notably in *The Bateman Household* (1860), where he recalled the Lake District and fell-walking, wrestling and skating. The key scene has the hero skating the lake in Wordsworthian rapture, and looking down at the glassy eyes of a student frozen under the ice. As my earlier comment on Payn's method would indicate, the whole novel was probably geared to this moment.

*Richard Arbour, or The Family Scapegrace* (1861) caught on largely because its central figure was a lion-tamer. Dickens's influence is strong throughout, in idiom as well as character. The hero, in tantrums as a baby, for example, would 'stiffen himself out like a ramrod, cast himself backwards upon the floor, without the least regard for the shock that was thereby inflicted upon his youthful head, and, in recumbent position . . . scream like a locomotive' (ch.4). Dick, the scapegrace, runs away to London, falls in with conspirators led by de Crespigny Gotsuchakoff, a pair of photographers, and at last a menagerie, where he becomes assistant to Tickerondua, the lion-tamer. Lyrical descriptions of the circus, the animals and the oddly assorted fairground characters are the best bit of the book, reflecting the mid-Victorian fascination with shows but also commenting ironically on the idiosyncratic and absurd in human nature. Dick ends up rather impressively as *aide-naturaliste* in the Jardin des Plantes in Paris.

The great success of *Lost Sir Massingberd* was partly owing to lucky timing and partly to its own virtues, particularly its humour. The novel appeared when the middlebrow public were avid for murder mysteries, in the climate of excitement generated by *Lady Audley's Secret* and *Aurora Floyd* (*East Lynne* came out a year later), and was greeted at once as a sensation thriller. In that category it met all the requirements, intrigue, suspense and a resolution achieved by grotesque means: the wicked old baronet's disappearance had been caused by his falling into a hollow oak in the forest with his arms pinned above his head. Unable to move or make anyone hear his piteous cries, he had died horribly. The situation plays out with nice appropriateness the novel's theme of a providence that rights the wrongs done to the physically timid heir to the Massingberd estate. It also calls up, with greater depth than the usual sensation novel, nightmare experiences of entrapment and helplessness (with all their psychological overtones) and the many myths associating trees with human beings.[59] Yet, for all that, the dynamics of its plot are laboured and the characters undeveloped. There is a staginess and artificiality not balanced by the usual domestic detail and scene-painting of the sensation novel. In fact *Lost Sir Massingberd* is not the run-of-the-mill sensation thriller at all but, like so many other Payn novels, really in a class of its own; it has to be read partly as parody of the form and partly as a reversion to the

Gothic story. Seen in that light, it takes on attractive qualities, although these were not perceived by the reviewers of the day. To begin with, its subtitle denotes 'a Romance of Real Life', sufficient clue to the mixing of modes Payn proposes, and this is followed by a rather strange preface in which the author creates the fiction that he must tell this tale before his nephew, who is bound to mar it.

> He writes in a snappy, jerky, pyrotechnic way, which they tell me is now popular, but which is not suited to my old-fashioned taste. . . . If I am somewhat old-world in my style, perhaps it may be forgiven me, in consideration of the reality of the circumstances narrated, and the very strong interest which I do not doubt they will arouse.

Apart from the playful use of the convention under which an author establishes the veracity of his story, this does seem a deliberate attempt to distinguish between the style of the contemporary sensation novel and another kind of 'old-fashioned' writing, which I should call neo-Gothic enlivened by Payn's high spirits. In this respect Payn deserves to be credited with some originality.

The narrator of *Lost Sir Massingberd*, Peter Meredith, is looking back on his youthful friendship with Marmaduke Heath, an ailing, timid boy who lived at Fairburn Hall with his uncle, Sir Massingberd, known locally as 'Giant Despair', one of the last blue-blooded villains of the Regency. Marmy, heir to the estate under entail, was being harried to death by the old tyrant. The narrator's quizzical perspective, hyperbolical diction, and eloquent evocation of doom and dread have the robust quality of fairytale. It is easy to see why Dickens thought well of its promise. 'Doubting Castle' and 'Giant Despair' conjure up fantasy of childhood fears, as in the scene where the two boys talking quietly in the churchyard among the tombstones suddenly face the baronet, a man of Herculean proportions with a curious U-shaped scar on his forehead and his lips contemptuously curled upwards in similar shape. His laugh is 'like the creaking of an iron hinge', his voice a low resonant boom. Sir Massingberd is a pantomime demon king, the boys two babes in the wood. Payn enjoys the fairytale world to the full, with lyrical passages contrasting the calm of Peter's secure home with the uproar of the

Massingberd seat, where dilapidated stone griffins guard the chipped steps and the visitor is announced by a great clangorous bell accompanied by the baying of Sir Massingberd's one-eyed dog, Grimjaw. Sir Massingberd's emporium is filled with tobacco-scented hangings, antlers, fishing-rods and Indian clubs; there are even picture frames that move sideways and secret staircases. It is the world of Thomas Love Peacock or Catherine Morland's imagined Northanger Abbey rather than that of Lady Audley.

Associating with the local gipsies (the occasion of some bravura description of walnut-stained children and iron pots), Peter Meredith gradually uncovers a blot in the scutcheon concerning Sir Marmaduke's seduction of one Sinnamenta many years ago. It is at this moment that Sir Massingberd disappears. Thus deprived of any further human conflict, Payn's plot might be expected to peter out in the third volume, but it does not. Instead Payn steps up the suggestions of a supernatural cause of Sir Marmaduke's absence. The names of the parts of the demesne sound a menacing refrain – Davit's Copse, Home Spinney, Old Plantation – as hands are procured to search the Chase and drag the waters. Peter's eye is drawn to the Wolsey Oak beyond the griffin-guarded gates, the wintry landscape making the kind of sympathetic parallels Henry James was to create in *The Turn of the Screw*.

A few leaves were still left to flutter down in eddies from the trees, or hop and rustle on the frosty ground, but their scarcity looked more mournful than utter bareness would have done. It was now the saddest time of all the year; the bleak east wind went wailing overhead; and underneath, the soil was black with frost.   (ch.32)

Wandering through the estate, chilled by its sombre aspect, Peter comes across yew trees clipped and cut in every conceivable form after the taste of the seventeenth century. 'One was almost tempted to imagine that they had been human once, and been turned into yew trees for their sins.' Park, woodland, knoll, coppice, the 'Old Plantation' where Sir Massingberd had last been seen alive (Payn writes a positive litany of trees) oppress the narrator with echoes of the past and premonitions of disaster, until breaking through the Spinney in a panic he comes across the dead body – of Grimjaw. Men with grappling irons drag the lake in vain, watched by the disapproving birds. 'I thought we had him then', said one, bringing up a heavy stone. 'It might have been his *heart*, for all that', declared another. Payn's fantasy orchestrates the macabre scene with the confusing evidence of poachers' and owls' cries remembered from that dreadful night when the baronet disappeared.

False clues and a laborious police investigation cause the pace to flag in the last few chapters, although Payn creates a Bow Street detective, a very presentable prototype Serjeant Cuff (long before Collins invented him), even to the detail of his suspicions antagonising the very people who have employed him. Marmy is married; a year goes by and happiness returns to Fairburn Hall. A new heir to the estate is born and the bones of the old baronet are found at last in Wolsey Oak. Peter calls to mind the gipsy curse: 'May he perish, inch by inch, within reach of the aid that shall never come, ere the God of the poor take him into His hand.' Payn concludes with a retort to those who will denounce his tale as impossible and absurd: 'To critics of this sort, I have only to express my regret that the mission of the author has in my case been reversed, and facts have fallen into such clumsy hands as to seem fiction' (ch.35). Sure enough, an American newspaper reported a true story that mimicked the death of Sir Massingberd exactly.[60]

It is easy to understand the popularity of *Lost Sir Massingberd*: it supplied novelty by depicting a crime without a body and thus intensifying the crossword-puzzle element so essential to the sensation mode, and its period flavour (events are supposed to occur in the early nineteenth century) helped the fairy tale atmosphere, as well as giving the novelist latitude to deal with Bow Street runners and the thrill of railway travel. The Gothic exuberance of the whole is well sustained with reminders of Scott and Byron, with dreams, hints of the supernatural, and a dash of George Borrow in the romany scenes. Today's reader, quite probably, would relish the *opéra bouffe* atmosphere and Payn's typically humorous narrative tone.

*Lost Sir Massingberd* was followed by *Married Beneath Him* (1865), an uneven though charming romance. Following a Trollopian model, Payn has two young men as rivals for the same girl. Jack

Meyrick, the Squire's son, may easily drift to the bad – and does; Fred Galton, son of the local doctor, loves Mary Perling, yet flirts with Eugenie de Lernay before he comes to his senses: 'Mr Frederick Galton is not a hero', writes Payn in Trollopian style. 'I never made any pretence of his being such a monstrosity' (II, ch.12). Mary, who 'did not think *vin ordinaire* of herself by any means', is ripe for love – 'She had devoured a couple of small circulating libraries' – but being of lower station she is highly disapproved of by Fred's uncle, the village curate of Casterton. So the romance must proceed in secret, 'and entailed all sorts of lies – white, piebald, and as black as Erebus' (I, ch.8).

So long as Payn conducts the tale in this spirited fashion all is well. The vacillating hero is decoyed for a while by Eugenie, while Mary pines modestly in the background. Some interest attaches also to Fred's aspiring to a literary career in London: there is a good interlude on the vanity of celebrities, a fracas between two rival authors in a clubroom and a realistic vignette concerning child decoys and robbery in Hyde Park. The conflict between Fred and his uncle, now custodian of the family fortune, deepens when it is divulged that the young man has secretly married Mary. But suddenly Payn abandons domestic realism for the worst sensationalism. Any serious questioning of social values, the *mésalliance*, the struggle of a young couple amidst poverty – all of which have been present so far in terse authorial comment – evaporates when Fred is embroiled in a murder. A body is found in the Serpentine (sensation novelists filled the Serpentine with corpses) and suspicion lights on Fred. Payn himself, fully aware of the third-volume dilemma – the need for a massive shock to the reader's nervous system – makes a rather shame-faced interpolation: 'As a debauched novel-reader whom nothing can interest short of *dénouement* feels a desire to plunge into, to being with, the conclusion of the third volume, so Frederick yearned to know the end of the whole matter, but did not dare to inform himself' (III, ch.60). Rather surprisingly, given his circumstances, Fred attends a hanging, and so great is his notoriety that there is even a request to the Home Secretary to model him in wax for the Chamber of Horrors. In an inspired moment Fred feigns madness, presumably to escape the hangman, and in a court filled with women jostling for a place Fred's equally imaginative counsel pleads homicide due to insanity on the basis of some of the young man's poems. 'Could a sane man write such verses?' he asks. By this time the novel is in Lewis Carroll territory, particularly when the crown attorney suggests that Fred's poems are no proof of madness – take *Sordello* or *Balder*, he reasons. Thus Fred is handed over to the custody of his family and removed to Switzerland, where it is quite clear that he is completely sane and did not by any stretch of imagination marry beneath him.

My reason for quoting this absurd denouement is to illustrate an aspect of Payn's work that puzzled critics. While it may be assumed that he often became careless about capitulating to stereotypes or destroying unity of tone, there is a consciousness about such violations that suggests he is teasing the audience, mocking the conventions he relies on:

> Without immediate reference to that unhappy skeleton in the cupboard who has been so very hardly worked by modern novelists, we may safely say, that there is commonly something 'going on' under most roofs which it is the interest of the party or parties concerned to keep exceedingly quiet. The more respectable – that is to say, the more extensive the household – the more numerous of course are those domestic secrets. In the boudoir or the housekeeper's room, in the heir's chamber or the tutor's garret, in the master's study or the groom's apartment over the stables – a shadow almost certainly abides in one or more of these, crouching down and cowering away from every onlooker.　(I, ch.8)

This enjoyment of the joke animates Payn's best sensationalism. It is a pity that he could not exercise it with greater judgement and finesse, or that the day of the comedy thriller had not yet arrived, though it gives a dimension of pleasure to the narrative even so. Some reviewers, Leslie Stephen in particular, were quick to praise this refreshing element, but others thought not only that Payn was guilty of laxity and cynicism, but also that he was not even playing fair by the conventions of the form. Often, I suspect, they missed the element of parody. At any rate, reviews indicate a certain puzzlement about his work throughout the sixties. The *Athenaeum* was obviously quite baffled by the tonal inconsistency of *The Clyffards of Clyffe*:

The romance is like a bad dream or a Victoria [*sic*] drama, with very well painted scenery. The descriptions of Nature are good and graphic, whilst the characters and incidents are utter nonsense. The conversations are carried on in a wild style, something between blank verse and bewitched prose. The story realizes all the objections which sensible parents and guardians make to novel-reading; it is idle, exciting, and foolish.[61]

*Mirk Abbey* (1865) is a prime example of what the critics objected to, functioning on one level as robust domestic comedy in a setting like those of Charles Lever, with horse races, trainers and gentlemen of the turf, and on another as a melodrama involving the book's central figure, the widowed Lady Lisgard, and her attempts to hide a first marriage for the sake of her sons' reputations. When her first husband appears from the lawless backwoods of British Columbia, Lady Lisgard is terrified, and spends much time in the library consulting books on wills, succession and illegitimacy. She and the colonial stranger, it appears, had been shipwrecked many years before and each had thought the other drowned. Lady Lisgard flees to London while the husband presents himself at Mirk Abbey to disclose the awful scandal just as Lady Lisgard's elder son is celebrating his majority. By chance the interloper blunders into a windmill, whirls aloft on the sails, and is heavily concussed. Meanwhile, unable to stay away, Lady Lisgard has returned to Mirk in disguise as Madame de Castellan. Not even her sons recognise her, and she is able to act as good fairy for a while until the inevitable settlements and reconciliations. In a note Payn defends himself from plagiarising *East Lynne* and maintains the feasible nature of his climax by explaining how easy it is to counterfeit age by the resources of the actor's make-up box. Notwithstanding this defence, the novel illustrates plainly how difficult it was to reconcile the absurdities of the thriller with circumstance and credible human beings. Was Payn parodying sensation fiction? Or was it accidental?

*The Clyffards of Clyffe* (1866) suggests that it was not. Here the excesses of sensational ingredients are matched by outsize characters and grandiloquent language. Payn's prefatory statement sets the tone: 'The Critical Reader who entertains a wholesome horror of "Sensation Novels" is respectfully requested to take notice that this work is avowedly "a Romance" – a species of fiction at one time freely permitted to the British

Novelist.' From the opening with its incantatory place names, *The Clyffards* strikes a note of parody. It is 1820 in the West Riding of Yorkshire. By gig through Donnerblick Scars to Hell Gate and Boden Pot, where the Boggart (Devil) walks, and where mad Guy Cliffard plunged to his death long years since, Clement Carr, part-proprietor of the nearby asylum, comes to visit his sister, Grace, who is married to Ralph Clyffard. The ancestral home is melancholy in the moonlight and Carr hears bloodhounds baying as the heavy iron gates open. Taking swiftly to the mantelpiece to avoid the dogs, he meets the son and heir, Rupert, and his blonde sister, whose voice is 'clear and musical as a struck stalactite' (I, ch.3). Not surprisingly, the plot is extravagantly sensational. Mrs Clyffard wants to possess the proud demesne of Clyffe and schemes to have her niece, Mildred, marry Rupert, who is touched with the Clyffard insanity. But Rupert's brother, Ray, is quite sane, hates Mrs Clyffard, and loves Mildred. With a convenient legend to fall back on, Mrs Clyffard disguises herself as the Fair Lady sewing a shroud and persuades her husband that Rupert must marry quickly. 'The doting fool is mine', she gloats after one visitation. In this atmosphere of medieval farce Payn interpolates anecdotes such as the tale of the Clyffard ancestor who buried his bloodhound in the chapel and was excommunicated.

Interspersed with this rigmarole are passages of vigorous realistic discription such as that of Morecombe Bay and the flats at low tide, and the caves where Mildred and Ray meet secretly. Indeed, in the second volume, when Mildred and Ray run away and take up residence on a wild southern coast, Payn is so caught up in local colour that he adds a note on the habits of the sea anemone (II, ch.12). Here the couple are tracked by another of Mrs Clyffard's henchmen, who plans a walk along the cliffs for Ray, savouring the outcome like 'an ogre sharpening his teeth before a baby-feast' (II, ch.4). He manages to hurl Ray over the cliff, but his plan to have Mildred cut off by the tide misfires. In a beautiful piece of melodrama Payn describes the villain on shore reaching after a crab in a hole in the rocks. Attempting to free his hand he dislodges a rock and his arm is imprisoned while the tide, like the rustle of a dress, creeps closer. Next day the villain's body is found with the wrist half cut through by a knife. Ray's deliverance at the Beacon Cliff is ingeniously accomplished: miraculously falling onto a ledge, he slides down to a cavern high

in the cliff where he finds foreign lace in bales: he has discovered
a smugglers' hideout. What spares this escape from banality are
Payn's anecdotes about men who grew up scaling the cliffs for
rare birds' eggs. So the cave is the Martins' Nest, and the
smugglers are the cliff fowlers, who perform courageous feats of
agility to conceal the contraband brought from France. His
anecdote about the fowling-trade is a digression, but its details
about swinging on the rope, the trust placed in the man at the
top, the rashness of the boys and the way of drawing lots by
feathers give vigour and actuality to a melodramatic scene.

In the final part of the novel the tension is undiminished, and
Payn's indulgence in improbable actions sustained with touches
of comedy. Rupert, now thoroughly mad, uses a razor blade as
some kind of magic mirror. Raymond scorns 'the ridiculous
notion of kidnappings, murders, private imprisonments, and all
the stage situations of romance' (III, ch.11), yet he is in the thick
of them. Truth, Payn insists, is indeed stranger than fiction, and
he gently chides his audience who 'read in *The Times* at breakfast,
every morning of their lives, some case or other much more
tremendous and astounding than any so-called "Sensational"
novelist would venture to put into fiction' (III, ch.11). This
sanctions fantastic events to come. Mildred is lured into a cave to
be saved by a loyal servant, while Mrs Clyffard, demented by the
failure of her schemes, causes Rupert to fall from the roof and
herself becomes a hopeless lunatic. All this purging of bad blood
gives new life to the surviving Clyffes, and the Hall takes its
rightful place in cheerful leadership of the community.

Comment on this novel was wide and generally favourable.
The *Morning Post* singled out Payn's poetic faculty perfectly
attuned to romance-writing: 'The story is weird, terrible, highly
poetical', suggesting a new dimension in the novelist's capacity.
Most perceptive of all, the *London Review* recognised the
distinction Payn was making between sensation and realistic
fiction in the heightening of scene-painting, narrative and
dialogue. What Payn achieves in *The Clyffards* (as the *Morning
Post* observed) was to bring back the Gothic romance.

In *A Perfect Treasure* (1869) Payn continues to explore the kind
of comedy thriller he returned to again and again (as in *The Confidential Agent*, 1880), and which a generation of later adventure
and crime writers, like Rider Haggard, John Buchan, A. E. W.
Mason and Baroness Orczy, were to exploit to the full. The

romantic, flamboyant plot combines with lifelike characters in realistic domestic interiors. Marmaduke Drake, whatever melodramatic events he becomes embroiled in, is also convincingly a young man struggling to become a writer. For the scrutiny of Mrs Blunt (clearly a portrait of Miss Mitford), he produces with pounding heart 'about ten pounds weight of poems', yearning to embark on 'that heart-breaking business' of becoming a real author. Mrs Blunt writes fine peppery letters and advises the sixteen-year-old that 'what is best is that which has been ripened in the brain, and been afterwards carefully pruned and trimmed' (ch.5). What he needs most, she counsels, is life experience, and almost at once Marmy is plunged into outlandish and mysterious adventures, revolving around his Uncle Theo's Hindu servant, Sangaree Tannajee (who clearly owes something to *The Moonstone*, published a year earlier). When Marmy finds him ferreting through a drawer, tone and dialogue have the exuberance of Kipling or Conan Doyle: 'Chorwallah [thief]!' he concludes, and the servant turns on him: 'Drop that ugly knife you scoundrel, drop it' (ch.10). Later, his uncle's desolation at the disappearance of the Hindu prompts Marmy to search for him. It transpires that the very ship on which Tannajee was sailing to India has foundered, and Marmy now becomes obsessed with recovering the body and trying to unravel the secret. Divers go down to the wreck and Marmy manages to substitute for one of them, since under the grotesque helmet 'there's no knowing one of us magnified tadpoles from another' (ch.18). Once again Payn draws on his journalist's file for the authentic description of diving apparatus and routines, colouring it in his fiction with appropriately Gothic imagery.[62] Marmy feels the impiety of his mission as well as the danger, 'long seaweeds swaying and curling like serpents beneath my feet', as he ventures into the twilight. He finds the ship 'like some monstrous whale' and the bodies of the drowned men move gently in the current, images of entrapment as well as grisly actualities he had already written about in an essay called 'Under the Sea'.[63] Marmy discovers the upright body of the Hindu fixing him with a glassy-eyed stare before sinking to the floor. A post mortem provides the solution to the mystery: the Hindu bore, like the toad – not in his head but in his stomach – a fabulous jewel, the fortune Uncle Theo had brought back many years ago from India with his servant's aid.

Payn's agile plotting and knack of diverting the reader with outrageous devices is also to be seen in *A Woman's Vengeance* (1872). Arthur Tyndall, a reckless young man, addicted to 'turf and bones' (horse-racing and dice) is engaged to Helen Somers. The first volume is largely taken up with low comedy directed mainly at Helen's Wagnerian mother, who has trouble with her aspirates, and with the antics during a boating expedition of Arthur's wild gambling friends. The breezy atmosphere is a rather inferior version of what Jerome K. Jerome was to produce in his classic of the river. So far there is no hint of the sensation novel. In the course of the cruise Arthur meets up with his childhood sweetheart, Alice Renn ('Jenny'), daughter of the innkeeper by the lock, and his old passion is aroused. But he marries Helen, whose jealousy when she learns about Jenny leads the novel in a darker direction. The mutual pain, vexation and discontents of the couple erupt in rows and remorse, quite convincingly drawn, although with masculine bias. At his best Payn observes the human comedy always with a cheerful worldly wisdom:

> When husband and wife whisper together in company, it is generally understood that they are not exchanging compliments. . . . (II, ch.12)

> 'There is no subject a man's word is less to be relied on, you know, than upon his banking account.' (II, ch.1)

As in so many cases of commercial fiction, the talented novelist has to choose between social and human insights and the factitious conventions of the popular romance. What up to now had been perfectly acceptable comedy of manners and realistic comment on a marriage going on the rocks is overwhelmed by the clichés of the sensation novel. In a fit of rage Helen throws Jenny over a slippery plank into the millrace, but then has second thoughts and tries to save her. Arthur, arriving in the nick of time, rescues both. Later, while on holiday in France, Helen and Arthur have a coach accident in which both are seriously injured. Recovering in hospital, Arthur is brought word that his wife has died. Clearly this is a major incident that provided the germ of the plot from which Payn worked backwards, elaborating clues and bizarre incidents, one of which is Arthur seeing Helen's ghost or double at a masquerade.

Returning to England, after a due interval Arthur resumes his friendship with Jenny and 'the resoldered pair set out along the well-remembered path, and renewed after that long desuetude their olden talk' (III, ch.3). Once they are married the ghost walks with a vengeance, particularly when Jenny finds a letter written by Helen prior to her death warning that her husband might well seek to murder her, perhaps by engineering a coaching accident. Totally forgetting that Arthur was himself within a hairsbreadth of death in the accident, Jenny starts to wilt and pine. When Helen's ghost appears before her, the shock causes her to have a miscarriage and her baby dies. Understandably Arthur comments, 'We two have some common enemy, malignant, remorseless, capable of inhuman atrocities' (III, ch.11). Eventually a remorseful Helen is revealed, to confess before she conveniently dies that she had been able to embark on her vengeance because of a confusion of name plates in the hospital which allowed her to assume another identity.

When the demand grew in the seventies and eighties for stories of more exotic cast in foreign settings, Payn adapted to suit the market, as in *By Proxy* (1878), which is among his best novels. Its organisation is rather better than usual and there is an intensity about the central character he seldom achieves. Two Englishmen are making their way by boat up a tributary of the Cha-Ho in northern China. Arthur Conway is a worn, tired-looking man with an air of having failed in life; 'Conway had missed his tip' is the general opinion. His companion, Ralph Pennicuick, on the other hand, is a much harder, more decisive character with a cruel streak in him: 'Steel Pen' or 'Black Beard' he is called behind his back. These two have an uneasy friendship which sets up a promising tension from the start. Against a convincingly drawn background of sacred shrines, priests and processions, Payn has Ralph steal a sacred jewel, the Shay-le, which brings a howling mob down on the travellers. The scene abruptly shifts to England, where Mrs Conway and her daughter, Nelly, live simply at Richmond. Mrs Conway is an embittered, querulous woman, thoroughly discontented with her lot and complaining about her absent husband. Nelly refuses to marry Pennicuick's son, Raymond, because she is poor and the Pennicuicks are wealthy. Meanwhile Black Beard languishes in jail doomed to the death of ten-thousand cuts, while Conway struggles to engineer his release by bribery. What Payn manages to convey in this exotic situation is a certain psychological complexity in the characters: Pennicuick has dared to desecrate the temple with a certain self-destructive bravado, while Conway broods with morbid intensity on his ill health, wastrel past and unhappy marriage. The incredible conclusion to this part of the novel is that by various stratagems Conway is substituted for Pennicuick, on the understanding that Ralph will provide money for Nelly so that she can marry Raymond.

Returning to England, Ralph Pennicuick changes his mind and breaks his promise to Conway. Henceforth he is to be haunted by guilt and remorse, and Payn skilfully develops outward signs of this inner conflict, including spectral visitation and confusion of identities. The false friend, reappearing in England as something of a hero, has robbed Conway of his identity, and as remorse breaks him down he begins in a way to resemble Conway physically. His son is shocked to find him greatly 'changed', 'a great alteration' in him; even his voice sounds different (ch.24). There is another ghost from the past too, for it begins to emerge that Mrs Conway bears the secret shame of having been attracted to Ralph, who had continued to pursue her after her marriage. Her guilt takes the form of feeling her husband's reproachful presence around her: 'Your father is alive, child', she tells Nelly (ch.22), and she now blames herself for having spoiled her husband's life. Such ironic echoes woven into the narrative point to the evil consequences of selfishness and greed.

Sensing that lies or misdeeds surround her husband's death, Mrs Conway calls on Ralph, which involves a painful dredging up of her past, and a quarrel in which she accuses him of treachery towards her, thereby ironically naming that greater betrayal of trust towards his friend that is gnawing at his conscience. Struck down by apoplexy, Mrs Conway imagines she sees her husband whispering 'Foul play' (II, ch.3), but of course her speech has failed her. Now Conway's presence grows more palpable to Ralph Pennicuick, a *Doppelgänger* constantly reminding him of his greed and egotism. Yet he is unable to overcome his pathological meanness, refusing to countenance his son's marriage: 'It is impossible . . . for a mean man to be otherwise than secretive. When pushed with relation to pecuniary affairs, he resorts to the expedient of the cuttle-fish; he darkens the whole matter; and when it comes to giving reasons for his economies, he will lie' (II, ch.6).

In an attempt to assuage his guilt Pennicuick stands for Parliament, but his spectral hauntings get worse; he has nightmares about China, and the bead of the chandelier above him glows like the Shay-le diamond. On the hustings a sign appears with the cryptic words, 'What has he Done? Inquire at Dhulang, China' (II, ch.13). Now the Press, scenting a story, begins to harass him and he receives a sketch depicting the execution at Dhulang, his face substituted for Conway's. Facing the material manifestation of Conway's presence, he suffers a stroke, and confesses his villainy to his son. Proper restitutions are made, Nelly becomes an heiress and can marry Raymond.

Another element of the story which bears on the theme of identity concerns Nelly's fidelity towards Raymond and her refusal to become a burden to him. Her generosity is the antithesis of his father's greed. Early in the story she has been befriended by Mr and Mrs Wardlaw, who act as her guardians rather in the manner of the Boffins in *Our Mutual Friend*. While they pretend to turn all human relationships into mercenary arrangements, they are in reality good-natured. They act, then, as parents towards Nelly 'by proxy', adding a further dimension to the title beyond the obvious one of Conway taking Pennicuick's place.

The final unravelling of the plot in the manner of sensation novels uses a familiar device. A strange man, Mr Pearson, had also made friends with Nelly and at one convenient moment had even come to her rescue when she had been cut off by the tide. He, it turns out, had been responsible for the hauntings, and at the end of the novel he comes face to face with Raymond to confess that he is Arthur Conway, who long ago had miraculously cheated his executioners with the aid of a Chinese sea captain. In fact, such a marvellous deliverance hardly detracts from the narrative wholeness and intriguing character conflict of this novel, particularly since the conventional happy endings are so much part of the long romantic tradition as to be acceptable in the general scheme of renewal and the triumph of good.

In his last years Payn worked nobly despite the mortifications and pains of arthritis; he writes with much pathos about old age, illness and the solace of home, friends and family in his late essays *The Backwater of Life*, published posthumously in 1899 with Leslie Stephen's short memoir. Payn ended his career in harness like the good journalist he was, with some charming anecdotal pieces such as *Gleams of Memory* (1894) and *Collections and Recollections* (1898) and novels which rang with the spirited humour and well-plotted adventure of the old days. Despite his infirmity he wrote *causerie* for the *Illustrated London News* for several years and contributed articles to *Nineteenth Century* and *The Times*. But at last he could no longer move around London.

Friends, anxious that he should not be denied his game of whist – his 'daily bread' as he called it – came twice a week for a rubber. As Leslie Stephen wrote, 'He could not leave his chair and I used to call for a chat on Saturday afternoons. He took his pains most bravely, always cheered up when friends came, and was full of interest and goodwill'.[64] *A Modern Dick Whittington* (1892) and *The Disappearance of George Driffell* (1896) satisfied his public and showed that the old hand had not lost its cunning; he could still tell a good story, the hallmark of his trade, for as Ernest Baker observed, 'The popular novelist, preacher, or after-dinner speaker is the man who can tell a story.'[65] In this and other respects he remained true to his profession and admirably representative of the mid-Victorian fiction industry and its middlebrow public.

It has been observed that to rescue even one good book from oblivion is a critic's richest reward. In the case of James Payn, Rhoda Broughton and Mrs Oliphant there is justification for salvaging several worthwhile novels. Only a sampling of their work and of the vast range of popular fiction has been surveyed here. Other writers of equal ability and interest must of necessity be passed over – M. E. Braddon, Mrs Henry Wood, Henry Kingsley, R. D. Blackmore, Sheridan Le Fanu and William Black (to name only a few) were intensely productive in the period covered by this study, and each warrants more than a few lines in literary histories customarily allotted to them.

For such writers, as for the trio comprehended here, traditional standards of literary criticism as to insight, discovery and innovation admittedly will find them lacking, although each comes close to distinction in a novel or two with certain touches of character or flashes of imaginative brilliance. At any rate, portions of their work engage the attention of any student interested in the broad field of Victorian fiction and could delight the ordinary reader. If only some enterprising publisher would undertake such projects as Ernest Baker's splendid twenty-volume series of *Half-Forgotten Books* issued in a more leisurely age.[66] Economies and production costs today make such publishing ventures unlikely, but the reader off the beaten track can at least take comfort in the reissue of minor fiction from time to time, such as Mrs Oliphant's *A Beleaguered City* in 1970 or Miss Broughton's *Not Wisely, but Too Well* in 1967. Richard Jefferies's *After London: or Wild England* and Marcus Clarke's *For the Term of His Natural Life* were welcome discoveries of 1980. It would be pleasant to contemplate a far wider range of novels from the heyday of Victorian popular fiction. For the argument still holds good that an age is often to be better appreciated by what is no longer read than by its standard works still on the shelves.

# Appendix

*Salem Chapel*, 2 vols (1863)

*Heart and Cross* (1863)

*The Perpetual Curate*, 3 vols (1864)

*Agnes*, 3 vols (1866)

*Miss Marjoribanks*, 3 vols (1866)

*A Son of the Soil*, 2 vols (1866)

*Madonna Mary*, 3 vols (1867)

*Francis of Assisi*, The Sunday Library (1868)

*The Brownlows*, 3 vols (1868)

*Historical Sketches of the Reign of George Second*, 2 vols (1869)

*The Minister's Wife*, 3 vols (1869)

*John, a Love Story*, 2 vols (1870)

*The Three Brothers*, 3 vols (1870)

*Squire Arden*, 3 vols (1871)

*At His Gates*, 3 vols (1872)

*Memoir of the Count de Montalembert, a Chapter of Recent French History*, 2 vols (1872)

*Ombra*, 3 vols (1872)

*May*, 3 vols (1873)

*Innocent, a Tale of Modern Life*, 3 vols (1873)

*A Rose in June*, 2 vols (1874)

*For Love and Life*, 3 vols (1874)

*The Story of Valentine and his Brothers*, 3 vols (1875)

*Whiteladies*, 3 vols (1875)

*Dress,* Art at Home Series (1876)

*Phoebe Junior, a Last Chronicle of Carlingford*, 3 vols (1876)

*The Curate in Charge*, 2 vols (1876)

*The Makers of Florence: Dante, Giotto, Savonarola and their City* (1876)

*Carità*, 3 vols (1877)

*Dante*, Foreign Classics for English Readers (1877)

*Mrs Arthur*, 3 vols (1877)

*Young Musgrave*, 3 vols (1877)

*The Primrose Path: a Chapter in the Annals of the Kingdom of Fife*, 3 vols (1878)

*Molière* (with F. Tarver), Foreign Classics for English Readers (1879)

*Within the Precincts*, 3 vols (1879)

*The Two Mrs Scudamores, Tales from Blackwood's Magazine* (1879)

*The Greatest Heiress in England*, 3 vols (1879)

*A Beleaguered City, being a Narrative of Certain Recent Events in the City of Semur, a Story of the Seen and the Unseen* (1880)

*Cervantes*, Foreign Classics for English Readers (1880)
*He That Will Not When He May*, 3 vols (1880)
*Harry Joscelyn*, 3 vols (1881)
*A Little Pilgrim in the Unseen* (1882)
*In Trust, the Story of a Lady and Her Lover*, 3 vols (1882)
*The Literary History of England in the End of the Eighteenth and Beginning of the Nineteenth Century*, 3 vols (1882)
*Hester, a Story of Contemporary Life*, 3 vols (1882)
*It Was a Lover and His Lass*, 3 vols (1883)
*Sheridan*, English Men of Letters (1883)
*The Ladies Lindores*, 3 vols (1883)
*Sir Tom*, 3 vols (1884)
*The Wizard's Son*, 3 vols (1884)
*Two Stories of the Seen and Unseen* ('Old Lady Mary'; 'The Open Door') (1885)
*Madam*, 3 vols (1885)
*Oliver's Bride, a True Story* (1886)
*A Country Gentleman and His Family*, 3 vols (1886)
*Effie Ogilvie, the Story of a Young Life*, 2 vols (1886)
*A House Divided against Itself*, 3 vols (1886)
*The Son of his Father*, 3 vols (1887)
*The Makers of Venice: Doges, Conquerors, Painters and Men of Letters* (1887)
*A Memoir of the Life of John Tulloch* (1888)
*Cousin Mary* (1888)
*The Land of Darkness, along with Some Further Chapters in the Experience of the Little Pilgrims* (1888)
*Joyce*, 3 vols (1888)
*The Second Son*, 3 vols (1888)
*Neighbours on the Green, a Collection of Stories* (1889)
*A Poor Gentleman*, 3 vols (1889)
*Lady Car, the Sequel of a Life* (1889)
*Kirsteen, a Story of a Scottish Family Seventy Years Ago* (1890)
*Royal Edinburgh: Her Saints, Kings, Prophets, and Poets* (1890)
*The Duke's Daughter; and The Fugitives*, 3 vols (1890)
*Sons and Daughters* (1890)
*The Mystery of Mrs Blencarrow* (1890)
*Janet*, 3 vols (1891)
*Jerusalem: Its History and Hope* (1891)
*A Memoir of the Life of Laurence Oliphant, and of Alice Oliphant, His Wife*, 2 vols (1891)

*The Railwayman and his Children*, 3 vols (1891)
*Diana Trelawney, the History of a Great Mistake*, 2 vols (1892)
*The Cuckoo in the Nest*, 3 vols (1892)
*The Heir Presumptive and the Heir Apparent*, 3 vols (1892)
*The Marriage of Elinor*, 3 vols (1892)
*The Victorian Age of English Literature* (with F. R. Oliphant), 2 vols
    (1892)
*Lady William*, 3 vols (1893)
*The Sorceress*, 3 vols (1893)
*Thomas Chalmers, Preacher, Philosopher and Statesman*, English
    Leaders of Religion (1893)
*A House in Bloomsbury*, 2 vols (1894)
*Historical Sketches of the Reign of Queen Anne* (1894)
*The Prodigals and Their Inheritance*, 2 vols (1894)
*Who Was Lost and Is Found* (1894)
*A Child's History of Scotland* (1895)
*The Makers of Modern Rome* (1895)
*Sir Robert's Fortune, the Story of a Scotch Moor* (1895)
*Two Strangers* (1895)
*'Dies Irae', the Story of a Spirit in Prison* (1895)
*Jeanne d'Arc: Her Life and Death*, Heroes of the Nations (1896)
*Old Mr Tredgold* (1896)
*The Two Marys (and Grove Road, Hampstead): Tales* (1896)
*The Unjust Steward, or, The Minister's Debt* (1896)
*Annals of a Publishing House: William Blackwood and his Sons, their
    Magazine and Friends*, 2 vols (1897)
*The Lady's Walk, a Tale* (1897)
'The Sisters Brontë', in Mrs Oliphant *et al.*, *Women Novelists of
    Queen Victoria's Reign* (1897)
*The Ways of Life, Two Stories* (1897)
*A Widow's Tale, and Other Stories* (1898)
*That Little Cutty, and Two Other Stories* ('Dr Barrère'; 'Isabel
    Dysart') (1898)
*The Autobiography and Letters of Mrs M. O. W. Oliphant*, arranged
    and ed. Mrs Harry Coghill (1899)
*Queen Victoria, a Personal Sketch* (1900)
*Stories of the Seen and the Unseen* ('The Open Door'; 'Old Lady
    Mary'; 'The Portrait'; 'The Library Window') (1902)

Mrs Oliphant also wrote over 200 articles for *Blackwood's
Magazine*.

*Rhoda Broughton (1840–1920)*

*Not Wisely, but Too Well: A Novel*, 3 vols (1867)
*Cometh Up as a Flower: An Autobiography*, 2 vols (1867)
*Red as a Rose is She: A Novel*, 3 vols (1870)
*Good-bye, Sweetheart!: A Tale*, 3 vols (1872)
*Nancy: A Novel*, 3 vols (1873)
*Tales for Christmas Eve* (1873), reissued as *Twilight Stories* (1879)
*Joan: A Tale*, 3 vols (1876)
*Second Thoughts*, 2 vols (1880)
*Belinda: A Novel*, 3 vols (1883)
*Betty's Visions and Mrs Smith of Longmains* (1886)
*Doctor Cupid: A Novel*, 3 vols (1886)
*Alas!: A Novel*, 3 vols (1890)
*A Widower Indeed*, with Elizabeth Bisland (1891)
*Mrs Bligh: A Novel* (1892)
*A Beginner* (1894)
*Scylla or Charybdis?: A Novel* (1895)
*Dear Faustina* (1897)
*The Game and the Candle* (1899)
*Foes in Law* (1900).
*Lavinia* (1902)
*A Waif's Progress* (1905)
*Mamma* (1908)
*The Devil and the Deep Sea* (1910)
*Between Two Stools* (1912)
*Concerning a Vow* (1914)
*A Thorn in the Flesh* (1917)
*A Fool in Her Folly* (1920)

Miss Broughton's short story 'Rent Day' appeared in *Temple Bar*, June 1893; and an article 'Girls Past and Present' in *Ladies Home Journal*, Sep 1920.

*James Payn (1830–98)*

*Stories from Boccaccio and Other Poems* (1852)
*Poems* (1853)
*Stories and Sketches* (1857)
*Leaves from Lakeland* (1858)

*Furness Abbey and Its Neighbourhood* (1858)

*A Hand Book to the English Lakes* (1858)

*The Foster Brothers, being a History of the School and College Life of Two Young Men* (1859)

*The Bateman Household* (1860)

*Richard Arbour, or, The Family Scapegrace*, repr. from *Chambers's Journal* (1861)

*Meliboeus in London* (1862)

*Lost Sir Massingberd: A Romance of Real Life*, 2 vols (1864)

*Married Beneath Him*, 3 vols (1865)

*People, Places and Things* (1865)

*Mirk Abbey*, 3 vols (1866)

*The Clyffards of Clyffe*, 3 vols, repr. from *Chambers's Journal* (1866)

*The Lakes in Sunshine: Being Photographic and Other Pictures of the Lake District of Westmoreland and North Lancashire*, with descriptive letterpress by J. P., 2 vols (1867–70)

*Lights and Shadows of London Life* (1867)

*Carlyon's Year*, 2 vols (1868)

*Blondel Parva*, 2 vols (1868)

*Bentinck's Tutor, One of the Family* (1868)

*Maxims by a Man of the World* (1869)

*A Perfect Treasure: An Incident in the Early Life of Marmaduke Drake, Esq.* (1869)

*A County Family*, 3 vols (1869)

*Found Dead*, 3 vols (1869)

*Gwendoline's Harvest*, 2 vols (1870)

*Not Wooed, but Won*, 3 vols (1871)

*Like Father, Like Son* (1871)

*A Woman's Vengeance*, 3 vols (1872)

*Cecil's Tryst*, 3 vols (1872)

*Murphy's Master, and Other Stories*, 2 vols (1873)

*The Best of Husbands*, 3 vols (1874)

*At Her Mercy*, 3 vols (1874)

*Walter's Word*, 3 vols (1875)

*Halves, a Novel, and Other Tales*, 3 vols (1876)

*Fallen Fortunes*, 3 vols (1876)

*What He Cost Her*, 3 vols (1877)

*By Proxy*, 2 vols (1878)

*Less Black than We're Painted*, 3 vols (1878)

*Under One Roof: An Episode in a Family History*, 3 vols (1879)

*High Spirits, being Certain Stories Written in Them* (1879)

*A Confidential Agent*, 3 vols (1880)

*From Exile*, 3 vols (1881)

*A Grape from a Thorn*, 3 vols (1881)

*Some Private Views, being Essays from the Nineteenth Century Review, with Some Occasional Articles from The Times* (1881)

*For Cash Only*, 3 vols (1882)

*Thicker than Water*, 3 vols (1883)

*Kit: A Memory*, 3 vols (1883)

*The Canon's Ward*, 3 vols (1884)

*Some Literary Recollections* (1884)

*The Talk of the Town*, 2 vols (1885)

*The Luck of the Darrells*, 3 vols (1885)

*In Peril and Privation: Stories of Marine Disaster Retold* (1885)

*The Heir of the Ages*, 3 vols (1886)

*Glow-worm Tales*, 3 vols (1887)

*Holiday Tasks: Being Essays Written in Vacation Time* (1887)

*The Eavesdropper: An Unparalleled Experience* (1888)

*A Prince of the Blood*, 3 vols (1888)

*The Mystery of Mirbridge*, 3 vols (1888)

*Notes from the 'News'*, repr. from the *Illustrated London News* (1890)

*The Word and the Will*, 3 vols (1890)

*The Burnt Million*, 3 vols (1890)

*Sunny Stories, and Some Shady Ones, etc.* (1891)

*A Stumble on the Threshold*, 2 vols (1892)

*A Modern Dick Whittington: or, a Patron of Letters*, 2 vols (1892)

*A Trying Patient, etc.* (1893)

*Humorous Stories about People, Places and Things* (1893)

*Gleams of Memory: with Some Reflections* (1894)

*In Market Overt* (1895)

*The Disappearance of George Driffell* (1896)

*Another's Burden* (1897)

*Collections and Recollections by One Who Has Kept a Diary* (1898)

*The Backwater of Life: or, Essays of a Literary Veteran*, with Introduction by Leslie Stephen (1899)

Payn also wrote *The Childhood of Charles Dickens* (privately printed, 1870).

# Notes

NOTES TO THE PREFACE

1 I am thinking of such studies as Margaret Dalziel, *Popular Fiction 100 Years Ago: An Unexplored Tract of Literary History* (London, 1957); P. J. Keating, *The Working Class in Victorian Fiction* (London, 1971); Victor E. Neuburg, *Popular Literature: A History and Guide* (Harmondsworth, 1977).

2 David Masson, *British Novelists and their Styles* (Cambridge, 1859) pp. 28–32; see *Athenaeum*, no. 1656 (23 July 1859) 107.

3 R. D. Altick, *The English Common Reader: A Social History of the Mass Reading Public* (Chicago, 1957) p. 299; *Macmillan's Magazine*, XIV (June 1866) 97, and XIII (Jan 1866) 203. See also K. M. Tillotson, 'The Lighter Reading of the Eighteen-Sixties', Introduction to Wilkie Collins, *The Woman in White* (Boston, Mass., 1969).

4 Alfred Austin, 'Our Novels', *Temple Bar*, XXIX (May–July 1870).


NOTES TO CHAPTER ONE: READING MANIA

1 'The Unknown Public', *Household Words*, XVIII (21 Aug 1858) 217–22; 'The Byways of Literature: Reading for the Million', *Blackwood's Magazine*, LXXXIV (Aug 1858) 200–16.

2 Quoted by Tillotson, Introduction to *The Woman in White*, p. ix.

3 Alfred Austin, 'The Novels of Miss Broughton', *Temple Bar*, XLI (May 1874) 197.

4 Altick, *The English Common Reader*, p. 83. By 1877, one contributor to *Good Words* found it impossible to define 'middle class' – XVIII (July 1877) 357. J. A. Banks notes at least seven levels above the lowest class; see *1859: Entering an Age of Crisis*, ed. P. Appleman, William Madden, Michael Wolff (Bloomington, Ind., 1959) p. 213.

5 James Payn, *Some Private Views* (London, 1881).

6 Ibid., p. 81.

7 Tillotson, Introduction to *The Woman in White*, p. ix.

8 *The Letters of Edward Fitzgerald*, ed. William Aldis Wright (London, 1894) II, 159; Max Sutton, *R. D. Blackmore* (Boston, Mass., 1979) p. 80; *The English Novel*, ed. L. Bartlett, W. R. Sherwood (Philadelphia, 1967) p. 304.

9 *Memorials of Two Sisters*, ed. Margaret Shaen (London, 1908) p. 296.

10 S. M. Ellis, *Mainly Victorian* (New York, 1969) p. 209 (first published 1925).

11  John Sutherland, *Victorian Novelists and Publishers* (London, 1976) p. 24. See also Guinevere Griest, *Mudie's Circulating Library and the Victorian Novel* (Bloomington, Ind., 1970). Cawthorn and Hutt's British Library in Cockspur Street had nothing like Mudie's trade, but its fiction stock corroborates my findings. The most popular minor novelists listed in an 1881 catalogue are: Mrs Oliphant (45 titles), Trollope (43), James Grant (38), G. P. R. James (36), W. H. Ainsworth (33), Mrs Henry Wood (29). Not far behind come Charlotte Yonge, Annie Thomas, F. W. Robinson, Anne Manning, Whyte Melville and Florence Marryat. There were many other circulating libraries in the country, like Bradford Circulating Library and Literary Society, founded in 1774, which survived until March 1981. Part of its stock, virtually unchanged for fifty years, gives a clear indication of the most popular three-deckers available to its subscribers: M. E. Braddon (23 titles), Mrs Oliphant (36), G. P. R. James (29) and James Payn (10).

12  Mrs Arthur Kennard, *There's Rue for You*, 2 vols (London, 1880).

13  George Moore, *Literature at Nurse; or Circulating Morals* (London, 1885).

14  Vineta Colby, *Yesterday's Woman: Domestic Realism in the English Novel* (Princeton, NJ, 1974) p. 4. For a contemporary classifying of novels see Masson, *British Novelists and their Styles*, pp. 214–28.

15  Anthony Trollope, *An Autobiography* (London, 1883) ch. 12.

16  Mrs Oliphant, *Phoebe Junior, A Last Chronicle of Carlingford* (London, 1876) III, 7.

17  Arnold Bennett, *Fame and Fiction, an Enquiry into Certain Popularities* (New York, 1975) pp. 62–3 (first published 1901).

18  Tillotson, Introduction to *The Woman in White*, p. v.

19  Q. D. Leavis, *Fiction and the Reading Public* (London, 1939); *Milton to Ouida: A Collection of Essays*, ed. Bonamy Dobrée (London, 1970).

20  Virginia Woolf, 'How Should One Read a Book?', *The Common Reader*, 2nd ser. (London, 1932) p. 263.

21  The reissue of G. M. Young's *Portrait of an Age* (London, 1962) drew attention to the historian's contention that 1860 was the date of that rift in English intelligence when learning began to fragment into specialism and the gap began to appear between literary culture and light entertainment.

22  In 1859 also, David Masson, in *British Novelists and their Styles*, states that the novel's capacity for greatness is no less than poetry's. In poetry, major events of 1859 were the first four poems of Tennyson's *Idylls of the King* and Fitzgerald's version of *The Rubaiyat of Omar Khayyam*.

23  Technological advances like the rotary press, chromolithography, improved and cheaper ways of producing paper, together with legislation easing taxes on paper (1862) were all contributory factors.

24  Alphonse Esquiros, *The English at Home* (London, 1861) p. 347.

25  The phrase used by Ernest Baker to describe the phenomenon is 'muscular blackguardism', in antithesis to the 'muscular Christianity' of Charles Kingsley and others; see Baker, *The History of the English Novel* (London, 1924–39) VIII, ch. 5. A similar celebration of male heartiness is to be seen in the school, university and sporting novels. The code of athleticism was severely criticised by Wilkie Collins in *Man and Wife* (1870). A gentle variant of the muscular outdoors novel was offered by George Borrow's

*Lavengro* (1851), in which the hero puts on the gloves with his gipsy friend, Jasper Petulengro. These rural adventures were continued in *Romany Rye* (1857).

26   Trollope, *Autobiography*, ch. 12.

27   School and university stories were popular well before Thomas Hughes's classics. College life with its bullying tutors, venial scouts and merry student pranksters exactly fitted the *Punch* style. See Theodore Hook, *Peter Priggins, the College Scout*, illustrated by 'Phiz' (1841); Charles Lister, *The College Chums* (1845). After Cuthbert Bede's contribution in the fifties and *Tom Brown's School Days* (1857) came many more, including Martin Legrand (James Rice), *The Cambridge Freshman or Memoirs of Mr Golightly* (1871); A. C. Hilton, *The Light Green: A Superior and High-class Periodical*, no. 1 (1872).

28   Francis Edward Smedley (1818–64), son of the high bailiff at Westminster, another celebrant of school and sporting life, was confined to a wheelchair. His heroes have a touch of the muscular Christian and also a certain warmth and humour, like Trollope's. *Frank Fairlegh* was a great success, achieving eight editions up to 1892. He also wrote (and 'Phiz' illustrated) *Lewis Arundel: or the Railroad of Life* (1852), *The Fortunes of the Colville Family* (1853) and *Harry Coverdale's Courtship and All That Came of It* (1855).

29   Cuthbert Bede was the pseudonym of the Revd Edward Bradley (1827–89), vicar of Stretton, Rutland, who became an expert in light literature and went about the Midlands lecturing on the subject for church funds. His quaint humour and lively style deserve to be better known. Among his best works are: *Photographic Pleasures, Popularly Portrayed with Pen and Pencil* (1855); *The Rook's Garden* (1865); *The White Wife* (1865); *Mattins and Muttons, or the Beauty of Brighton* (1866); and historical novels, *Boscobel* (1872) and *Fotheringhay and Mary, Queen of Scots* (1866). See *Dictionary of National Biography*, XXII (Supplement), ed. Sidney Lee (London, 1909) 250–1.

30   George Alfred Lawrence (1827–76) was a prolific author whose romantic adventure stories were much in vogue in the period covered by this study. The son of Alfred Charnley Lawrence, rector of Sandhurst, Kent, and Emily Mary Finch-Hatton, sister of the ninth Earl of Winchilsea, he was educated at Rugby and Balliol College, Oxford, and called to the bar in 1852, but forsook law for literature and a roving life. See *Dictionary of National Biography*, XI, ed. Sidney Lee (London, 1909) 695–6; Ernest Baker, *Half-Forgotten Books* (London, 1903) vol. 4, and introduction to *Guy Livingstone*.

31   'Thorough' suggests a link with Charles I's attempts to retain absolute power as monarch and govern without parliament.

32   S. M. Ellis, *Wilkie Collins, Le Fanu and Others* (London, 1931) p. 198.

33   Gordon H. Fleming, 'George Alfred Lawrence and the Victorian Sensation Novel', *University of Arizona Bulletin*, XXIII, no. 16 (4 Oct 1952) 29.

34   Baker, *Half-Forgotten Books*, vol. 4, p. vi.

NOTES TO CHAPTER TWO: THE FICTION INDUSTRY

1   *Saturday Review*, XXXVII (7 Feb 1874) 182.

2   Ibid., XLV (27 June 1878) 783. See also 'The Unknown Public', *Household Words*, XVIII (21 Aug 1858) 217–22; 'The Byways of Literature', *Blackwood's Magazine*, LXXXIV (Aug 1858) 200–16; 'Cheap Literature', *British Quarterly Review*, XXIX (Sep 1859) 313–45.

3   Payn, *Some Private Views*, p. 81.

4   Ibid., p. 92.

5   The *Annual Register* for 1863 cites issues from the London press alone of 81 quarterly, 359 monthly, 254 weekly and daily publications.

6   Royal A. Gettman, *A Victorian Publisher: A Study of the Bentley Papers* (Cambridge, 1960) p. 84.

7   Edmund Downey, *Twenty Years Ago* (London, 1905) pp. 246–7.

8   See Leonard Huxley, *The House of Smith, Elder* (London, 1923).

9   Sir Edward Cook, *Literary Recreations* (London, 1918) p. 93.

10  Malcolm Elwin, *Old Gods Falling* (New York, 1939) p. 149.

11  Quoted in Walter E. Houghton, 'Victorian Periodical Literature and the Articulate Classes', *Victorian Studies*, XXII, no. 4 (Summer 1979) 407.

12  Leslie Stephen, Introduction to James Payn, *The Backwater of Life or Essays of a Literary Veteran* (London, 1899) p. xxxii.

13  Kenneth Robinson, *Wilkie Collins* (London, 1951) p. 236. Some comparative circulation figures are helpful: among the leading quality journals, *Quarterly Review* 8000; *Edinburgh Review* 7000; *Westminster Review* 4000; *North British Review* 2000. *Blackwood's Magazine* had a sale of 10,000, and *Fraser's Magazine* 8000. Compare, among the popular magazines, *Temple Bar*, with 30,000 under Sala, levelling off to about 15,000 by 1884, and, earlier, *Household Words*, averaging 40,000. See Houghton, *Victorian Studies*, XXII, no. 4, 391; Altick, *The English Common Reader*, appendix C, pp. 391–6.

14  Payn, *Some Private Views*, p. 93.

15  W. H. Colles, Authors' Syndicate Correspondence, Humanities Research Center, University of Texas, Austin.

16  Sutherland, *Victorian Novelists and Publishers*, p.22.

17  For further information on this important aspect of book production, see N. John Hall, *Trollope and his Illustrators* (London, 1980); Forrest Reid, *Illustrators of the 'Sixties* (London, 1928); Gleeson White, *English Illustration: 'The Sixties' – 1855–70* (Bath, 1970) (first published 1897).

18  But in 1864, George Ford estimated, some 300 new novels appeared; quoted in *Wilkie Collins*, ed. Norman Page, Critical Heritage (London, 1974) p. 16.

19  Sutherland, *Victorian Novelists and Publishers*, pp. 24, 227.

20  Houghton, in *Victorian Studies*, XXII, no. 4, 389.

21  Most of these figures are from Altick, *The English Common Reader*, appendices, pp. 379–85; M. Elwin, *Victorian Wallflowers* (London, 1934) p. 238.

22  Mrs Oliphant *et al.*, *Women Novelists of Queen Victoria's Reign* (London, 1897) p. 248.

23  Thomas Seccombe, 'Cuthbert Bede', *Dictionary of National Biography*, XXII (Supplement), 250–1.

24  Downey, *Twenty Years Ago*, p. 7.

25  Ibid., p. 9.

26  Ibid., p. 14.

27  Gettman, *A Victorian Publisher*, p. 62.

28  Victoria Glendinning, *Sunday Times*, 7 June 1981, p. 12.

29  Downey, *Twenty Years Ago*, pp. 12, 16.

30  Gettman's version of the transaction has the novel bringing in £300 a year for twenty years (*A Victorian Publisher*, pp. 76–7).

31  Ibid., p. 96.

32  S. M. Ellis, *William Harrison Ainsworth and his Friends* (London, 1911) II, 237. Geraldine Jewsbury (1812–80), novelist and close friend of the Carlyles, published her first book, *Zoe, the History of Two Lives*, in 1845. Besides novels she wrote children's books and short tales for *Household Words*. For many years she was a contributor to the *Athenaeum*. See *Dictionary of National Biography*, X, ed. Sidney Lee (London, 1908) 821–3.

33  James Payn, 'A Reader's Error', *Some Literary Recollections* (London, 1884) pp. 236–8. Payn also forced an unsuitable happy ending on George Gissing's *A Life's Morning* (1888); see Baker, *History of the Novel*, IX, 138.

34  Sutherland, *Victorian Novelists and Publishers*, p. 13.

35  See F. D. Tredrey, *The House of Blackwood 1804–1954* (Edinburgh, 1954).

36  Sutherland, *Victorian Novelists and Publishers*, p. 17.

37  *Autobiography and Letters of Mrs M. O. W. Oliphant* (1899), ed. Mrs Harry Coghill (Leicester, 1974) p. 24.

38  Quoted V. and R. A. Colby, *The Equivocal Virtue: Mrs Oliphant and the Literary Market Place* (New York, 1966) p. 158.

39  Mrs Oliphant, *Autobiography and Letters*, pp. 291–2.

40  Downey, *Twenty Years Ago*, pp. 24–5.

41  Payn, *Some Literary Recollections*, p. 72.

42  Ibid., p. 36. Ainsworth at first paid Mrs Henry Wood nothing for her stories in *Bentley's Miscellany*, but eventually stumped up £60 a year (Ellis, *William Harrison Ainsworth*, p. 237).

43  Payn, *Some Literary Recollections*, p. 39.

44  Payn, *Gleams of Memory: With Some Reflections* (London, 1894) p. 186.

45  Tinsley, *Random Reflections of an Old Publisher* (London, 1900) II, 105–6.

46  Payn, *Some Literary Recollections*, pp. 219–20.

47  The Authors' Syndicate, a branch of the Society of Authors, had a very capable business manager in W. H. Colles. It acted as clearing-house, literary agency and general adviser to its members. Colles was co-author with H. Cresswell of *Success in Literature* (London, 1911).

48  Ouida was Marie Louise de la Ramée (1838–1908). Her pen name came about from a childish mispronunciation of her name. Her novels of military and fashionable life were excoriated in some quarters, frequently laughed at for their extravagance, but she had a devoted circle of readers. F. C. Burnand parodied her in *Punch* in 1878. After 1860 she lived in Italy, vigorously resenting it when other lady novelists such as Rhoda Broughton chose to holiday in her vicinity in Florence. She published forty-four works of fiction. See *Dictionary of National Biography*, 1901–1911, ed. H. W. C. Davis and J. R. H. Weaver (London, 1909) pp. 487–8.

49  *Cornhill Misc.*, Humanities Research Center, University of Texas, Austin.

50  Gettman, *A Victorian Publisher*, pp. 79, 243.

51 Michael Sadleir, *Things Past* (London, 1944) p. 104; Gettman, *A Victorian Publisher*, p. 152.

52 Ethel Arnold, 'Rhoda Broughton as I Knew Her', *Fortnightly Review*, CXIV (2 Aug 1920) 275.

53 Gettman, *A Victorian Publisher*, p. 195.

54 Sadleir, *Things Past*, p. 99.

55 Ibid., p. 100.

56 Gettman, *A Victorian Publisher*, pp. 139–40, 243.

57 For further details of sales figures see Altick, *The English Common Reader*, pp. 383–6.

58 Robinson, *Wilkie Collins*, p. 168.

59 *Wilkie Collins*, ed. Page, p. 16.

60 Some hack novelists with marketable value did fairly well out of the arrangement. Mrs J. H. Riddell, for example, was a drawing-card after modest successes with *Too Much Alone* (1860) and *City and Suburb* (1861) and was staggered when Tinsley, who had never paid her less than £400 per novel, offered £800 for *George Geith of Fen Court* (1864). See Tinsley, *Random Reflections*, p. 96.

61 Payn, *Some Literary Recollections*, p. 239.

62 Take the case of Annie Tinsley (1826–85), who wanted to be a poet. 'Married life soon knocked the poetry out of me', she wrote grimly. Her husband was an incompetent lawyer so she turned to hack writing to support the family. She was one of the unlucky women novelists in the competitive publishing world: in 1858 Smith, Elder bought the copyright of *The Cruellest Wrong of All* and sold it to Chapman & Hall, who brought out six cheap editions. The same thing happened to her *Darkest before Dawn* (1864). See Henry Peet, *Mrs Charles Tinsley (Annie Tinsley) Novelist and Poet* (Frome and London, 1930). Miss Braddon faced similar hardships in her life, but unlike Annie Tinsley found her fame and fortune through writing. See Robert Lee Wolff, *Sensational Victorian: The Life and Fiction of Mary Elizabeth Braddon* (New York, 1979).

63 This was regularly matched by Annie Thomas (Mrs Pender Cudlip), who boasted that she could turn out a three-volume novel in six weeks (Tinsley, *Random Reflections*, pp. 249–50). She held her own for thirty years.

64 Trollope, *Autobiography*, ch. 7. See also Gordon N. Ray, 'Trollope at Full Length', *Huntington Library Quarterly*, XXXI (4 Aug 1968) 320.

65 Payn, *Some Literary Recollections*, p. 240.

66 Sutton, *R. D. Blackmore*, p. 80.

67 R. C. Terry, *Anthony Trollope: The Artist in Hiding* (London, 1977).

68 Rachel Anderson, *The Purple Heart Throbs: The Sub-Literature of Love* (London, 1974) p. 18.

69 Helen Black, *Notable Women Authors of the Day* (London, 1906) p. 44.

70 Mrs Oliphant, *Autobiography and Letters*, p. 107.

71 Lady Ritchie, *From the Porch* (London, 1913) p. 33.

72 Payn, *Gleams of Memory*, p. 97. Steady production was the rule for most stars of the circulating library. In the seventies Ouida produced nine novels, Mrs Henry Wood ten, Miss Braddon sixteen. See Walter de la Mare, 'Some Women Novelists of the "Seventies" ', in *The Eighteen-Seventies,* ed. H. Granville-Barker (Cambridge, 1929) p. 51.

73 Tinsley, *Random Reflections*, p. 250. See also Gettman, *A Victorian Publisher*, p. 232; Edgar Johnson, *Charles Dickens: His Tragedy and Triumph* (New York, 1952) II, 394; Gordon Ray, 'Trollope at Full Length', *Huntington Library Quarterly*, XXXI (4 Aug 1968) 319.

74 Barbara Silberg, 'Rhoda Broughton', unpublished dissertation, Pennsylvania State University, 1977 (Ann Arbor, Mich.: University Microfilms, 1980) p. 40. I am indebted to this thesis for useful background on the authoress.

75 F. A. Mumby and I. Norrie, *Publishing and Bookselling* (London, 1974) p. 246.

76 Silberg, 'Rhoda Broughton', p. 27.

77 For a detailed discussion of Trollope's business with his publishers, see Sutherland, *Victorian Novelists and Publishers*, ch.6.

78 Gettman, *A Victorian Publisher*, pp. 111–14.

79 Griest, *Mudie's Circulating Library*, p. 79.

80 Downey, *Twenty Years Ago*, pp. 17–18.

81 Griest, *Mudie's Circulating Library*, p. 87.

82 Amy Cruse, *The Victorians and their Books* (London, 1935) p. 315.

83 Griest, *Mudie's Circulating Library*, pp. 88 and 26.

84 Ibid., p. 75.

85 Ibid., p. 32.

86 Ibid., p. 165.

87 Ibid., p. 27.

88 See my Introduction to Anthony Trollope, *Why Frau Frohmann Raised her Prices, and Other Stories* (New York, 1981).

89 Michael Sadleir, 'Anthony Trollope and his Publishers', *Library* (Oxford), V (1925) 235.

90 Trollope, *Autobiography*, ch.18.

91 Silberg, 'Rhoda Broughton', p. 12.

92 Sadleir, *Things Past*, p. 86.

93 Colby and Colby, *The Equivocal Virtue*, p. 164.

94 Quoted Eileen Bigland, *Ouida: The Passionate Victorian* (London, 1950) p. 153.

95 In the Preface to her *The Story of Barbara: Her Splendid Misery and Her Gilded Cage* ([1881?]), Miss Braddon mentions a copyright suit over the novel's title, explaining the present one 'now given to a book that was written to amuse the public, and not to exercise the copyright lawyers'. Bentley once found himself with a writ for £20,000 from Messrs Gilbey for an alleged libel on their sherry in Rhoda Broughton's *Joan*.

96 It was not until the closing years of the century that some copyright protection for American publication began to emerge.

NOTES TO CHAPTER THREE: LOOKING-GLASS OR MAGICAL MIRROR: REVIEWS OF POPULAR NOVELS

1 *Saturday Review*, XX (9 Dec 1865) 742–3.

2 Amongst the most perceptive were Meredith Townsend and R. H. Hutton

in the *Spectator*, H. F. Chorley in the *Athenaeum*, Mrs Oliphant in *Blackwood's Magazine*, Leslie Stephen in the *Cornhill Magazine*, Walter Bagehot and E. S. Dallas in *The Times*.

3    Studies on the art of the novel include: J. C. Jeaffreson, *Novels and Novelists from Elizabeth to Victoria* (London, 1858); Masson, *British Novelists and their Styles* (1859); G. L. Craik, *A Compendious History of English Literature*, 2 vols (London, 1861); James Hannay, *A Course of English Literature* (London, 1866); and Hippolyte Taine, *A History of English Literature*, 3 vols (New York, 1877). Such works, of course, ignored minor fiction.

4    Although reviews began to turn towards questions of style and literary merit after mid-century, articles in the popular weeklies still comprised vast amounts of plot paraphrase.

5    Sensation fiction is the cause of acrimony. The earliest reference to 'sensation novelists' has been noted by B. F. Fisher in the *London Review* (16 Feb 1861), in respect of American writers, although in a general way 'sensation' had been applied to Wilkie Collins in 1855 reviews of *Antonina* and *Basil*; see *Nineteenth Century Literary Perspectives: Essays in Honour of Lionel Stevenson*, ed. C. de L. Ryals (Durham, NC, 1974).

6    Thomas Arnold, 'Recent Novel Writing', *Macmillan's Magazine*, XIII (Jan 1866) 202.

7    Ibid., p. 205.

8    Ibid., p. 207.

9    *Saturday Review*, XXI (9 June 1866) 681.

10    See Matthew Arnold, *Essays in Criticism*, 1st ser. (London, 1865), and *Culture and Anarchy* (London, 1869).

11    F. T. Palgrave, 'On Readers in 1760 and 1860', *Macmillan's Magazine*, I (Apr 1860) 488.

12    David Masson, 'Three Vices of Current Literature', ibid., I (May 1860) 1.

13    Robert W. Buchanan, 'Society's Looking-Glass', *Temple Bar*, VI (Aug 1862) 130–2.

14    *Spectator*, XXXIV (28 Dec 1861) 1428.

15    *Saturday Review*, XIX (4 Feb 1865) 146.

16    Ibid., XII (5 Oct 1861) 360.

17    Ibid., XV (17 Jan 1863) 84.

18    Ibid.

19    *Quarterly Review*, CXIII (Apr 1863) 486.

20    *Saturday Review*, X (25 Aug 1860) 249.

21    Ibid., VIII (31 Dec 1859) 816.

22    Ibid., XIX (27 May 1865) 639. Trollope, as usual, had the balance right when he declared that a novel should instruct in morals while it amuses: see 'On English Prose Fiction as a Rational Amusement' (1870), in *Four Lectures*, ed. Morris L. Parrish (London, 1938); 'Novel Reading', *Nineteenth Century*, V (Jan 1879) 24–43; 'The Teaching of Novels', *The Times*, 14 Nov 1873, p. 10; *Autobiography*, ch.12.

23    *Saturday Review*, XXIX (2 Apr 1870) 458.

24    Ibid.

25    *Quarterly Review*, CXIII (Apr 1863) 482.

26    *Athenaeum*, no. 1635 (26 Feb 1859) 284.

27    *Saturday Review*, XIX (4 Feb 1865) 145.

28 'Immoral Books', *Saturday Review*, XXII (24 Nov 1866) 637.
29 W. R. Greg, *Literary and Social Judgements*, 4th edn (London, 1877) p. 190.
30 *Saturday Review*, XXVIII (25 Dec 1869) 831.
31 *Athenaeum*, no. 2114 (2 May 1868) 623.
32 Ibid.
33 *Saturday Review*, XXII (24 Nov 1866) 637.
34 Mrs Oliphant, 'Novels', *Blackwood's Magazine*, XCIV (Aug 1863) 170.
35 *Saturday Review*, VII (8 Jan 1859) 43.
36 Juliet Pollock, 'Novels and their Times', *Macmillan's Magazine*, XXVI (Aug 1872) 358.
37 Mrs Oliphant, 'Novels', *Blackwood's Magazine*, CII (Sep 1867) 257–80.
38 Alfred Austin, 'The Vice of Reading', *Temple Bar*, XLII (Sep 1874) 251–7.
39 Mrs Craik, 'To Novelists and a Novelist', *Macmillan's Magazine*, XIII (Apr 1861) 441–7.
40 Mrs Oliphant, 'Novels', *Blackwood's Magazine*, XCIV (Aug 1863) 170.
41 Trollope, *Autobiography*, ch.13.
42 'Criticism on Novels', *Saturday Review*, XLIV (1 Dec 1877) 676.
43 Ibid., XXXIV (28 Sep 1872) 417.
44 Ibid., XXXV (3 May 1873) 595.
45 Ibid., XXXII (2 Dec 1871) 785.
46 Ibid., XXXIII (29 June 1872) 835.
47 Ibid., XXXI (7 Jan 1871) 29.
48 *Athenaeum*, no. 2710 (4 Oct 1879) 430.
49 *Athenaeum*, no. 2714 (1 Nov 1879) 355.
50 Ibid., no. 2710 (4 Oct 1879) 430.
51 Mrs Oliphant, *Autobiography and Letters*, p. 107.
52 Barbara Cartland, in *Guardian*, 27 July 1981, p. 8.

NOTES TO CHAPTER FOUR: QUEEN OF POPULAR FICTION: MRS OLIPHANT AND THE CHRONICLES OF CARLINGFORD

1 Quoted in Q. D. Leavis, Introduction to *Autobiography and Letters*, p. 10. See also Ritchie, *From the Porch*, p. 13; and A. C. Benson, *Memories and Friends* (London, 1924) p. 79.
2 Introduction to *A Widow's Tale, and Other Stories* (Edinburgh and London, 1898). See also L. P. Stebbins, *A Victorian Album* (London, 1946) p. 189.
3 Tredrey, *The House of Blackwood*, p. 179.
4 Colby, *The Equivocal Virtue*, p. 199.
5 Leavis, Introduction to *Autobiography and Letters*, p. 10.
6 Isabel Clarke, *Six Portraits* (London, 1935) p. 197. See also Tredrey, *The House of Blackwood*, p. 136. Mrs Oliphant was awarded a Civil List pension of £100 in 1868, some small reward for her labours. As she observed, 'I have worked a hole in my right forefinger' (*Autobiography and Letters*, p. 427).
7 *Dictionary of National Biography*, XXII (Supplement) 1102–6.
8 Stebbins, *A Victorian Album*, p. 160.
9 *Autobiography and Letters*, p. 44.

10  Ibid., p. 64.
11  Ibid., p. 78.
12  Ibid., p. 6.
13  Ibid., p. 141.
14  Benson, *Memories and Friends*, p. 79.
15  *Autobiography and Letters*, p. 147.
16  Ibid., p. 6.
17  Ibid., p. 5.
18  Ibid., p. 8.
19  Ritchie, *From the Porch*, p. 23.
20  Benson, *Memories and Friends*, p. 74.
21  Ritchie, *From the Porch*, p. 24.
22  Alexander Innes Shand, 'Contemporary Literature', *Blackwood's Magazine*, CXXV (Mar 1879) 338.
23  Austin, in *Temple Bar*, XXIX (July 1870) 489.
24  Shand, in *Blackwood's Magazine*, CXXV (Mar 1879) 337.
25  Today's feminist criticism is giving long overdue attention to this aspect of Victorian fiction. See Françoise Basch, *Relative Creatures: Victorian Women in Society and the Novel, 1837–67* (London, 1974); Ellen Moers, *Literary Women* (New York, 1977).
26  Trollope had begun to find fame with *The Warden* (1855) and *Barchester Towers* (1857), while Mrs Gaskell had already succeeded with *Cranford* (1853). A ready market existed for stories in rural communities. Anne Thackeray was one of several readers who made the comparison with George Eliot: see Ritchie, *From the Porch*, pp. 6, 13. Mrs Oliphant had no illusions: 'No one even will mention me in the same breath' (*Autobiography and Letters*, p. 7).
27  For discussions on religious issues relating to these novels, see M. Maison, *Search Your Soul Eustace: A Survey of the Religious Novel in the Victorian Age* (London, 1961); V. Cunningham, *Everywhere Spoken Against: Dissent in the Victorian Novel* (Oxford, 1975); and Robert Lee Wolff, *Gains and Losses: Novels of Faith and Doubt in Victorian England* (New York, 1977).
28  *The Rector*, ch.1. Serialisation of *The Rector* and *The Doctor's Family* was in *Blackwood's Magazine*, Oct 1861–Jan 1862.
29  *Salem Chapel* was first serialised in *Blackwood's Magazine*, Feb 1862–Jan 1863.
30  *The Perpetual Curate* appeared in *Blackwood's Magazine*, June 1863–Sep 1864.
31  *Autobiography and Letters*, p. 191.
32  Ibid.
33  An instance of Mrs Oliphant's shrewd observation of the strategies forced upon wives to placate male ego concerns her friend Ellen Blackett, wife of the publisher. See *Autobiography and Letters*, p. 82.
34  A pictorial treatment is to be found in Arthur Hughes's painting *The Long Engagement* (1859), Birmingham City Museum and Art Gallery. See W. R. Greg, 'Why Are Women Redundant?', *National Review*, XIV (Apr 1862), which, among several suggestions concerning the surplus female population, argues that encouraging men to marry late incites cads to commit immoral acts.

35　*Miss Marjoribanks* was serialised in *Blackwood's Magazine*, Feb 1865–May 1866.
36　Baker, *History of the English Novel*, X, 200.
37　*Phoebe Junior, a Last Chronicle of Carlingford* was not serialised, but appeared in three volumes under Hurst and Blackett's imprint, 1876.
38　A discrepancy; in *Salem Chapel* she was Lady Western.
39　See the *Athenaeum*, no. 2539 (24 June 1876) 851.
40　*Saturday Review*, XLII (22 July 1876) 113.
41　The brazen Copperhead bears a resemblance to Trollope's Melmotte; *The Way We Live Now* had appeared the previous year.
42　The *Athenaeum* found him repulsive, declaring that he should have been killed off early in the story – no. 2539 (24 June 1876) 851.
43　Herbert Paul, *Men and Letters* (London, 1901) p. 154.

NOTES TO CHAPTER FIVE: DELIGHTFUL WICKEDNESS: SOME NOVELS OF RHODA BROUGHTON

1　Sir Clements Robert Markham (1830–1916), the famous Artic explorer, wrote widely on exploration, sea-faring history and the monarchy. His best-known books were *King Edward VI: His Life and Character* (1907), *The Life of Admiral Sir Leo McClintock* (1909) and *The Lands of Silence* (1921).
2　*Notable Women Authors of the Day*, published in book form in 1906. The collection included Jean Ingelow, Adeline Sergeant, Edna Lyall, Florence Marryat and Lynn Linton.
3　Ibid., p. 44.
4　Ibid.
5　Sadleir, *Things Past*, p. 93.
6　Ibid., p. 84.
7　*The Times*, 7 June 1920, p. 17.
8　Rhoda's grandfather was Sir Henry Delves Broughton. Her father was presented to the living of Broughton, Staffs, in 1855. Her mother, Jane Bennett, daughter of a Dublin QC, had a sister who married the novelist Joseph Sheridan Le Fanu in 1844. See *Dictionary of National Biography*, Supplement, 1912–1921, ed. J. R. H. Weaver (London, 1927) pp. 69–70.
9　See Compton Mackenzie, *My Life and Times* (London, 1964) III, 161.
10　Black, *Notable Women Authors*, p. 41.
11　*The Times*, 7 June 1920, p. 17.
12　Percy Fitzgerald *Memoirs of an Author* (London, 1895), I, 167.
13　Ethel Arnold, in *Fortnightly Review*, CXIV (2 Aug 1920) 275.
14　The short stories *Tales for Christmas Eve* (1873), later reissued as *Twilight Stories* (1879), have a Pinteresque quality, especially one called 'The Man with the Nose'.
15　Quoted Sadleir, *Things Past*, p. 91. See also Ellis, *Mainly Victorian*, p. 210.
16　Leon Edel, *The Life of Henry James* (New York, 1972) V, 32; and Thomas Anstey Guthrie, *A Long Retrospect* (London, 1936) p. 144.
17　Ethel Arnold, in *Fortnightly Review*, CXIV (2 Aug 1920) 267.
18　Quoted in Cruse, *The Victorians and their Books*, p. 333.

19    Sadleir, *Things Past*, p. 94 (undergraduates, of course, vied for invitations to tea); and Clarke, *Six Portraits*, p. 217.

20    Sadleir, *Things Past*, p. 116. See also John Sparrow, 'An Oxford Caricature and Provocation', *Encounter*, XXXIX (July 1972) 94.

21    Comment by Tamie Watters, ibid., XXXVI (Apr 1971) 41.

22    *The Times*, 7 June 1920, p. 17.

23    Quoted by Estelle Gilson, correspondence in *Encounter*, XXXVII (Aug 1971) 92. See also *The Diary of Sir Edward Walter Hamilton 1880–1885*, ed. Dudley W. R. Bahlman (Oxford, 1972) II, 400; and Lady Constance Battersea, *Reminiscences* (London, 1922) p. 391.

24    Ethel Arnold, in *Fortnightly Review*, CXIV, 264.

25    Percy Lubbock, *Mary Cholmondeley* (London, 1928) p. 42. See also Percy Lubbock, *Portrait of Edith Wharton* (London, 1947) p. 73; and Forrest Reid, 'Minor Fiction in the "Eighties" ', *The Eighteen-Eighties*, ed. Walter de la Mare (Cambridge, 1930) p. 122.

26    Edel, *Henry James*, V, 31. Lord Houghton's receptions were celebrated. Thomas Hardy first met Rhoda at luncheon there with Robert Browning in 1883. See Florence E. Hardy, *The Life of Thomas Hardy 1840–1928* (London, 1962) p. 159 (first published 1928).

27    Battersea, *Reminiscences*, p. 391.

28    Edel, *Henry James*, V, 33. For a description of her in old age see Walter Sichel, 'Rhoda Broughton', *Bookman*, LII (Aug 1917) 138; and Marie Belloc Lowndes, Foreword to *A Fool in Her Folly* (London, 1920).

29    Edel, *Henry James*, V, 33.

30    Lubbock, *Mary Cholmondeley*, pp. 39–40.

31    Ibid.

32    A collection of twenty letters at the Humanities Research Center, University of Texas, Austin. The Hon. Florence Ellen Hungerford Milnes (1855–1923) was the daughter of Richard Monckton Milnes, first Baron Houghton. Her mother was daughter of the second Lord Crewe. In 1882 she married the Hon. Arthur Henry Henniker-Major. A great beauty, she was said to have partly inspired the character of Sue Bridehead in *Jude the Obscure*. Hardy was her devoted friend for thirty years. A writer herself (she published six novels, three collections of short stories and a four-act comedy), she collaborated with Hardy in the tale 'The Spectre of the Real'. In 1896 she was elected President of the Society of Women Journalists. See *One Rare Fair Woman: Thomas Hardy's Letters to Florence Henniker 1893–1922*, ed. Evelyn Hardy and F. B. Pinion (London, 1972).

33    Andrew Lang, *Old Friends: Essays in Epistolary Parody* (London, 1890) pp. 108–16.

34    Quoted in Silberg, 'Rhoda Broughton', p. 1, from Bonamy Dobrée and Edith Batho, *The Victorians and After, 1830–1914* (London, 1938) pp. 274, and 301.

35    Sadleir, *Things Past*, p. 116.

36    Baker, *History of the English Novel*, X, 211.

37    *The Times*, 7 June 1920, p. 17.

38    *Not Wisely* was serialised in *Dublin University Magazine*, Aug 1865–July 1866.

39  Rhoda denies the similarity by explicit reference to G. A. Lawrence's hero in ch.4.

40  *Cometh Up* was serialised in *Dublin University Magazine*, July 1866–Mar 1867. Rudyard Kipling notes in the short story 'Baa Baa, Black Sheep' that the boy Punch was forbidden to open this novel on account of its 'sinfulness' – *Wee Willie Winkie, and Other Stories* (London, 1915) p. 294 (first published 1895).

41  *Athenaeum*, no. 2088 (2 Nov 1867) 569, and no. 2060 (20 Apr 1867) 514.

42  *Spectator*, XL (19 Oct 1867) 1172–4.

43  This was the first of many books to be serialised in *Temple Bar*. It appeared May 1869–Mar 1870; see Ellis, *Mainly Victorian*, p. 209.

44  *Athenaeum*, no. 2210 (5 Mar 1870) 640; Sadleir, *Things Past*, p. 104.

45  Elisabeth Lynn Linton, 'Miss Broughton's Novels', *Temple Bar*, LXXX (June 1887) 199.

46  F. C. Burnand's parody *Gone Wrong*, by Miss Rhody Dendron, uses the multiple-narrative device of this novel in *Punch*, LXX (25 Mar–3 June 1876).

47  Austin, in *Temple Bar*, XLI (July 1874) 201.

48  A reference to an article fiercely critical of the modern woman by Elisabeth Lynn Linton (1822–98) in *Saturday Review*, XXV (14 Mar 1868) 339–40.

49  Austin, in *Temple Bar*, XLI (July 1874) 202.

50  Sadleir, *Things Past*, p. 106. The *Saturday Review* was vigorously condemning vain, silly heroines 'doing outrageous things with quite seraphic intentions' – XXXV (29 Mar 1873) 429.

51  *Saturday Review*, XLII (4 Nov 1876) 575.

52  *Spectator*, XLIX (30 Dec 1876) 1646. The *Athenaeum* similarly advised her to leave the cheap and vulgar to lesser writers such as Florence Marryat and Annie Thomas – no. 2559 (11 Nov 1876) 767.

53  Edel, *Henry James*, V, 32.

54  Silberg, 'Rhoda Broughton', p. 70.

55  *Second Thoughts* was her first novel to be issued in two volumes. Attractively bound in cloth with a floral print of pink and blue flowers on a black ground, it was a departure from Bentley's earlier issues of her books.

56  E. F. Benson, *As We Were: A Victorian Peep Show* (London, 1930) p. 312, attributed to Howard Sturgis. The earliest reference I have found to this aphorism is by Ethel Arnold, in *Fortnightly Review*, CXIV (2 Aug 1920).

57  Among her later books, *Mamma* (1908) and *A Fool in her Folly*, published posthumously in 1920 and dealing with unhappy love affairs, convinced Sadleir that they relived 'the tragedy which set its mark on her for ever' (*Things Past*, pp. 86–7). They may equally have simply been a return to one of her most successful plots.

58  Battersea, *Reminiscences*, p. 391.


NOTES TO CHAPTER SIX: HIGH SPIRITS: JAMES PAYN, BEST OF THE JOURNALISTS

1  Although most literary histories mention him among minor novelists, the only article solely about the author is Leslie Stephen's Introduction to his memoir *The Backwater of Life* (1899).

2    Huxley, *The House of Smith, Elder*, p. 127.

3    The memoirs are: *Some Private Views* (London, 1881); *Some Literary Recollections* (London, 1884); *Gleams of Memory, with Some Reflections* (London, 1894); and *The Backwater of Life*. His *Collections and Recollections, by One Who Has Kept a Diary* (London, 1898), not listed in the British Library catalogue, also contains biographical material. See also *Dictionary of National Biography*, XXII (Supplement) 1125–8.

4    *The Times*, 31 Mar 1898, p. xiv.

5    *Dictionary of National Biography*, XXII (Supplement) 1126.

6    Alexander Innes Shand, *Days of the Past: A Medley of Memories* (London, 1905) p. 173; Horace Pym, *A Tour Round my Bookshelves* (London, 1891) p. 85; see also *Fifty Years of Fleet Street: The Life and Recollections of Sir John R. Robinson*, ed. Frederick M. Thomas (London, 1904) p. 352.

7    Arthur Conan Doyle, *Memories and Adventures* (London, 1930) pp. 306–7 (first published 1924).

8    Masson, *British Novelists and their Styles*, p. 253.

9    'I had been " devoted to literature" of a kind that is injuriously called "light" from childhood, and had spoilt reams of good paper with juvenile compositions' (*Gleams of Memory*, p. 65).

10    Leslie Stephen, *The Mausoleum Book*, Introduction by Alan Bell (Oxford, 1977) p. 105.

11    See *Meliboeus in London* (Cambridge, 1862), eighteen articles first published in *Chambers's Journal*; the article 'In Our Back Garden' appeared in *People, Places and Things* (London, 1865). See also *Stories and Sketches*, papers from *Household Words* and *Chambers's Journal* (London, 1857).

12    The Society of Authors was founded in 1883. Tennyson was President and Walter Besant Chairman. Board members included George Meredith, Edmund Gosse, Rider Haggard, Walter Herries Pollock and G. A. Sala. The Authors' Syndicate operated in the Strand under the direction of W. M. Colles.

13    Walpole, 'Novelists of the Seventies', in *The Eighteen-Seventies*, ed. Granville-Barker, p. 32. See also Oliver Elton, *A Survey of English Literature 1830–1880* (London, 1920) II, 319–20; Laurie Magnus, *English Literature in the Nineteenth Century* (New York, 1909) p. 278.

14    From information supplied by the author's grandson, Mr William Payn.

15    W. Robertson Nicol, *A Bookman's Letters* (London, 1913) p. 227.

16    *Some Literary Recollections*, p. 10.

17    *Some Private Views*, p. 18. Some of his school experiences are treated in *The Foster Brothers* (1859) and *Less Black than We're Painted* (1878).

18    *Some Literary Recollections*, p. 34.

19    Ibid., p. 21.

20    The authoress left a charming recollection of her protégé at this time in poor health: 'exactly the charming lad that so often goes off in consumption – full of beauty, mental and physical, and with a sensibility and grace of mind such as I have rarely known'. See Vera Watson, *Mary Russell Mitford* (London, 1949) p. 297.

21    They had twelve children. Their eldest daughter, Alicia Isobel, married George Buckle, editor of *The Times* (1884–1912) and biographer of Disraeli.

22    *Some Literary Recollections*, pp. 69–70.

23 *Days of the Past*, p.174.
24 See *Some Literary Recollections*, ch.5.
25 Ibid., p. 173.
26 *Days of the Past*, p. 147.
27 *Some Literary Recollections*, p. 195.
28 Ibid., p. 198.
29 Fitzgerald, *Memories of an Author*, I, 144. The occasion was a meeting at the home of Edward Bulwer-Lytton of the Guild of Literature and Art.
30 *Some Literary Recollections*, pp. 242–3.
31 Ibid., p. 196.
32 Correspondence with Wilkie Collins, Humanities Research Center, University of Texas, Austin.
33 Frederick Maitland, *The Life and Letters of Leslie Stephen* (London, 1906) p. 356.
34 Noel Annan, *Leslie Stephen* (London, 1951) p. 76.
35 *Cornhill Misc.*, Humanities Research Center, University of Texas, Austin.
36 For further evidence of Payn's editorial work, see Elwin, *Old Gods Falling*, pp. 149, 316; Downey, *Twenty Years Ago*, p. 137; and Hester Thackeray Ritchie, *Thackeray and his Daughters: The Letters and Journals of Anne Thackeray Ritchie* (New York, 1924) p. 177.
37 Hesketh Pearson, *Conan Doyle* (London, 1974) p. 11 (first published 1943). See also Adrian Conan Doyle, *Sir Arthur Conan Doyle Centenary* (London, 1959) p. 113.
38 Charles Higham, *The Adventures of Conan Doyle* (New York, 1976) p. 84.
39 The drama was presented at Aberdeen on 10 April 1899, and subsequently at the Garrick Theatre, London, 10 June 1899.
40 *Autobiography of Sir Walter Besant* (London, 1902) p. 261.
41 'The Compleat Novelist', *The Backwater of Life*, pp. 151–2.
42 *Gleams of Memory*, p. 112.
43 *The Backwater of Life*, p. 159.
44 Ibid., pp. 107–8.
45 *Some Literary Recollections*, pp. 261–2.
46 Reviewing *A Woman's Vengeance* in *Saturday Review*, XXXIV (12 Oct 1872) 475–6. See also *Athenaeum* review of *Blondel Parva*, no. 2142 (14 Nov 1868) 636.
47 *The Backwater of Life*, pp. 154–5.
48 Ibid., pp. 156–7.
49 See *Some Private Views*, p. 106; and compare *The Backwater of Life*, pp. 154–5.
50 *Gleams of Memory*, p. 62.
51 MS of *Married Beneath Him*, MS 812, Department of Special Collections, University of Chicago Library.
52 *Some Private Views*, p. 250.
53 *Saturday Review*, XXXI (7 Jan 1871) 29.
54 Noel Annan, *Leslie Stephen*, p. 295; R. L. Stevenson, 'The Morality of the Profession of Letters', *Fortnightly Review*, XXIX (Apr 1881) 513–20, quoted in David Skilton, *Anthony Trollope and his Contemporaries: A Study in the Theory and Conventions of Mid-Victorian Fiction* (London, 1972) p. 35.
55 Payn called Leigh Hunt his literary godfather; his very first poem was

published in *Leigh Hunt's Journal*. He did not meet him, 'but as a boy I had an admiration for him that was akin to love' (*Some Literary Recollections*, p. 34).

56  *High Spirits, being Certain Stories Written in Them* (London, 1879). The *Athenaeum* greeted it enthusiastically as the work of 'a mind that looks cheerfully on all things, and apprehends the comic in them instinctively and by preference' – no. 2710 (4 Oct 1879) 430.

57  It did attract one review that rankled. Fitzjames Stephen in the *Saturday Review* took exception to its democratic opinions and attacks on the 'bloated aristocracy' (*Some Literary Recollections*, p. 190).

58  *Athenaeum*, no. 1636 (5 Mar 1859) 318–19.

59  Payn had many precedents: Virgil, *Aeneid*, III. 27–42; Ariosto, *Orlando Furioso*, VI. 26–53; Fradubio in Spenser's *The Faerie Queene*, I. ii. 30–44. Shakespeare's Ariel is freed from a tree in *The Tempest*.

60  The *Philadelphia Ledger* published a story some time after the novel appeared about a soldier who, escaping from Indians in 1791, hid in a large oak, where he became trapped and starved to death (*Some Literary Recollections*, pp. 260–1).

61  *Athenaeum*, no. 1989 (9 Dec 1865) 801. See also ibid., no. 1942 (14 Jan 1865) 50.

62  Payn took much material from Alponse Esquiros, *English Seamen and Divers* (London, 1868).

63  *Stories and Sketches* (1857).

64  Stephen, *The Mausoleum Book*, p. 105.

65  Baker, *History of the English Novel*, VIII, 185–6.

66  Published by Routledge (London, 1903–6).

# Index